Afterlife
Knowledge
Guidebook

A Manual for the Art of Retrieval
and Afterlife Exploration

EXPLORING THE AFTERLIFE
SERIES

Bruce Moen

HAMPTON ROADS
PUBLISHING COMPANY, INC.

for the evolving human spirit

Cover design by Jane Hagaman
Cover art by Rosalie James
Illustrations on pages 20, 23, 112, and 115 © Anne Dunn Louque

Hampton Roads Publishing Company, Inc.
1125 Stoney Ridge Road
Charlottesville, VA 22902

434-296-2772
fax: 434-296-5096
e-mail: hrpc@hrpub.com
www.hrpub.com

If you are unable to order this book from your local
bookseller, you may order directly from the publisher.
Call 1-800-766-8009, toll-free.

Library of Congress Cataloging-in-Publication Data

Moen, Bruce.
  Afterlife knowledge guidebook : a manual for the art of retrieval and afterlife
exploration / Bruce Moen.
       p. cm.
  Summary: "Presents a complete system of concepts, techniques, and exercises
for exploring the afterlife safely and reliably on your own"--Provided by
publisher.
  Includes bibliographical references.
  ISBN 1-57174-450-9 (6 x 9 tp : alk. paper)
  1. Future life. 2. Astral projection. I. Title.
  BF1311.F8M535 2005
  133.9'01'3--dc22

                                        2005004236

                        ISBN 1-57174-450-9

                    10 9 8 7 6 5 4 3 2 1
        Printed on acid-free, recycled paper in Canada

Dedication

To Rebecca, whose love and guidance made this possible.

To Duncan Roads and Ruth Parnell of *NEXUS* magazine for their encouragement and insistence that I create the workshop that evolved into this *Afterlife Knowledge Guidebook.*

To those of you who use what is written here to begin practicing the Art of Retrieval—exploring our afterlife by being of service to fellow human beings trapped after death in the solitary isolation of their own delusions.

To all Helpers physical and nonphysical who make this work and afterlife exploration possible.

Contents

Part IV: Retrieval-Based Exploration

Prologue

Becalmed on a hot, muggy Minnesota day, sitting in a small rowboat on a quiet lake, Dad and I were fishing. Our conversation turned to some of the things I'd discovered about where we go and what we do after we die. Dad said, "Well, we just can't know until we die." But years later as I sat with Dad, now comatose, in a hospice, swiftly moving toward the end of his physical lifetime, I watched Mom, who'd died years earlier, come to visit with Dad to make his transition smoother. During our first visit after he died Dad's first words were, "Well, Bruce, I guess you were right about this place being here."

For centuries we have been told by our religions that knowledge of our after-life is unattainable, and by science that its existence is a fantasy. Those same sources once told us to believe the Earth is both flat and the center of the Universe. Ordinary human beings like Columbus and Galileo explored for them-selves and found the truth. But if we are to find the truth about our existence beyond physical death we need real evidence. How and where do we find it?

Evidence comes through direct experience. This book provides concepts, techniques, and exercises you can use to gather your own verifiable evidence and prove it to *yourself.* Proving to yourself that our afterlife exists is just the beginning of an adventure that can take you to knowledge and understand-ing of the origin of our being.

So how do you accumulate real evidence? I suggest using this Basic Premise.

1. Find a way to communicate with a person known to be deceased.

2. Gather information from this deceased person that you can have no other way of knowing.

3. Verify this information to be true, accurate, and real.

4. If you continue gathering such evidence, the weight of it will lead you to the truth.

That might seem like an impossible task. Yet, since I began teaching my "Exploring the Afterlife Workshop" in 1999, hundreds of ordinary folks with no special gifts or psychic talents have learned to accomplish it routinely.

This guidebook is a compilation of the proven methods that have evolved from my teaching the workshop. Their effectiveness is demonstrated by the fact that in every workshop participants experience direct, validated communication with the deceased. Hundreds of people have used the Basic Premise to prove to themselves they will continue to exist beyond physical death. They have communicated with deceased friends, loved ones, and strangers, and have gathered information they have been able to verify as accurate. Many go beyond simple verification to explore the nature of our afterlife existence. Some use the same methods to explore far beyond mere human existence.

While the concepts, techniques, and exercises are simple, the path to Afterlife Knowledge is at once simple and complex. I am fond of saying that learning to explore our afterlife is so easy that the hardest thing is to believe you are doing it. Our beliefs—beliefs we take on from our culture, religion, parents, science, and other sources—change the simple to the complex. They can alter, block, and distort our perception. As your verified experiences eliminate these effects, your perception beyond physical reality greatly improves. Communication with the deceased and others There becomes a matter of routine. You know beyond doubt that we exist beyond physical reality.

It's my hope that your curiosity to know more will drive you to continued exploration of our afterlife and beyond. It's my hope that you will share what you find with others, spreading Afterlife Knowledge as far and wide as possible.

The Art of Retrieval

I began actively exploring our afterlife in 1992 after attending a six-day residential program called Lifeline at The Monroe Institute in Faber, Virginia. Lifeline was developed by out-of-body traveler and author Robert A.

Monroe, the institute's founder, from his out-of-body explorations of many nonphysical realms, including our afterlife.

Monroe claimed to have discovered areas in which the newly deceased appeared to be isolated and trapped, due to the circumstances of their death or their beliefs or other factors. Monroe's descriptions of their existence bore a strong resemblance to the feeling of being trapped within a dream. He discovered that it was possible to assist these people to become aware of their situation and move to a better afterlife environment. Monroe called this assistance *retrieval*.

For three and a half years after attending Lifeline I gathered my evidence through supposed contact with the deceased. (These experiences are recounted in *Voyages into the Unknown* and *Voyage Beyond Doubt*, the first two books in my Exploring the Afterlife Series.) As I learned more about how and why people become trapped, my motivation for retrieval changed to compassion for these stuck human beings. Some are just isolated and lonely. Some are confused. Some are in a constant state of sadness, or fear, or even terror. The realization that many would remain trapped until retrieved became the driving force in my practice of the Art of Retrieval.

This *Afterlife Knowledge Guidebook* will teach you a simple, effective, inexpensive system to prove to yourself our afterlife is real through practicing the Art of Retrieval. It is my hope that long after you have proven this to yourself, and explored far beyond our afterlife, your compassion for these stuck human beings will drive you to continue the practice.

How to Use This Book

The information and exercises in this book are a progression of learning through your own direct experience. Each chapter builds upon the knowledge and understanding you gain through your experiences from previous chapters. I urge you not to skip any chapters or jump ahead to begin working on material or exercises that your previous experience has not prepared you for.

My reason for urging you not to skip is simple. Changing the beliefs we hold about what is real and what is not is critical to the process of learning how to explore our afterlife. Your beliefs about what is real may change as a result of your experiences. Each chapter of this book is part of a *process* intended to bring experiences that conflict with your beliefs. To the extent that you can accept the evidence of your own conflicting experiences as real, the beliefs that distort, color, and block your perception will be removed. As conflicting beliefs are removed, perception beyond physical reality improves, providing clearer perception of further evidence.

Along with exercises, I share some of my and other people's experiences with each exercise. This is a two-edged sword. Reading about someone else's experience *after* you've had your own can provide some level of validation of your experience. But if you read about others' experiences *before* you've had your own, it becomes too easy to discount your own experience as having happened only because it was similar to what you read. I urge you not to read ahead.

Before you begin using this *Afterlife Knowledge Guidebook* I strongly suggest you purchase a notebook to record your experiences, understandings, questions, and wonderings. And, I strongly suggest you *use it*. Learning to explore our afterlife and beyond is a *process*. Recording your experiences, thoughts, and understandings as they occur can be an immensely valuable part of this process. As your Afterlife Knowledge grows, you may look back on previous experience and see it in a new light, gaining even more understanding.

The first things I suggest you write in this notebook are answers to the questions listed below. This helps set the intent that will guide you through the process. Take your time. Think about how you'd clearly state your answers before you write them down. Be clear and concise. Write more than just a few words.

> *Why did you purchase the* Afterlife Knowledge Guidebook?
> *What do you want to get out of using the information and exercises?*
> *What is it that you want to know?*

The frame of mind in which you approach this material is important. What works best is an open-minded approach, in which you delay judging your experiences and arriving at solid conclusions. Think of it as if you are gathering the pieces of a huge jigsaw puzzle. As you find each piece you may have no idea where it fits, or if it even belongs to your puzzle, but it's probably best not to throw any pieces away.

PART I

Concepts of Consciousness

1

A Concept of Consciousness

A university professor friend of mine says that when academics discuss the survival of consciousness beyond death they make little progress because they get stuck trying to define consciousness. As an engineer I'm more interested in the practical side of things. If a simplified concept makes progress possible, it can be used as a tool to complete a task.

Believers in the religion of science accept that the origin of consciousness lies within the physical brain. When the brain dies, there is no longer a place for consciousness to exist, so for such scientists, when your brain dies, you cease to exist. Most religions claim that consciousness continues to exist after death in a state dictated by their own rules and beliefs. In other words, you continue to exist in their version of eternal Heaven or eternal Hell.

In my view, neither science nor religion has much to offer regarding a useful concept of consciousness. To simplify your exploration, I'd like to share a concept of consciousness I find practical. Our physical universe is said to be very large. Astronomers say that the farthest reaches of our physical universe are at least 15 billion light years—about 8,790,000,000,000,000,000,000 miles—from the Earth. The number is incomprehensible. It's a very large physical universe.

I suggest that everything that exists within our physical universe is a form, or manifestation, of whatever consciousness is. Whatever consciousness is, it must be at least as large as our physical universe just to contain · it all. And by this concept, every object within our physical universe—the

Earth, the Moon, the planets, the Sun, the stars, and galaxies—can be thought of as small *areas of consciousness* within one larger Consciousness. Likewise, a rock, a tree, a squirrel, a lake, a human being, or a mountain within our universe can be conceptualized as small *areas of consciousness* within Consciousness.

My own explorations beyond physical reality suggest that ours is not the only universe that exists, though it may be more accurate to define these other universes as *nonphysical dimensions*. To their inhabitants these dimensions are just as real as our universe is to us. My concept of consciousness would say that all of these other dimensions and everything in them are also small *areas of consciousness* within the same, single, larger Consciousness that contains our physical universe. My concept of Consciousness is now much bigger than our physical universe, and each of these *nonphysical dimensions* and all objects and occupants can be thought of as *areas of consciousness* within a single, larger Consciousness. I find this concept useful because I don't have to precisely define what consciousness is. Instead, I am free to explore whatever consciousness might be and let my discoveries build a clearer understanding of what it actually is. Besides, it allows me to talk about how it is that we can explore beyond physical reality.

If we wanted to know about an area of consciousness within our physical universe—say, the Moon—we could observe it through a telescope. We could send a rocket with cameras and sensors to make observations. We could land humans to walk on it, gather samples, observe it, and experience it. Each of these methods of exploring can be thought of as *shifting our focus of attention* to the area of consciousness called the Moon. Once our *focus of attention* is shifted to the Moon we can gather information about it by observing our surroundings within this *area of consciousness* called the Moon. The way in which this *Afterlife Knowledge Guidebook* teaches exploration beyond physical reality is, conceptually, the very same.

All that we need do to explore nonphysical realities is to first learn how to *shift our focus of attention* from one area of consciousness to a different area of consciousness within one all-encompassing Consciousness. Then we need to understand how to observe our surroundings from within that nonphysical area of Consciousness. That might sound simplistic to some readers, but that's an engineer's concept. It's a simplified way of thinking about something that can be used to make progress toward a goal.

Throughout this guidebook we'll use this concept of shifting one's focus of attention as a means of exploring beyond physical reality. I use *Focused Attention* as the label for the method of exploration I'm teaching. You can use what you learn in this book to explore those areas of consciousness called our afterlife. You can also use what you learn here to explore areas of consciousness beyond our human afterlife—way beyond.

Trust

A word about trust. As you begin learning to explore our afterlife you face the most basic trust issue all human beings must face:

Can I trust that the information my senses bring into my awareness from my surroundings is real?

Learning to explore our afterlife requires that we learn to use what might be called our *nonphysical senses*. As I learned to use them, trust was a continuing issue.

Early in life every human being went through this process of learning to trust the information our senses bring. Perhaps thinking about how we made it through this process before can serve as a model for how we can do it again. Think of your physical birth as entry into an unfamiliar reality, in a body equipped with unknown, unfamiliar senses. Before we could use physical senses to explore and interact, we had to first realize that we had them. We had to then find ways to determine if what these senses told us about the physical world surrounding us was real or fantasy. I got insight into that process by watching my infant daughter learn to become aware of and trust her physical senses.

When I first shook a baby rattle close to her, its sound didn't get much of a reaction from her. She just continued waving her arms, sucking her toes, or whatever she was doing. But with repeated experience, I noticed the look on her face change to a quizzical, wide-eyed look that expressed the feeling of "What's that?" That look was my first indication that the rattle's physical reality sound was entering my daughter's awareness. It was the beginning of her realization that she had the physical sense we call hearing. Her physical sense of hearing was bringing her into connection with physical reality. With repeated experience, the look on my daughter's face acquired that quizzical, wide-eyed look just by my bringing the rattle where she could see it. I could move the rattle slowly back and forth in front of her and watch her eyes follow its motion. That showed me that she was becoming aware of the rattle by using her physical sense of sight. Now, her physical sense of sight too was bringing her into connection with physical reality. Shaking the rattle enough that it made its sound, where she could see it, I watched her begin to associate the sight and sound of the rattle as being connected to the physical world object.

As my daughter grew and gained enough control of her physical body to move it where she wanted it to go, bringing the rattle into her view brought an interesting response. She'd grab the rattle in her tiny little hand and shake it. Then I'd see a huge smile of satisfaction form on her cute, tiny little face. Reaching for the rattle expressed her trust in her sense of sight. Shaking the rattle to hear its noise was her verification that what her sight and hearing were bringing into her awareness was real.

Our afterlife exists within a nonphysical reality in which our physical world senses are completely useless. To explore and learn about our afterlife, you first need to realize that you *have* nonphysical senses. Ultimately, you will need to trust these senses enough to try to verify and validate what these senses bring into your awareness.

One of my earliest, biggest mistakes was to expect that perception within nonphysical realities, using nonphysical senses, would be the same as perception within physical reality using physical senses. Like my daughter with her baby rattle, only through repeated experiences did I develop these nonphysical senses to a useful, reliable level and develop trust in what my new nonphysical senses were telling me. I had to find a way to grab the baby rattle and shake it. I had to find ways to verify what my nonphysical senses were telling me.

For the first three and a half years of my exploration of our afterlife, I was more than half convinced that at some point I'd realize that I was subconsciously creating some grand, self-deceptive fantasy. As you learn to explore our afterlife, don't be surprised if you find yourself asking, "Am I making this all up? Is this just my imagination?" My intent in writing this *Afterlife Knowledge Guidebook* is to help you answer these questions far more quickly than I did.

The Hemi-Sync Model of Consciousness

My basic nonphysical-reality navigation tool I learned while participating in programs at The Monroe Institute (TMI). I call it a Hemi-Sync Model of Consciousness:

Once you can identify the feeling of any area within consciousness, merely remembering and reexperiencing that feeling will automatically shift your awareness back to that area of consciousness.

Hemi-Sync is a patented audio technology using specific sound patterns that have been demonstrated to automatically shift one's awareness to specific areas of consciousness. Robert Monroe, out-of-body traveler, author, founder of The Monroe Institute, and the inventor of Hemi-Sync, labeled various areas of consciousness Focus 10, Focus 12, etc. Program participants shift their awareness to various focus levels using Hemi-Sync sounds, and then they learn to do so without the sounds. The trainers told us that each focus level has a specific *feeling* and that after the Hemi-Sync sound patterns guide you to experience the feeling, remembering that specific feeling automatically shifts your awareness to that specific area of consciousness, or focus level. Of course I did not believe the trainers. I was certain that without the magic Hemi-Sync sound patterns I would never get to any of the focus levels. But in time, experience taught me the TMI trainers were right, which resulted in what I call the Hemi-Sync Model of Consciousness.

Each state of consciousness has specific feelings associated with it, and you will learn to return to any area of consciousness by remembering its feeling. As you focus your attention on sensing any *feeling* associated with the exercises in this book, you learn to shift your focus of attention to specific areas of consciousness. People exist, in our afterlife, in specific areas of consciousness. The Hemi-Sync Model of Consciousness is a tool you learn to use to go There.

State-Specific Memory

While we're on the subject of navigating consciousness, I've got a useful tip for you. Many times I returned from an afterlife exploration with only tiny fragments of memory of the experience, and to bring more memory of the exploration back into my awareness was a little like waking up and trying to remember a dream. I've come to understand this phenomenon as something Charles Tart, a consciousness researcher, calls "State-Specific Memory." The concept of State-Specific Memory means:

The memory of an event is stored within the area of consciousness in which that event occurred.

Awakening from sleep can be thought of as a shifting of your focus of attention from one area of consciousness—let's call it *dream consciousness*—to another area of consciousness, physical-world consciousness. As you begin the process of waking up, while you're dreaming, the dream is vivid. Your awareness is focused within dream consciousness and that is where the dream is occurring. It's all clear in your mind just before you begin waking up. For example:

It feels hot and humid. There is the sound of pesky insects buzzing around in the air. You are in a small hut in a jungle looking at a man tied to the chair he is sitting in. Two men with rifles, bayonets fixed, stand at attention behind the chair. Another man, standing in front of the chair, is interrogating the man sitting in it. A lit cigarette hovers a fraction of an inch above the left forearm of the man tied in the chair.

As you begin to wake up a little, the colors and sounds begin to fade, and as you wake up a little more, the whole scene begins to fade. A little more, and you can still remember what you were dreaming about, but the details are starting to get fuzzy. A little more, and you might remember only that you were dreaming. The concept of State-Specific Memory explains this, and suggests a way to remember the dream.

The dream occurred within dream consciousness, and that is the area of consciousness where the memory of the event is stored. Waking up is the process of shifting your awareness away from dream consciousness to physical-world consciousness. Once you're fully awake, it's difficult to remember the dream because your awareness is now located within physical reality, instead of where the memory of the dream is stored.

If you try to remember that dream from a physical consciousness perspective, it's really tough. If you want to remember more of the dream, you will need to find a way to shift your awareness back to the area of consciousness in which the dream occurred. The Hemi-Sync Model of Consciousness provides a simple way to do that.

As you try to remember the dream, you might suddenly realize that you are remembering the feeling of a hot, muggy day. You probably don't know *why* you're experiencing that, just that you *are*. Focus your attention on that feeling. Remember that feeling as best you can, to the point of reexperiencing it. As you do, your attention begins to shift back toward the area of consciousness in which the dream occurred. You might get a flash image of a burning cigarette and a feeling of anxiety without knowing why. Focus your attention on any feelings that accompanied the image. While you are focusing attention on these feelings, the image of two soldiers, rifles at their sides, might flash through your mind. As you focus on the feelings associated with any of the images you get, your awareness shifts further and further toward dream consciousness. As you do, your attention shifts further toward the area of consciousness in which the dream occurred and memory of the dream is stored. As you continue this process, at some point you will have shifted enough of your awareness back into dream consciousness that you will remember the dream. Suddenly, you're back in the hut in the jungle. All the images of the dream come flooding into awareness and you remember the entire dream.

You have shifted your awareness back to the area of consciousness in which the dream occurred and where its memory is stored. At that point it is less a matter of remembering the dream than of reexperiencing it. You can focus your attention on any facet of the dream and it comes clearly and fully into awareness. In the same way, you can use this concept to remember more of the details of your afterlife exploration experiences.

I'd like to add a little more to what I mean by feelings.

Many folks have had the experience of smelling a specific odor, or hearing an old song on the radio, and immediately remembering a past experience, perhaps long forgotten. For many it's more like reexperiencing that long-forgotten event. I include things like smells, songs, an itch, and other such memory triggers in the definition of "feelings" in the Hemi-Sync Model of Consciousness. Also, perhaps the concept of State-Specific Memory makes it easier to understand why things like certain smells or songs cause us to immediately remember or reexperience past events. When we smelled that smell or heard that old song, we were within a specific area of consciousness. Experiencing that certain smell again seems to automatically shift our awareness back to the area of consciousness in which the events we experienced are stored. Then, out pops full detailed memory of those events. While you are trying to remember your dreams or afterlife exploration experiences, sometimes a smell, an itch, or other such "feeling" provides the means of shifting one's awareness back to the area of consciousness where the event occurred.

Making Written Notes

Whether you're learning to remember dreams or afterlife exploration experiences, making notes immediately after the experience is a good first step. If you've ever read much about learning to remember your dreams you know that most sources recommend that you write down anything and everything you can remember immediately upon waking. I agree with this completely. Shifting one's awareness from dream consciousness to physical world consciousness is not an instantaneous process. Immediately upon waking some portion of our awareness is still aware within dream consciousness. The notes we make immediately upon waking can be used to facilitate remembering more.

The way I wrote my books can serve as an example. Many times I would return from an afterlife exploration experience able to remember only enough for three or four short lines of notes. When it came time to write about that experience for one of my books I was faced with writing an entire chapter with only those skimpy notes. I found that if I read a line from my notes, focusing my attention on any feelings that resulted as I read it, I'd remember more of the experience. My writing became a process of focusing attention on feelings that happened during my exploration experiences and then remembering more of the details. From a few skimpy notes I could easily remember enough of the experience to write a detailed description several pages in length. This was part of what led me to understand and utilize Dr. Tart's concept of State-Specific Memory.

Making Verbal Notes

With practice it's possible to describe your afterlife exploration experiences into a tape recorder. I use a small, inexpensive, voice-activated tape recorder with a lapel microphone for this purpose. The advantage I find in using a tape recorder is that it records not only the content of my notes, but also the subtleties of voice inflections, pace, etc. Later, when I am listening to my tape-recorded notes, these subtleties seem to automatically elicit reexperiencing the feeling and emotional content of the explorations. It's as if the feelings that I was experiencing at the time are somehow recorded right along with my voice. Focusing attention on my recording automatically shifts my awareness to the feelings and back to the area of consciousness in which the experience occurred, making memory of the experience much easier. And that is just what I'd expect to happen using the combination of the Hemi-Sync Model of Consciousness and State-Specific Memory as tools of consciousness exploration. I strongly suggest you consider using a tape recorder, especially in later exercises in this book.

Some Implications of State-Specific Memory

During a workshop, after I lectured about State-Specific Memory, one participant volunteered a story that I'd like to pass along. While in college, his roommate was a pot smoker. This guy did all of his studying for tests under the influence of marijuana. He discovered that the only way he could remember enough of what he studied to pass the tests was to be stoned on pot while taking the test. To me this illustrates the concept of State-Specific Memory. It also is a comment on the misguided use of drugs as an attempt to enhance one's exploration experiences. The memory of what the roommate studied was stored in an area of consciousness you might call "stoned on pot consciousness." And the only way he could gain access to the memory of what he studied was to be in the state of consciousness where the memory was stored, stoned on pot.

Too often those who teach in the metaphysical arena suggest that a specific diet, incense, drug, chemical, magic powder, state of poverty, or other *prop* is necessary for the student's success. These props usually only serve to shift awareness to states or areas of consciousness unnecessary for success. To remember the successful experiences, the student will most likely have to continue to use the prop. To successfully explore beyond physical reality and remember our experiences, shifts of consciousness are required. I personally prefer that these shifts not require the use of chemicals, diets, magic powders, drugs, etc. Such props are unnecessary and often counterproductive.

2

Relaxation and Energy Gathering

Almost every practice intended to develop awareness beyond physical reality begins by teaching the student how to relax. Why do you suppose that is so? Using the Hemi-Sync Model of Consciousness I could say that awareness of our physical-world surroundings (Here) constantly generates a set of feelings that keeps our awareness focused Here. What our eyes see and our ears hear tend to keep our awareness anchored within physical reality.

Think of perception There as trying to have a conversation with a friend in a crowded, noisy restaurant. The distractions of the restaurant tend to pull your awareness away from the conversation, anchoring your awareness within the noise of the restaurant. If you can find a way to close down your awareness of the surrounding distractions it will be easier to hear what your friend is saying.

Loosening our anchors to physical reality makes it easier to perceive within nonphysical realities. Closing our eyes closes down a portion of our awareness of the physical world's visual noise. Choosing a relatively quiet, comfortable environment closes down a portion of our awareness of the physical world's auditory noise. After reducing awareness of "outside noise" there is one more anchor to loosen, our physical-world thoughts. If we are focusing our attention on our grocery list, or that the car needs an oil change, we are still anchored. Relaxation is a way of freeing our awareness from these anchors to perceive beyond physical reality.

To quiet the "internal dialogue" you don't need to learn exotic meditative techniques. All that's necessary is that you learn to relax. The simplest way I know to teach you to relax is a simple breathing pattern. The only thing special about this breathing pattern is that it is done *very slowly, without stopping or holding your breath.*

By *very slowly* I mean that it should take approximately five to ten seconds to inhale and five to ten seconds to exhale. By *without stopping* I mean that at no point during your relaxation breathing should you be holding your breath. Instead, just breathe in slowly until your lungs are *comfortably* full, then without stopping or holding your breath, begin slowly exhaling until your lungs are comfortably empty, then, without holding your breath begin slowly inhaling again.

What I mean by *comfortably* full or empty is that a relaxation breathing pattern need not induce any feeling of strain. You don't need to force yourself to inhale or exhale the last tiny bits of air you can get in or out of your lungs. The point at which you change from inhaling or exhaling could best be defined as the point at which you just begin to feel strain. If while first learning this relaxation breathing pattern you find you reach the point of feeling strain after a slow count of three or four, you're breathing too fast. Just slow the pace of the next breath until it takes a slow count of six to ten to reach that point of feeling any strain. I don't mean to imply that you should always be mentally counting as you breathe. It's useful as you are first learning this relaxation breathing pattern, but once you feel the proper, slow pace, mental counting can be dispensed with.

How many of these Deep Relaxing Breaths you need to take can vary from time to time. With practice, three are all that most folks find necessary. That's why this exercise is called "Three Deep Relaxing Breaths (3DRB)." You have done enough Deep Relaxing Breaths when you can *feel* some change in your level of relaxation. If you are fairly relaxed before you begin 3DRB it might only take one or two. If you're fairly agitated before you begin 3DRB it might take six or more. The whole point of this exercise is to *feel* that change in your level of relaxation, to actually *feel* it.

While a deeper level of relaxation is probably better then a very shallow one, there is no need to get carried away. You don't need some fall-out-of-your-chair level of relaxation. All that is necessary is that you feel some change in your level of relaxation. A little more is better, but experience shows it's not all that necessary.

Remember the Hemi-Sync Model of Consciousness. One object of the Three Deep Relaxing Breaths (3DRB) exercise is for you to *identify the feeling of relaxation.* Get to know what relaxation feels like, so that just by remembering

13

that feeling you reexperience it. By *identifying the feeling* I do not mean for you to sit there analyzing what relaxation feels like, wondering if you're feeling it deeply enough. I mean feel it to the point that the very act of remembering the feeling of being relaxed causes you to experience relaxation.

As you are doing the 3DRB exercise below, focus your attention on what it feels like to be relaxed. Each time you practice this exercise, just before you begin the breathing pattern, intend to remember the feeling of relaxation. You will know you are "getting it" when just by intending to remember the feeling of relaxation you notice a change in your level of relaxation. Relaxation can be thought of as an area or state of consciousness within the vast field of consciousness you're going to learn to explore. Shifting your focus of attention to relaxation consciousness is a first step.

3DRB Exercise: Description

Choose a quiet setting. Begin by sitting on a chair. If you'd like to do this exercise while lying down, I suggest you save that for later. By *later* I mean after you've learned to cause a change in your level of relaxation by just remembering the feeling. One simple advantage of sitting instead of lying down is that it's easier to avoid falling asleep. Remembering one's experiences that occur in the area of consciousness called *asleep consciousness* is more difficult than remembering experiences that occur in *awake and relaxed consciousness*.

In your quiet setting, begin by moving your body into a comfortable sitting position. As you begin to shift your focus of attention to relaxation consciousness you may discover that the position you're sitting in isn't as comfortable as you thought. Feel free to move your body into a more comfortable position at any time during the exercise.

Next, close your eyes—a simple way to reduce visual distractions.

Then begin the slow, deep relaxation breathing pattern. Breathe in through your mouth or nose, whatever is most comfortable to you. I suggest that the first few times you do this exercise you slowly, mentally count to six while inhaling and exhaling. This mental counting is just to help you get a feel for the slow pace and can be dispensed with soon. You don't need to time this, or be too concerned with doing it for exactly the right amount of time, but an inhale or exhale shorter than about five seconds is too short and more than ten seconds is overkill.

It's time to change from inhaling to exhaling when your lungs are comfortably full. While it's hard to describe that comfortably full feeling, there is a point at which you begin to have the *urge to exhale*. This urge to exhale *feel-*

ing usually happens before you're straining to take in more air. While exhaling, there will come a point when you might notice the feeling of an *urge to inhale*. That feeling seems to be just right as the point to change from one to the other. If you find that you're experiencing tension or strain at the end of your inhale or exhale, you're going too far. Again, don't drive yourself crazy trying to analyze this to death. There's lots of margin for error.

Repeat this relaxation breathing pattern until you can sense some change in your level of relaxation. With practice you'll have changed your level of relaxation enough for afterlife exploration with Three Deep Relaxing Breaths.

Remember, this exercise is intended to help you relax, to turn down the noise level, and it's intended to give you the opportunity to experience the *feeling* of the state of consciousness called relaxation consciousness so you can return to that state again at any time just by remembering what it *feels* like to be relaxed.

Afterlife Knowledge Exercise Scripts

This *Afterlife Knowledge Guidebook* has written scripts for all the exercises. These are provided to make it easy for you to make your own audio exercise recordings on tape, compact disk (CD), or your format of choice. Using an audio recording helps eliminate one more physical reality anchor (remembering the instructions), providing better focus of attention on the intent of the exercise. After each instruction in the script you'll notice instructions like (wait 10 sec). This is intended to give you time to perform the action before giving the next instruction. Don't drive yourself crazy striving to get the timing exact; it's a guideline, not a rule. For most exercises a soft, soothing voice is preferable.

A complete set of recordings of all the *Afterlife Knowledge Guidebook* exercises in the author's voice is available for purchase on CDs at the www.afterlife-knowledge.com web site.

Three Deep Relaxing Breaths Exercise: Script

This is the Three Deep Relaxing Breaths Exercise. (Wait 5 sec)

As you get ready to begin this exercise, adjust the volume setting of this recording so that you can comfortably and easily hear and understand my voice. You may do this exercise either sitting or lying down. (Wait 15 sec)

When you're ready to begin, please close your eyes. (Wait 15 sec)

To begin this exercise, move your body into a comfortable, relaxed position in your quiet place. (Wait 30 sec)

In a moment I will ask you to begin a long, slow, deep inhale and continue as I count from one to six. Then, without stopping or holding your breath, begin a long, slow exhale, and continue as I count back down to one. If you feel the urge to change from inhaling to exhaling, or exhaling to inhaling, before I complete the count, slow down the pace of your next breath. (Wait 5 sec)

Begin slowly inhaling. (Wait 1 sec)

One (Wait 1 sec)

Two (Wait 1 sec)

Three (Wait 1 sec)

Four (Wait 1 sec)

Five (Wait 1 sec)

Six (Wait 1 sec)

Begin slowly exhaling.

Six (Wait 1 sec)

Five (Wait 1 sec)

Four (Wait 1 sec)

Three (Wait 1 sec)

Two (Wait 1 sec)

One (Wait 1 sec)

Breathe normally. (Wait 10 sec)

Again, inhale slowly, as I count.

One (Wait 1 sec)

Two (Wait 1 sec)

Three (Wait 1 sec)

Four (Wait 1 sec)

Five (Wait 1 sec)

Six (Wait 1 sec)

Begin slowly exhaling, as I count.

Six (Wait 1 sec)

Five (Wait 1 sec)

Four (Wait 1 sec)

Three (Wait 1 sec)

Two (Wait 1 sec)

One (Wait 1 sec)

Breathe normally. (Wait 20 sec)

Continue these Deep Relaxing Breaths at your own pace, while you mentally count from one to six with each inhale and then back to one with each exhale. (Wait 1 min)

As you continue your Deep Relaxing Breaths, focus your attention on the feel of its slow, relaxing pace. (Wait 1 min 30 sec)

Breathe normally as you focus your attention on the feeling of being relaxed. (Wait 30 sec)

Take in more deep, relaxing breaths without mentally counting. Just feel the slow pace of these Deep Relaxing Breaths. I'll be quiet now while you do this. (Wait 1 min)

Again, allow yourself to breathe normally as you focus your attention on the feeling of being relaxed. (Wait 20 sec)

In future exercises, when I ask you to take in Three Deep Relaxing Breaths, remember the feeling of being relaxed and use the breathing pattern you have just learned to easily return to this deeply relaxed state. (Wait 10 sec)

When you're ready, open your eyes and give yourself a few moments to fully return from the exercise. Then immediately begin to write about your experience and use the questions in the debriefing section for this exercise in the *Afterlife Knowledge Guidebook* as a starting point to record your experience in detail in your notebook.

Debriefing, 3DRB Exercise

Take a few moments to record your experience in your notebook.

Did you notice a change in your level of relaxation?
What does it feel like to be within the state of consciousness called Relaxation?
Are there physical body cues that tell you you're relaxed? What are they?
Are there internal cues that tell you you're relaxed? What are they?

More Practice

Repeat this exercise at least two more times using the exercise recording. Each time you do, focus your attention on the feeling of the slow pace and the feeling of relaxation. Record your experience in your notebook after each practice session.

Still More Practice

Repeat this exercise without using the exercise recording. As you do, focus your attention on remembering the feeling of being relaxed. When you are able to induce the feeling of change in your level of relaxation within three breaths, you're ready to move on to the next exercise in this book. When you can induce that change by merely remembering the feeling of relaxation to the point of reexperiencing it, you are an advanced student.

Hints and Tips

Some folks find it easier to experience the feeling of relaxation more fully during this exercise by imagining, or pretending, their inhaling breath is gathering up all the tensions in their body, and then imagining that the exhaling breath carries those tensions out of the body. Experiment with this, focusing your attention on any feelings you experience.

Some folks find it easier to experience the feeling of relaxation more fully with this exercise if they open their eyes, stand up, and walk around a little after each time they complete the exercise. I think that this works because walking around for a few moments brings back some of the feelings of the anchors and tensions of physical reality. Walking around sharpens the contrast between feeling anchored or tense and feeling relaxed.

When you use this 3DRB exercise it is important that you feel at least some change in your level of relaxation. If you don't actually feel a change in your level of relaxation, repeat the 3DRB exercise until you do. Relaxation is a state of consciousness you'll need to learn to shift your focus of attention to for afterlife exploration.

Using Relaxation in Future Exercises

From now on when you hear the instruction, "Take in Three Deep Relaxing Breaths" or see "3DRB" it means:

1. Sit in a comfortable position in a quiet place.

2. Close your eyes.

3. Remember the feeling of relaxation.

4. Take in a slow, deep breath until your lungs are comfortably full.

5. Without hesitating or stopping the flow of your breath, begin a slow exhale, remembering and reexperiencing the feeling of being relaxed.

6. Continue this breathing pattern for at least Three Deep Relaxing Breaths or until you can actually feel a change in your level of relaxation.

Energy Gathering

You could think of your conscious awareness as a rechargeable flashlight that shines brightest just as it comes off the charger. To use Focused Attention to its best advantage, just like the flashlight, it's helpful to first put your conscious awareness on the charger. That is what Energy Gathering is all about.

As with relaxation, many esoteric disciplines teach some form of Energy Gathering, though that's not usually the term they use to describe it. The form I use and teach is a modification of a technique taught in programs at The Monroe Institute. Energy Gathering uses a specific breathing pattern, the same, slow paced, deep breathing pattern you learned in the relaxation exercise. Energy Gathering can be done any time you'd like to give your awareness a boost, and we're going to use it extensively in future exercises.

The description of this exercise might at first sound complicated, but it's really a simple, powerful exercise that you can do while standing, lying down, or walking around. Since people in my workshops are most often sitting in chairs, I'll describe it that way. I suggest you first learn Energy Gathering sitting in a chair and then later experiment with other positions.

Energy Gathering Exercise: Description

There are two parts to this Energy Gathering Exercise: establishing the flow and building the level. Imagination plays a role in both parts of the exercise.

Establishing the flow begins with getting into a comfortable position in your chair. Both feet on the floor seems to work best as it reduces the tension-inducing, distracting strains of crossing your legs. It doesn't matter much where you do this, as long as you're in a comfortable position. You can sit in a disciplined yoga position, or comfortably slouch if you like. While it's helpful to keep your spine and legs fairly straight, it's not really necessary. You can loosen or remove anything that's too tight or binding, like tight belts, collars, and shoes. They can be an uncomfortable, distracting, physical-reality anchor.

The exercise begins with 3DRB (Three Deep Relaxing Breaths). Remember the feeling of relaxation as you continue the breathing pattern

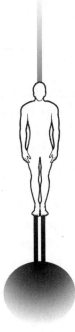

until you sense some change in your level of relaxation. Then it's time to begin using your imagination.

While continuing to take deep, relaxing breaths, begin thinking about clean, clear, bright, shiny, sparkling bits of energy floating in a vast pool below your feet. Imagine it. Notice I don't say you need to *visualize* or *see* this pool of energy, just imagine or pretend that it is there. It is completely unnecessary for you to visualize or actually see it. All that's necessary is to think about it, imagine it, or pretend it is there below your feet.

Then, focus your attention on the bottoms of your feet. I know, some of you are wondering, what does he mean? To illustrate, take off your shoes and socks and put your feet on the floor. Focus your attention on what the floor feels like against your feet. Does it feel warm or cool? Smooth or rough? Soft or hard? Answering these questions requires that you focus your attention on the bottoms of your feet.

To establish the flow, with your attention at the bottoms of your feet, begin thinking about that pool of clean, clear, bright, shiny, sparkling energy below your feet. Then, as you begin inhaling, using the same, slow, deep breathing pattern as for relaxation, imagine a column of this energy coming up from the pool and entering your body through the bottoms of your feet. As you continue slowly inhaling, imagine this energy flowing upward through your body. If you timed your breath just perfectly (which I emphasize is completely unnecessary) when your lungs are comfortably full, this flow of energy is just beginning to emerge from your body, flowing upward out the top of your head. Without stopping or holding your breath, slowly exhale, imagining this flow of energy exiting the top of your head and continuing to flow upward in a column, out of sight, above you. Then, once again begin thinking about the pool of clean, clear, bright, shiny, sparkling energy below your feet. Focus your attention at the bottoms of your feet, and repeat the cycle. The pace of Energy Gathering Breathing is the same as that of 3DRB. Inhaling and exhaling should each take about five to ten seconds.

Establishing the Flow Exercise: Script

This exercise is to establish the flow for Energy Gathering. (Wait 5 sec)

Before beginning this exercise look at the image in the Energy-Gathering chapter in the *Afterlife Knowledge Guidebook*. If you haven't done so, or if you can't clearly remember it from a previous viewing, stop this recording and review that image to facilitate doing the exercise. (Wait 10 sec)

As you get ready to begin this exercise adjust the volume of this recording so that you can comfortably and easily hear and understand my voice. You may do this exercise either sitting or lying down. (Wait 15 sec)

When you're ready to begin, close your eyes. (Wait 15 sec)

To begin this exercise, move your body into a comfortable, relaxed position in your quiet place. (Wait 30 sec)

Remember the feeling of relaxation, as I guide you through the slow pace of the first deep relaxing breath. If you feel the urge to change the direction of your breathing before I complete the count, just slow the pace of your next breath. The slow breathing pace used here is the same as you will use to establish the flow of energy later in the exercise. (Wait 10 sec)

Begin slowly inhaling.

One (Wait 1 sec)

Two (Wait 1 sec)

Three (Wait 1 sec)

Four (Wait 1 sec)

Five (Wait 1 sec)

Six (Wait 1 sec)

Begin slowly exhaling.

Five (Wait 1 sec)

Four (Wait 1 sec)

Three (Wait 1 sec)

Two (Wait 1 sec)

One (Wait 1 sec)

Breathe normally. (Wait 10 sec)

Take in Three Deep Relaxing Breaths, or as many as you need to feel some change in your level of relaxation. (Wait 45 sec)

Allow yourself to breathe normally as you focus your attention on the feeling of being relaxed. (Wait 15 sec)

In a moment I will guide you through the breathing pattern to establish the flow of energy from a vast pool of clean, clear, bright, shiny, sparkling energy below your feet, into your body through the bottoms of your feet, up through your body, and out through the top of your head. Use the same slow breathing pace, without stopping, as you use for Three Deep Relaxing Breaths. (Wait 5 sec)

Remember the image of establishing the flow of energy from below in the *Afterlife Knowledge Guidebook.* (Wait 15 sec)

Be willing to imagine or pretend the pool of energy and this flow. (Wait 5 sec)

Begin thinking about a vast pool of clean, clear, bright, shiny, sparkling energy below your feet. (Wait 15 sec)

Think about a column of that clean, clear, bright, shiny, sparkling energy flowing upward from the pool toward the bottoms of your feet. (Wait 10 sec)

Focus your attention at the bottoms of your feet. (Wait 5 sec)

Breathe this energy in through the bottoms of your feet. (Wait 1 sec)

Up through your body. (Wait 2 sec)

And out through the top of your head. (Wait 2 sec)

As you exhale, pretend this column of energy continues flowing upward, out of sight. (Wait 4 sec)

Breathe normally. (Wait 10 sec)

Again, think about that pool of clean, clear, bright, shiny, sparkling energy below you, and a column of this energy rising upward from it toward the bottoms of your feet. (Wait 5 sec)

Focus your attention at the bottoms of your feet. (Wait 5 sec)

Breathe this energy in through the bottoms of your feet, up through your body, and out the top of your head. (Wait 1 sec)

As you exhale imagine the column of energy continuously flowing upward, out of sight. (Wait 10 sec)

Continue taking in these Energy Gathering Breaths to establish the flow, on your own, at your own pace, imagining each of the steps as you do so. Be willing to imagine or pretend this flow. (Wait 1 min)

Quietly, in the background, continue these Energy Gathering Breaths, as you focus your attention on any feeling or sensation of a flow entering your body through the bottoms your feet, moving upward through your body, out through the top of your head, and continuing upward out of sight. (Wait 20 sec)

Return to breathing normally and focus your attention on the feeling of establishing the flow of energy from below. (Wait 30 sec)

In future exercises, when I ask you to take in Three Energy Gathering Breaths to establish the flow from below, remember the image and feeling of establishing the flow and use the breathing pattern you have just learned to do this calmly and easily. (Wait 5 sec)

When you're ready, open your eyes, give yourself a few moments to fully return from the exercise. Then immediately begin to write about your experience and use the questions in the debriefing section for this exercise in the

Afterlife Knowledge Guidebook as a starting point to record your experience in detail in your notebook.

Debrief

Take a few moments to record your experience in your notebook.

What was your experience of imagining the pool of energy?

Did you notice any sensations or feelings with your attention focused on your feet during the exercise?

Did you notice any sensations or feelings as you breathed this energy up through your body and out the top of your head?

Did you notice any sensations or feelings as you exhaled and imagined the column of energy continuing to flow upward out of sight?

If so describe them in detail.

Building the Level Exercise: Description

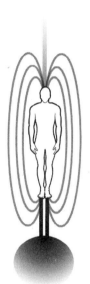

Once the flow of energy has been established, the next step in Energy Gathering is to build the level of energy—putting your conscious awareness on the charger—by recirculating a portion of the energy flowing out the top of your head back down around the outside of your body as you exhale. With each succeeding inhalation, both the recirculating energy and more energy from the pool are inhaled in through the bottoms of your feet and up through your body. Imagination again plays a role in this exercise.

Think of the column of energy flowing up out of sight as having a thin, outside layer. As you begin to exhale, imagine this thin layer peeling away from the column, its flow turning downward. As you continue to exhale, imagine this thin layer of energy completely surrounding your body and showering down toward your feet, outside your body. The drawing might make this a little easier to imagine.

Building the Level Exercise: Script

This is the Building Up the Level of Energy from Below exercise. (Wait 5 sec)

Before beginning this exercise look at the image in the Energy Gathering chapter in the *Afterlife Knowledge Guidebook*. If you haven't done so, or if you can't clearly remember it from a previous viewing, stop this recording and review that image to facilitate doing the exercise. (Wait 10 sec)

As you get ready to begin the exercise, adjust the volume of this recording so that you can comfortably and easily hear and understand my voice. You may do this exercise either sitting or lying down. (Wait 15 sec)

When you're ready to begin, close your eyes. (Wait 15 sec)

To begin this exercise, move your body into a comfortable, relaxed position in your quiet place. (Wait 30 sec)

Remember the feeling of relaxation and take in Three Deep Relaxing Breaths, or as many as you need to feel some change in your level of relaxation. (Wait 45 sec)

Breathe normally as you focus your attention on the feeling of being relaxed. (Wait 15 sec)

Remember the image of establishing the flow of energy from below in the *Afterlife Knowledge Guidebook*. (Wait 15 sec)

Begin thinking about a vast pool of clean, clear, bright, shiny, sparkling energy below your feet. (Wait 15 sec)

Think about a column of that clean, clear, bright, shiny, sparkling energy flowing upward from the pool toward the bottoms of your feet. (Wait 15 sec)

Focus your attention at the bottoms of your feet. (Wait 10 sec)

On your next inhale, slowly breathe this energy into your body through the bottoms of your feet. (Wait 1 sec)

Up through your body. (Wait 2 sec)

And out through the top of your head. (Wait 2 sec)

Then, as you exhale, pretend the column of energy continues flowing upward out the top of your head and out of sight. (Wait 10 sec)

Breathe normally. (Wait 15 sec)

Remember the image and feeling of establishing the flow of energy from below as you take in at least Three Energy Gathering Breaths to establish the flow. (Wait 45 sec)

Breathe normally and focus your attention on the feeling of establishing the flow of energy. (Wait 20 sec)

Now that the flow of energy is established, in a few moments I will guide you through the exercise to build up the level of energy. (Wait 5 sec)

Remember the image of building up the level of energy from below that you saw in the *Afterlife Knowledge Guidebook*. (Wait 15 sec)

Slowly exhale, as you remember how the image shows a thin layer of the column of energy above the head turning and showering down all around the outside of the body. (Wait 10 sec)

Breathe normally. (Wait 10 sec)

With your next slow exhale, remember how the image shows this showering energy flowing downward around your body and below the feet. (Wait 10 sec)

As you continue, use the same breathing pace and pattern as in previous exercises: that is, slowly and without stopping or holding the breath. (Wait 5 sec)

Slowly inhale, as you remember how the image shows the showering energy turning upward toward the feet, and then into the body through the bottoms of the feet. (Wait 10 sec)

Breathe normally. (Wait 15 sec)

Continue remembering this image as I guide you through three cycles of the building up the level of energy from below exercise. (Wait 5 sec)

When you are ready, at the beginning of your next exhale, imagine energy from the column above your head peeling off and showering down as you continue slowly exhaling. Then as you begin to inhale, breathe this, and more energy from the pool, in through the bottoms of your feet, up through your body, and out the top of your head as you continue slowly inhaling. (Wait 10 sec)

As you exhale, imagine another layer of energy peeling off from the column and showering down around you. (Wait 10 sec)

As you inhale, breathe in all the showering energy, and more from the pool, up through your body, and out through the top of your head. (Wait 10 sec)

Again, as you exhale, imagine yet another layer of energy showering down around you. (Wait 10 sec)

And again, as you inhale, breathe all the showering energy and more from the pool in through the bottoms of your feet, up through your body, and out through the top of your head. (Wait 10 sec)

Breathe normally. (Wait 10 sec)

Take in three more Deep Relaxing Breaths. (Wait 30 sec)

Take in three more Energy Gathering Breaths to establish the flow from below. (Wait 30 sec)

At your own pace, begin and continue the breathing pattern to build up the level of energy from below, imagining each of the steps as you do so. (Wait 20 sec)

Be willing to imagine or pretend this flow. (Wait 1 min 30 sec)

Quietly, in the background, continue building up the level of energy, as you focus your attention on any feeling or sensation of this ever-increasing level of energy. (Wait 1 min)

25

Return to breathing normally and focus your attention on the feeling of building up the level of energy. (Wait 30 sec)

In future exercises, when I ask you to take in Three Energy Gathering Breaths to build up the level from below, remember the image and the feeling of building up the level and use the breathing pattern you have just learned to do this calmly and easily. (Wait 10 sec)

When you're ready, open your eyes, give yourself a few moments to fully return from the exercise. Then immediately begin to write about your experience, using the questions in the debriefing section for this exercise as a starting point to record your experience in detail in your notebook.

Debrief

Take a few moments to record your experience in your notebook.

What was your experience of imagining the pool of energy this time?

Did you notice any new sensations or feelings with your attention focused on your feet during the exercise?

Did you notice any sensations or feelings as you breathed this energy up through your body and out the top of your head?

Did you notice any sensations or feelings as you exhaled and imagined the column of energy continuing to flow upward out of sight?

Describe your experience of the showering and recirculating energy.

The Complete Exercise for Energy Gathering from Below: Description

When I began using this Energy Gathering Exercise, I tended to think that energy was entering my body only during my inhale, and exiting or recirculating only during the exhale. Energy Gathering is actually a continuously flowing, ever-increasing level of energy. There is a specific feeling, or set of feelings, associated with this continuously flowing, ever-increasing level of energy, and identifying that feeling is the object of this next exercise. In this next exercise you'll use two techniques to help you identify the feeling of a continuously flowing, ever-increasing level of energy. The first of these techniques will be for you to imagine that the flow of showering energy recirculates around and through your body three times with each inhale and each exhale. To do this you might pretend that as you inhale, your eyes follow a point in the flow of this energy as it flows in through the bottoms of your feet, up through your body, out the top your head, showers down around you, and reenters through your feet three times as you inhale. Then imagine this again as you exhale. The second technique you will use in this exercise to help you experience the feeling of a continuous flow of energy will be to shift your focus of attention to various areas of your body at different points in the breathing pattern. This is how people in my workshops learn to identify the feeling. Once you can identify this feeling and remember it, Energy Gathering becomes a simple matter of remembering that feeling.

By now you've become familiar with relaxation, establishing the flow, and building the energy level. Therefore, I'll say less during the exercise, to give you the opportunity to practice without the distraction of my voice.

The Complete Exercise for Energy Gathering from Below: Script

This is the complete exercise is for Three Energy Gathering Breaths from Below. (Wait 5 sec)

Before beginning this exercise, look at the image in the Energy Gathering chapter in the *Afterlife Knowledge Guidebook*. If you haven't done so, or if you can't clearly remember it from a previous viewing, stop this recording and review that image to facilitate doing the exercise. (Wait 10 sec)

As you get ready to begin the exercise, adjust the volume of this recording so that you can comfortably and easily hear and understand my voice. You may do this exercise either sitting or lying down. (Wait 15 sec)

When you're ready to begin, please close your eyes. (Wait 15 sec)

To begin this exercise move your body into a comfortable, relaxed position in your quiet place. (Wait 30 sec)

Remember the feeling of being relaxed. (Wait 20 sec)

At your own pace take in Three Deep Relaxing Breaths, or as many as you need to feel some change in your level of relaxation. (Wait 45 sec)

Remember the image of establishing the flow of energy from below in the *Afterlife Knowledge Guidebook*. (Wait 15 sec)

At your own pace, remembering each of the steps as you do this, take in Three Energy Gathering Breaths to establish the flow from below. (Wait 45 sec)

Remember the image of building up the level of energy from below in the *Afterlife Knowledge Guidebook*. (Wait 15 sec)

At your own pace, remembering each of the steps as you do this, take in Three Energy Gathering Breaths to build up the level. (Wait 45 sec)

Continue building up the level of energy from below. (Wait 30 sec)

As you continue building up the level of energy from below, imagine or pretend that your eyes follow a point in this flow as it circulates around and through your body three times with each inhale and three times with each exhale. (Wait 30 sec)

As you continue building up the level of energy, shift your focus of attention to the top of your head as you begin your inhale. Feel the energy flow into your feet and out the top of your head at the same time. (Wait 30 sec)

As you continue building the level of energy, shift your focus of attention to the bottoms of your feet as you begin your exhale. Feel the energy flow into your feet and out the top of your head at the same time. (Wait 30 sec)

As you continue this Energy Gathering Exercise, focus your attention on the feeling of a continuous, ever-increasing flow and level of energy through and around your body. This is the feeling of Energy Gathering from Below. (Wait 30 sec)

In future exercises, when I ask you to, take in Three Energy Gathering Breaths from Below, remember the image and feeling of a continuous, ever-increasing flow of energy through and around your body, and use the breathing pattern you have just learned to calmly and easily do this. (Wait 10 sec)

When you're ready, please open your eyes and give yourself a few moments to fully return from the exercise. Then immediately begin to write about your experience and use the questions in the debriefing section for this exercise in the *Afterlife Knowledge Guidebook* as a starting point to record your experience in detail in your notebook.

Debrief

The object of following a point in the flow three times around as you inhale and exhale, and of moving the focus of your attention to the opposite end of your body in the previous exercise, is to experience any feelings that indicate a continuous flow of energy into your body. As you practice the Energy Gathering Exercise, there will come a point in which you will realize you can feel, or pretend to feel, both flows of energy, up through your body and showering down around you, simultaneously. That is the feeling you are looking for in this exercise. That feeling is Energy Gathering

Take a few moments to record your experience in your notebook.

What was your experience of imagining the pool of energy this time?
Did you notice any new sensations or feelings with your attention focused on your feet during the exercise?

Did you notice any sensations or feelings as you breathed this energy up through your body and out the top of your head?

Did you notice any new sensations or feelings as you exhaled and imagined the column of energy continuing to flow upward out of sight?

Describe your experience of the continuous, ever-increasing flow of energy.

How Many Times?

Many folks ask how long and how often they should do the Energy Gathering Exercise. When you begin practicing the Energy Gathering Exercise, I recommend three- to four-minute sessions. As you continue these practice sessions, there may come a point, after you've experienced the feelings and sensations of the flow of energy, when you notice those feelings are not as obvious and seem not to be present. That is an indication that gathering energy is becoming an easy, natural shift of your focus of attention to gathering energy consciousness.

Tips and Hints: Read Only after Completing the Above Exercises

While doing these (or any) exercises it's easy to forget that the state of relaxation is beneficial to experiencing the effects of the exercise. As you continue to do these exercises take note of your level of relaxation. If a little tension has crept in during the exercise, take in 3DRB or as many as you need to feel a change in your level of relaxation before continuing. I can't tell you how many times I forgot to do this and only realized after the exercise why it wasn't working.

To sense what the flow of energy feels like as it comes up through your feet and continues moving up your legs, close your eyes and pay close attention to the feeling of air entering your nostrils and passing through them as you breathe in. It might almost be described as a hollow, airy feeling. Many workshop participants describe the feeling of energy flowing into their feet and up their legs and body as similar. Many workshop participants describe the feeling of the flow of energy as a tingling sensation in the feet, legs, or elsewhere in the body.

Sometimes imagining—pretending—that you feel something flowing upward through your body helps make you aware of the actual flow. Pretending has a way of opening one's perception to experience unfamiliar things. It's okay to pretend.

In the Energy Gathering Exercise my experience of feeling the continuous flow of energy was easier if I focused my attention both on the bottoms of my feet and on the top of my head at the same time. The resulting "vacuum cleaner feeling" felt as if I, with my attention focused at the top of my head during the inhale, could feel something being "sucked" into the bottoms of my feet. With my attention at the bottoms of my feet during the exhale there was a feeling of something blowing out of the top of my head. Focusing my attention on both of these feelings at once establishes the flow and buildup of energy in my body.

Some workshop participants say something like: "Gee, the first few times I did the Energy Gathering Exercises I could actually feel the sensations of the flow of something like you described. But I don't think I'm gathering energy anymore because I'm not feeling it the same way." I explain this by asking folks to remember the last time they moved to a new house. The first few nights in that new house, you heard every little plink, plunk, and thud. After spending enough nights in your new house you no longer heard those noises. Do you think those noises stopped happening? Probably not. Something in us seems to automatically and carefully focus our attention on anything new in our environment. Once that part of us is satisfied that it understands the new thing, it ignores the repeated experience of that once-new thing. Just as those noises in the new home no doubt continued after we lost awareness of them, in my experience Energy Gathering continues to happen during the exercise after we no longer feel those "first experience" feelings.

If you felt any sensation you could describe as a flow or movement of "something" anywhere inside or outside your body at any point during this exercise, you've experienced a feeling of Energy Gathering. That is a key to understanding how to gather energy very quickly in future exercises. Gathering Energy is a state of consciousness and, again, the Hemi-Sync Model of Consciousness says, if you remember the feeling to the point of reexperiencing it, your awareness will automatically shift to that Gathering Energy state of consciousness. With practice, just remembering the imagery and feeling of Energy Gathering causes Energy Gathering to begin. As your awareness becomes satisfied that it understands Energy Gathering, it may begin to ignore the sensations and just gather energy on automatic pilot.

As you continue practicing Energy Gathering, you may notice patterns in the flow of energy through your body or showering down around the outside your body. There are flows within the flow. Workshop participants have reported swirls, spirals, turbulence, colors, and many other patterns.

Using Energy Gathering in Future Exercises

From now on when you hear the instruction, "Take in Three Energy Gathering Breaths from Below" or see "3EGB," it means:

Begin thinking about that vast pool of clean, clear, bright, shiny, sparkling energy below you.

Remember the feeling of establishing the flow of energy.

Establish the flow.

Remember the feeling of letting energy shower down around you.

Begin recirculating energy.

Remember the feeling of gathering energy.

Gather energy.

3

Affirmations

An affirmation is a clear, concise, complete, positive, present-tense statement of a desire. Affirmations define the target for awareness, so precision is important. Ambiguously worded affirmations yield ambiguous results, and wordy affirmations dilute the statement of your desired outcome. Incomplete affirmations leave room for unintended results.

One of my favorite stories about miswording an affirmation comes from a close friend. While she was single, she used affirmations to find the *right man*. Her affirmations listed the qualities this *right man* would have. Each time she made up a new list she learned more about how to be clear, concise, and complete. One of her lists included things like: crazy in love with me, can't live without me, worships the ground I walk on, and wants to always be near me. She forgot a word. She met a man who was crazy in love with her, couldn't live without her, worshipped the ground she walked on, always wanted to be near her—and was already married. It took a while to get rid of this guy. When wording an affirmation, take the time to write it down. Give it some thought. Make it clearly, concisely, and completely define your desire.

Affirmations should use positive wording. Saying, "I want to be rich" has a completely different feeling from "I don't want to be poor." In my view it's the feeling generated by an affirmation that's important, and positively worded affirmations feel, well, more positive.

An example of positive wording of an affirmation that might be useful in afterlife exploration is, "I desire clearer perception." A negatively worded example of the same affirmation could be, "I don't want my perception blocked." If you say both of those statements to yourself, perhaps you'll understand what I mean by the different feeling quality of each one. Go with what feels good.

Tense (past, present, or future) also affects the outcome. For example, the affirmation, "My perception is going to improve" doesn't actually say that your perception has to ever actually improve, just that it's always *going to* improve. Your affirmation can be fulfilled by your perception remaining in a state in which it is *going to improve* at some future time, instead of actually *being* improved. This might sound like a silly distinction but I've experienced the nonresults of future-tense wording of my affirmations enough times to learn to be careful.

An example of a present-tense affirmation is, "Whenever I desire to explore the afterlife my perception is clear." That little verb *is* brings the affirmation statement into the present tense. (This affirmation implies some future time—"whenever"—because I didn't want to be bothered to state this affirmation at the beginning of every exploration session. This wording automatically applies to those specific future times.)

Sometimes results are immediate and sometimes they're not. Reviewing the wording of an affirmation may give clues as to why the results are taking so long to occur.

In my experience the affirmations that take more time often turn out to be a *process* instead of a *destination*. That process may have more necessary steps than those defined in the wording. An example: Let's say that, back when I was a single man, my affirmation stated my desire that I meet the perfect woman. Perhaps, in order for me to recognize a perfect woman when I saw one, I needed some preparation. Maybe my beliefs about what a perfect woman is are the reason I'm already twice divorced. Maybe I needed to grow a little, understand more, who knows? After stating my affirmation to meet the perfect woman I might begin having some of those *growing experiences* that tend to leave bumps and bruises as I learn more about what the perfect woman is. I might whine and complain that my affirmation is not working, when in truth my affirmation stated a desire that is fulfilled through a process rather than a single event. In this case the *growing experiences* I'm having were unknowingly implied in my affirmation. When you start getting upset that your affirmations seem not to be happening, give some thought to experiences you're having that might be part of the *process* of fulfilling your affirmation. (As for me, my relationship with my wife, Pharon, demonstrates I must have learned much from that process.)

I used to state affirmations repeatedly, thinking this was somehow adding power and speeding the time in which my affirmation would be fulfilled. So when Rebecca (my friend and teacher about whom I've written in previous books) suggested that I state my affirmation just once and then let it go, it took a little thinking for me to understand why. As I analyzed it, I realized that the only reason to repeatedly restate the affirmation is doubt that the process is actually working. Stating an affirmation once, letting it go, and not giving it another thought is in a way an affirmation of the affirmation process itself.

Placing Intent

Someone once told me that intent is everything, and I tend to believe it. If it *is* true, then *placing* intent is the beginning of everything. Learning to place intent is a powerful tool of afterlife exploration—and in many other areas of life, as well.

Placing intent and affirmations are closely related. The affirmation defines the target for my missile of awareness. Placing intent is the launch button, guidance system, and rocket fuel that fly my awareness to that target. Placing intent is one of the closest things to magic I've encountered. Some day a total stranger may ask you to visit a deceased loved one, another total stranger. Properly placed intent will guide you easily and effortlessly into contact and communication with that person. As I say, it's almost magical.

Placing intent is a specific area of consciousness. An affirmation expressed while your attention is focused within placing intent consciousness is given added power. Once you learn how to place intent, you have a powerful tool you can use during your afterlife explorations and elsewhere in your life. Considering its importance, I encourage you to take the time to learn the lesson in this exercise.

I have written about Rebecca teaching me about placing intent in my previous books. She described it as a *feeling*, and suggested I think about a flower bud sitting on the top of my head, and then experience the feeling of that bud as it blossoms into a beautiful flower.

After I understood placing intent I could see why Rebecca described it the way she did. But at the time I needed a simpler, more concrete way to learn it. I had to approach this lesson from my logical, rational, engineer's perspective. Finding a way to directly experience this feeling of placing intent, in order to be able to shift my awareness to that state of consciousness at will, had to be simpler and more rational than trying to figure out what a flower bud is feeling as it blossoms.

Logic told me that if placing intent is the beginning of everything, then shifting my awareness to the area of consciousness that is placing intent must precede everything I do. Logically, the feeling of placing intent must occur while my awareness is shifted there, whether I'm aware of that feeling or not. Even something as simple as bending my index finger must be preceded by shifting to placing intent consciousness. I had to first consciously or subconsciously place the intent to bend the finger. Then nerves get activated, impulses get sent to muscles, and the finger bends.

I decided that if I could focus my attention on any feeling that occurred *just before* I bent my index finger, I might become consciously aware of the feeling of placing intent. Once I could identify that feeling, causing myself to remember/reexperience that feeling in the future would automatically shift my awareness to placing intent consciousness. Stating my affirmations There would add power to their fulfillment. (The Hemi-Sync Model of Consciousness strikes again.) All this logical, rational rigmarole gave birth to the Silly Little Finger Bending Exercise that I used to teach myself how to place intent.

Once I came up with this exercise, I did it everywhere and often. Sitting in my cubicle at work I'd take some Deep Relaxing Breaths, gather some energy, relax my hand, and focus all my attention on any feelings associated with bending my index finger. I probably did this 20 to 30 times a day, off and on for weeks.

At first I'd feel something and think, "There it is!" only to discover I was just feeling the muscles tensing up in my arm or my finger. After lots of false alarms that my awareness misidentified as placing intent, and then ignored, I finally caught a whiff of the placing intent feeling, just an instant before anything physical happened. Each time I'd catch the slightest flash of the feeling it became easier to identify and know it the next time. Once I identified that feeling, thinking back to Rebecca's flower bud description, I could see what she was trying to describe. Flower buds probably do experience that feeling as they blossom into flowers.

When you learn the feeling of placing intent you'll discover all kinds of uses for it. And, if you can remember the feeling associated with an effect, remembering that feeling leads to reexperiencing the effect. So, let's get started learning about the feeling of placing intent.

The Silly Little Finger Bending Exercise: Description

There are two basic ways to do the Silly Little Finger Bending Exercise—the open-air technique and the contact pressure technique. The sketches below illustrate the hand and finger positions for these two techniques.

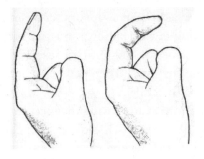

The open-air technique.   The contact pressure technique.

The contact technique shortens the time between when you start to bend your finger, and when you know it has bent, because the change in contact pressure tells you the finger bent.

I recommend that you bend the index finger on your nondominant hand in this exercise. That is, if you're right-handed bend the index finger on your left hand, and vice versa. Either finger will do nicely, but if you use your nondominant hand, the feeling of placing intent seems to stand out a little better.

Learning to properly place intent is a subtle yet powerful tool. We'll be using it in future exercises and learning more about its uses as you continue. I recommend that you repeat this exercise often.

The Silly Little Finger Bending Exercise: Script

This is the Silly Little Finger Bending Exercise. (Wait 5 sec)

As you get ready to begin the exercise adjust the volume of this recording so that you can comfortably and easily hear and understand my voice. You may do this exercise either sitting or lying down. (Wait 15 sec)

When you're ready to begin, please close your eyes. (Wait 15 sec)

To begin this exercise move your body into a comfortable, relaxed position in your quiet place. (Wait 30 sec)

Remember the feeling of relaxation and take in Three Deep Relaxing Breaths, or as many as you need to feel some change in your level of relaxation. (Wait 45 sec)

Breathe normally as you focus your attention on the feeling of being relaxed. (Wait 20 sec)

Remember the image of establishing the flow of energy from below in the *Afterlife Knowledge Guidebook*. (Wait 15 sec)

Remember each of the individual steps and the feeling of establishing the flow of energy as you take in at least Three Energy Gathering Breaths to establish the flow from below. (Wait 45 sec)

Remember the image of building up the level of energy from below in the *Afterlife Knowledge Guidebook*. (Wait 15 sec)

Remember the image and feeling of a continuous, ever-increasing flow of energy through and around your body as you take in at least Three Energy Gathering Breaths from Below. (Wait 45 sec)

Move your nondominant hand to a comfortable resting position. You can rest it in your lap, rest it in your other hand, or in any other comfortable, relaxed position. Being able to fully relax your arm, hand, and fingers makes it easier to identify the feeling of placing intent. (Wait 15 sec)

Focus your attention on your index finger, and feel any sensations like air moving across its skin, tension in any of its muscles, coolness, or warmth. Experience what it feels like where it is. (Wait 20 sec)

While continuing to focus your attention on your index finger, bend it. Feel what it feels like to bend your finger and then bring it back to its original position. Do this at least three times just to get familiar with what normal finger bending feels like. (Wait 20 sec)

Take in Three Deep Relaxing Breaths, at your own pace. (Wait 30 sec)

Take in Three Energy Gathering Breaths from Below, at your own pace. (Wait 30 sec)

Once again, focus your attention on your index finger. (Wait 10 sec)

Know that you are going to bend it. (Wait 5 sec)

When you're ready, begin this Silly Little Finger Bending Exercise. With your attention focused to experience any feeling that occurs just the instant before it bends, bend your finger, and then repeat this process. I'll sit quietly while you do this. (Wait 2 min)

When you're ready, please open your eyes and give yourself a few moments to fully return from the exercise. Then immediately begin to write about your experience and use the questions in the debriefing section for this exercise in the *Afterlife Knowledge Guidebook* as a starting point to record your experience in detail in your notebook.

Debrief of Finger Bending Exercise

Take a moment to record in your notebook what you experienced.

If you experienced any feelings associated with the instant before your finger bent, describe them.

Describe where in your body you "felt" these feelings.

Tips and Hints: Read Only after Completing the above Exercises

It took me more than a few times doing this exercise before I caught a whiff of the feeling I was looking for. Lots of things happen when you bend your finger, some physical, some nonphysical. I mistakenly thought I'd experienced the feeling of placing intent several times before I actually got it.

If I were to describe the feeling of placing intent some of the words I'd use would be: anticipation, apprehension, expectancy, a feeling like something is about to happen, a feeling like I KNOW without a doubt that it's about to happen.

Other experiences of feeling placing intent are quite common. One happens in your car. You're first in line, stopped at the red light, with lots of cars behind you chomping at the bit to get moving the instant the light turns green. You can almost feel the tension of the people in the cars behind you, and you know if you don't get moving the instant the light turns green you'll be hearing horns honking. You're waiting, feeling a little anxious, perhaps even feeling a little nervous, for that light to turn green. When the light turns green there's a feeling that passes through you just the instant before any muscles move. Before your foot moves off of the brake pedal, before your foot moves to step on the gas. That feeling you experience the instant before a muscle moves is the one you're looking for. It's the feeling that says GO before your foot moves down on the gas pedal.

A workshop participant left the workshop without having identified the feeling of placing intent. She wrote me an e-mail a week or so later to tell me how she got it. She lives in the country, and she and her daughter were walking to the mailbox when she spotted a soda can in the road. Without giving it much thought she decided to kick the can. If you are walking, you have to focus your attention on getting your body and leg in just the right position to kick the can without stopping. She did that little stutter-step you do to get your foot in the right position as you're walking toward the can, and at the last possible instant decided not to kick the can. In that instant she knew the feeling of placing intent.

Some folks say that it's almost like a nonphysical finger that bends just before the physical finger does. They say it's as if they are about to bend their finger, and then just the instant before their physical finger bends, they feel a nonphysical finger bend first. Some claim to actually get a visual impression of the nonphysical finger bending.

Some folks identify the feeling of placing intent the first time they do the exercise. Some folks get it after a few times. And then there are folks like me. I did this exercise daily for weeks before I found that feeling.

If you're like me, plan on doing this exercise daily, during your normal, routine activities. At least three or four times a day do the Silly Little Finger Bending Exercise. Pick a place to do it where you won't get a lot of stares and questions about what you're doing. During a meeting with your boss at work is probably not a good time to practice. The restroom is actually a pretty good place to practice; it's quiet, you're alone, you're sitting down, you're relaxed, and the exercise only takes a few moments.

Above all, keep at it. Experiencing and identifying this feeling is an important tool of afterlife exploration. Think of placing intent as another area of consciousness you can learn to shift your focus of attention into; call it *Placing Intent Consciousness* if you like. Once you have identified the feeling of being in that area of consciousness, returning is just a matter of remembering that feeling to the point of reexperiencing it. The Hemi-Sync Model of Consciousness strikes again!

How to Use Placing Intent

You can use placing intent in many situations. For example, you can use it when stating an affirmation, or initiating contact with a deceased loved one, or in conjunction with retrievals and exploring the afterlife. You can use it to get a parking spot close to the front door next time you go to the grocery store. You can use it to help you fulfill any desire.

To do so, think of placing intent as a specific area of consciousness that you can enter by remembering/reexperiencing its feeling. If you express your desire for something when you are within that area of consciousness, *seemingly magical* things can happen. If you were using placing intent in conjunction with an affirmation, the process would go something like this:

Give some thought to carefully wording the affirmation in clear, concise, complete, positive, and present-tense words.

Write down the final version of the affirmation and memorize it.

Sitting in a comfortable position, in a quiet place, close your eyes.

Take in 3DRB and 3EGB.

Remember the feeling of placing intent to the point that you reexperience the feeling, either before, during, or after you state your affirmation.

Repeat your affirmation in your mind, once.

Let go of any thoughts about your affirmation.

Take note of other feelings you experienced while repeating your affirmation.

Here's a secret. If you just can't seem to capture the feeling of placing intent, just the act of remembering yourself doing the Silly Little Finger Bending Exercise can be used to place intent.

While it might be ideal to experience the feeling of placing intent for the entire time you're stating your affirmation, I haven't found that at all necessary. Reexperiencing the feeling even for less than a second before, during, or after stating your affirmation is quite adequate.

With continuing practice, focusing your attention on reexperiencing the feeling of placing intent, you can learn to extend the time you are within placing intent consciousness. If you decide to practice to extend the length of time, you may discover a nearby area of consciousness I call Pure Doubtless Intent. Absolutely amazing things can happen. With one's attention focused within this area of consciousness I'm certain that walking on water or flying through the air would only be a matter of expressing the desire. But, for the purposes of afterlife exploration such an effort is completely unnecessary. I suggest you experiment and practice at least to the point of learning to recognize and remember the feeling of placing intent for a second or so.

Doubt

Working through the exercises using affirmations and placing intent often brings up questions about the effect of doubt. I still have trouble with doubt, but a lot less than I used to.

Here's what would happen. I'd have my affirmation written down clearly, concisely, completely, and in present-tense, positive wording. I'd shift my awareness to the feeling of placing intent and start mentally stating my affirmation. Then I'd hear myself say, *This isn't going to happen. This stuff never works.* And sure enough, my affirmation wouldn't be fulfilled. I was certain my doubt had something to do with canceling my affirmation, but didn't understand how that worked.

At first I thought I'd have to find a way to not think about doubt while stating my affirmation. Good luck! That's like someone saying to you, *don't think about a black dog.* What's the first thing that happens? You start thinking about a black dog. Trying to *not* think about doubt while stating an affirmation works the same way. No mental gymnastics to avoid feeling doubt ever worked, yet sometimes my affirmations were fulfilled even though I'd felt doubt as I placed my intent; I knew there had to be more to it. If affirmations had to be placed doubtlessly I'd never have gotten anywhere.

I eventually realized that the very belief that doubt would cancel my affirmation could, by itself, cancel my affirmation. Such a belief automatically sabotages the entire effort. Figuring this out took way longer than I'd care to admit. Then, in one of those *light-bulb-coming-on-in-your-mind* moments, I came to understand what happens when we feel doubt while placing intent.

If I experience the feeling of doubt as I'm placing intent for my affirmation, I am placing intent for *both* my affirmation and my doubt to manifest.

Let's say I need a new car. I craft a real whiz-bang affirmation, take my 3DRB and 3EGB, shift my awareness to placing intent consciousness, and just as I begin to state my affirmation I suddenly start feeling doubt. I hear myself saying, *This is ridiculous! I'm going to walk into a car dealership and pick out the car I want. Then the loan officer is going to take one look at my income and laugh me out of his office!* Here's what would have happened before I understood the effect of feeling doubt. . . .

I'd walk into the car dealership, pick out the car, get to the loan officer, and he'd take one look at my income level and start laughing. And as I'd be walking out of his office I'd be saying to myself, *See! I knew it! This affirmation stuff is a lot of crap! I'm not going to be able to buy a car!* As I now understand it, what canceled the affirmation was not my feeling doubt, but my saying those last few sentences to myself, ending with *I'm not going to be able to buy a car!*

Using my present understanding, this same car-shopping scenario would go like this. . . .

I walk into the car dealership, get to the loan officer, he takes one look at my income level and starts laughing. And as I'm walking out of his office I'll be saying to myself, *This is great! I remember I was feeling doubt when I placed the intent for buying a car. Those feelings of doubt just manifested. That means my affirmation process is working! I am definitely going to be getting a new car!*

41

To restate my present understanding of the effects of doubt:

If I experience the feeling of doubt as I'm placing intent for my affirmation, I am placing intent for *both* my affirmation and my doubt to manifest.

Since anything you are feeling as you place intent becomes part of the result, placing intent can be tricky. Don't worry about it, just keep practicing and notice what happens. Use your experiences as a way to learn how things work. One can learn a great deal either by doing things correctly or by making mistakes. Experiences that demonstrate fulfillment of your placed intent, with or without doubt included, are the best way I've found to deal with doubt.

Affirmations and placing intent can be used to define the targets of your curiosity and take your awareness to sources of information to satisfy that curiosity. They are simple, effective, powerful little tools.

Earlier I described a state of consciousness I called Pure Doubtless Intent consciousness. My visits there have been rare, but enough to know it exists. Suffice it to say that I believe that if a person intended for a live elephant to appear on top of the Empire State Building in New York City, and that person was in an absolutely pure doubtless state when that intent was placed, people all over New York City would be hearing the elephant trumpet, and reading about the elephant that fell from the sky and landed at the base of the Empire State Building. As I stated earlier, in my opinion understanding how to place intent in such a doubtless state would make walking on water, levitation, and flying through the air common occurrences.

Placing Intent in Future Exercises

When you hear the instruction, "place intent" in future exercises it means:

1. Remember performing the Finger Bending Exercise.

2. Remember the feeling of placing intent to the point of reexperiencing it and allow your focus of attention to shift to that area of consciousness.

4

Beliefs

Experience has taught me that beliefs are the basic building material of our world. Rarely does anything enter my awareness without first passing through the distortion, coloring, filtering, and editing of the beliefs I've come to hold. Since birth I've interpreted all experience through my growing set of beliefs to construct the worldview in which I live. This has a profound effect on my capability to *accurately* perceive within physical and nonphysical realities. Understanding how beliefs operate to alter your perception is one of the keys to learning to explore our afterlife.

The single most important key factor to success in afterlife exploration is understanding and dealing with the effects of your beliefs upon your perception.

It wasn't until I began to recognize and effectively deal with this belief factor that I began to make progress in my attempts to prove to myself our afterlife even exists. Once I began to effectively deal with this factor the pace of my progress greatly accelerated. Years of teaching afterlife exploration demonstrates that dealing with this belief factor is critical.

Most of us believe that the answer to any question can be deduced through empirical measurement, experimentation, and observation. We often refer to this answer as "the truth," as if such a truth is objective, unchanging, and universally applicable. We accept this "truth" until a new question casts doubt on our conclusion. At this point, scientists break into two camps, one believing that the original conclusion remains "the truth," and one believing that further experimentation, observation, and data analysis may uncover a new truth that is the "real truth" or at least closer to whatever the "real truth" is.

For scientists to give up belief in the old truth and accept a new truth as the real truth, any scientist must be able to exactly replicate the experiment and its results. If no other scientist can replicate the experiment and its results, the new truth is judged to be untrue, and the integrity of a scientist continuing to espouse the new truth is deemed questionable.

But, what if only a very small number of scientists are able to replicate the results? Usually, the replication is explained away as a function of collusion, delusion, experimental error, or coincidence.

Most of us believe that the scientific method's benchmark of universally replicable results can be applied to a question like, "Does the afterlife really exist?" There was a time when I believed that. But I've discovered that a distinction exists between what might be called physical and nonphysical realities. Within physical reality, experiments can measure properties, and these measurements can be replicated. But in my quest to discover the truth about our afterlife's existence, I've discovered that replication of results by all investigators is no longer a reliable standard. Experience convinces me that the beliefs of the experimenter actually become part of any such experiment and are the determining factor in its results. I call this the belief factor. That is, the beliefs of the experimenter can be the determining factor in the results of such experiments.

As an example of this belief factor, I'd point to a series of remote staring experiments run by two Ph.D. researchers. A detailed description of this experiment is in *The Journal of Parapsychology* (vol. 61, no. 3, Sept. 1997: p. 197).

Dr. Marilyn Schlitz, of the Institute of Noetic Sciences (IONS), attempted to duplicate the results of a remote staring experiment previously run in the 1930s, to determine if it was true that a person being surreptitiously stared at by another person could detect the staring. The original experiment had answered that question in the affirmative, and Dr. Schlitz's experiment confirmed that result.

Dr. Richard Wiseman, reading about Dr. Schlitz's experiment, ran the identical experiment, but his results clearly indicated that no such statistical correlation existed! At this point something interesting happened. Drs. Schlitz and Wiseman agreed to run exactly the same experiment, under exactly the same conditions, in exactly the same location. They went to great lengths to eliminate any possible source of differences in their results.

Each test subject (randomly selected from the same pool to eliminate potential differences in test subject populations) was seated in front of a video camera, wired with electronic sensors to detect changes in electrical skin conductance, and left alone to read a book (to provide some distraction from their part in the experiment). A second test subject was seated in a different room that had a television monitor that could be made to display the video camera image of the first test subject.

Drs. Schlitz and Wiseman used exactly the same computer and software to randomly select the timing and conditions of thirty-two testing sessions with each pair of test subjects. During sixteen of these sessions the second test subject was directed to stare at the image of the first test subject on the television monitor. During the other sixteen sessions the second test subject was directed to not stare at the image. During these test sessions either Dr. Schlitz or Dr. Wiseman was seated in a third room, remote from both test subjects, thus eliminating any possibility of physical contact or collusion between themselves and the test subjects. The researchers both ran the same number of experiments with sufficient pairs of test subjects that the results would be statistically significant.

Analysis of the data from Dr. Schlitz's experimental runs clearly demonstrated a statistically verified correlation between staring of the second test subject and changes in the electrical skin conductance of the first test subject. Her data shows that the person being stared at *can* detect remote staring. Analysis of Dr. Wiseman's data clearly demonstrated that there was no statistically verifiable correlation between remote staring and detection. His data shows that the person being stared at *cannot* detect remote staring. Drs. Schlitz and Wiseman ran this experiment more than once with the same result. The only difference these researchers could point to in an attempt to explain this impossible result was this:

Dr. Schlitz believed that detection of remote staring was possible, while Dr. Wiseman did not.

Their experiment demonstrates that some subtle, as yet not understood, mechanism (I call it the belief factor) can actually alter the results of rigorously controlled sessions with test subjects so that the resulting data will conform to the experimenter's beliefs. A direct implication of this belief factor effect is that scientists attempting to replicate the results of the remote staring detection experiment will tend to replicate the results of the scientist whose beliefs they share. This in turn means that the belief factor can change what you experience (and perceive) to conform to your beliefs. If you don't understand that this is possible, and don't learn how to effectively deal with it, the probability of successful afterlife exploration is very, very low.

For example, if you were taught to believe that the *spirit world* is filled with demons, your deceased grandmother could be standing right in front of you and the belief factor can cause you to see a hideous demon instead. If you were taught to believe that the spirit world is fraught with the danger of losing your soul to Satan, your deceased son or daughter could be there in front of you, desperately trying to reach out and touch you to let you know he or she is okay. The belief factor could cause you instead to see one of Satan's minions, pitchfork, tail, fiery eyes, and all. If you've been taught to believe that there is no afterlife, you may explore time after time and find nothing at all. This is why I say the truth is such an important key. Knowing that it exists and understanding how it functions are the keys to eliminating its effects.

The next most important key to your success is understanding that the truth can completely block your perception so that you perceive nothing when what you experience or perceive conflicts with your beliefs. This effect is illustrated in an experience recounted in my second book, *Voyage Beyond Doubt*, in a chapter entitled "Grandma and the Skunk."

Shortly after I moved to Virginia to study with my friend Rebecca, she told me that recently she had been on a long drive, late at night, with a couple of hours' driving still ahead when suddenly the smell of skunk filled her car. Rebecca is kind of peculiar, in my view, because she loves the smell of skunk. As it built up in the car that night she thought to herself, *some poor little skunk's been run over,* but then realized that her long-deceased grandmother was now sitting in the back seat of the car. She started carrying on a conversation and Grandma told her that no skunk had been run over. Instead, she had brought the smell into the car with her. Grandma and the skunk smell reappeared every 20 minutes for the rest of her drive, in order to help Rebecca stay awake.

Several weeks after Rebecca told me this, I was visiting Rebecca at her house, way out in the countryside. Suddenly the strong scent of skunk filled the living room, so strong I felt my eyes beginning to water. I was convinced a skunk had somehow gotten into the house, and I worried about being bitten by a rabid skunk.

Rebecca told me that it was just her Grandma, visiting, bringing the smell.

"That's impossible!" I said, with an engineer's college-educated certainty. "She couldn't do a thing like that!" In the next *millisecond* the smell of skunk completely disappeared. I don't mean it gradually dissipated. I mean, it went away like the light from a bulb when you flip the switch. One instant it was there with all its eye-watering power, and in the next instant it was gone. I jumped up and started running from room to room. I *knew* it was impossible for such a strong smell to instantly disappear from every room at once, but I couldn't detect the odor anywhere in the house. Later Rebecca asked me if I had learned anything from Grandma's visit. "You were smelling the odor of a skunk so strongly you said it felt like your eyes would start watering. Something happened, and then you couldn't smell it any more. What do you supposed made it go away in an instant?"

"I had just expressed my doubt about the possibility of a nonphysical person being capable of inducing the smell of a skunk in my nose," I replied.

"Would you say you were expressing your *belief* that such a thing was impossible?"

"Yes, you could put it that way. I don't believe it's possible."

"Yet, you claimed the way it disappeared from the house is also impossible, didn't you?"

Based on my understanding of chemical concentrations in air, and with the lack of air movement through the house, it was also impossible. In the absence of air movement, on a still night, it could take hours for the last vestiges of the smell to be gone. But, for the smell to be as strong as it was, a skunk would have had to have sprayed in the house. In either case, it was impossible for the smell to have disappeared so quickly.

"And yet, you experienced both things, didn't you?"

"Yes, and that's not possible either!" I stammered.

"What possible explanation could there be for your experience?" Rebecca asked, with a sly grin.

"It's not physically possible. I suppose that leaves open the possibility that it might be nonphysically possible."

"Keep going."

"If it was a nonphysical smell, I sensed it before I had any time to make a judgment about it based on my beliefs. I experienced a nonphysical skunk smell that you claim your grandmother brought with her, or created or something. But my experience conflicted with what I've come to accept as *true reality*, and so I denied the possibility. As soon as I denied it was possible, the smell disappeared from my experience. My denial of the possibility of my own direct experience prevented me from continuing to experience it. The nonphysical reality of that smell can only be perceived if I'm willing to accept that my own direct experience is real. If I deny its existence, I have no way to experience or detect it."

At that time, I wasn't convinced there was an afterlife—meaning, I still held beliefs that conflicted with its existence. Rebecca's grandmother and the nonphysical skunk smell she brought led me to some understanding of the profound power of beliefs to distort and block my perception.

All of us have taken on beliefs about the afterlife, from our religions, schools, science, our parents, friends, and culture. Most of us have accepted beliefs that now block our perception beyond physical reality. The one thing that will prevent you from learning to explore beyond physical reality and prove to yourself that our afterlife is real will be your inability to eliminate whatever beliefs conflict with our afterlife's existence. A primary task in learning to explore our afterlife is eliminating the beliefs that distort and block your perception.

How do we do that? The most effective way I've found can be summed up in this concept:

Having an experience that conflicts with a belief and accepting that experience as real eliminates the belief and the distortion and blockage of perception that belief causes, thus opening perception.

Within that statement is a paradox. In order to eliminate a belief that blocks perception one must have an experience that this belief, itself, is blocking from perception. The belief that ghosts do not exist will tend to prevent you from seeing ghosts. But, in order to eliminate that belief, you have to see a ghost. Paradox.

Grandma and the Skunk showed me one way around this paradox. The smell of skunk entered my perception and experience before I was told of its source. As long as I did not know the supposed origin of this smell I could perceive it. Only after Rebecca told me that the source was her deceased grandmother were my beliefs confronted by the experience. And only after I expressed disbelief (by saying *"that's impossible"*) was my perception of that smell immediately and completely blocked. It's almost as if my beliefs are not enforced under special circumstances, which I call *windows of opportunity.*

During a window of opportunity we can perceive experiences that would normally conflict with our beliefs and trigger a perceptual blockage. That window remains open until some part of our awareness realizes the experience conflicts with a belief and (immediately and automatically) attempts to pull the curtain over the window. But, even though the belief eventually blocks the conflicting experience, *we have still had that experience.* To the extent we can accept any part of the experience as real, some or all of the belief will be removed, thereby removing some or all of the perceptual blockage the belief causes and further opening perception to future experience. Here's an example of a fairly common window of opportunity experience.

Suddenly you begin thinking about a friend you haven't spoken to in a long time, casually wondering if he still drives as recklessly as your last ride with him. In the next moment the telephone rings and before you pick up the phone you *know* it's your friend calling. Sure enough, you pick up the phone, say hello, and it's your friend on the line. If you're the kind of person who believes there is no such thing as telepathic communication, what will you do with this window of opportunity experience? If you're like me you'll probably witness your beliefs attempting damage control.

You might find yourself explaining it away as a lucky guess, or an amazing coincidence. That might prevent you from exploring this experience any further—until your friend starts talking about the car accident he was in today. More flukes, lucky guesses, or meaningless events?

Explaining it away leads to the status quo. The other path, withholding judgment and accepting the experience as real, leads to the ability to communicate telepathically. But it may take many experiences to completely eliminate the belief using only random *window of opportunity* type experiences.

Fortunately, you can intentionally open these windows using simple, effective techniques. One workshop participant (I'll call her Jane), hearing my lecture on beliefs, asked for a specific technique she could use to trigger belief-conflicting experiences. As she put it, "I don't know what beliefs I have that are blocking my perception, or what kind of experiences I need to have to eliminate them." So her question was, *if I don't even know what the beliefs are, how can I find a way to open a window of opportunity?*

I suggested that she shift her awareness to placing intent consciousness, and express her desire to have an experience that would conflict with her afterlife beliefs. I was sure it sounded simplistic, but unbeknownst to me, during a workshop break she found a quiet place and gave some thought to wording an affirmation to express her desire. She then remembered the feeling of placing intent she'd experienced during the Silly Little Finger Bending Exercise, and said, *I desire to have an experience that will conflict with my beliefs about the afterlife.* A week or two after the workshop Jane e-mailed me to share the results.

She had awakened during the night and had seen a cloud of lighted fog floating in her bedroom doorway. As she focused her attention on the cloud, it transformed into an apparition of her deceased mother-in-law, Nadine.

During their ensuing conversation Jane asked Nadine to show, tell, or give her something that would prove she was really talking to a dead person. Nadine said that she'd left something for her son, Jane's husband, at the hospital where she worked as a nurse before her death. Nadine suggested they call the hospital to find out what it was.

The next day Jane pestered her husband until he called the hospital to find out if it was true his mother had left something there for him. It took a little digging and the usual run-around, being passed from one hospital clerk and administrator to another. But he discovered that his mother had been paying into an annuity for him, in his name, for several years. No one in the family knew this annuity existed until Jane's husband made that phone call. No doubt it would have eventually become known, when the hospital administrator got around to it, but Jane was convinced she'd gotten the information from Nadine—who was known to be deceased. Getting previously unknown information from Nadine's apparition that was later verified as accurate forced Jane to accept that Nadine continues to exist after physical death. Jane further shared with me that since that incident her perception of and ability to communicate with those in our afterlife had greatly improved. She had an experience that conflicted with her afterlife beliefs and accepted that experience as real, removing the blockage and expanding her perception.

Beliefs and Identity

It took me quite a while to understand why—if improving perception beyond physical reality is a simple matter of eliminating beliefs—it is so difficult to accomplish. Finally my *Punky* experience, described in *Voyage Beyond Doubt*, showed me the relationship between my beliefs and my identity.

About three and a half years after I began to actively seek proof of our afterlife's existence, a friend whom I'll call Rosalie asked me to check on her recently deceased father, whom I will call Joe. I still harbored beliefs conflicting with our afterlife's existence, but I agreed to try to contact him. My mind's eye images showed me Joe in a hospital bed, in the company of his wife, Sylvia, who had predeceased him. I wanted desperately to get something from him that would prove—as much to myself as to Rosalie—that my visit was real. So, I asked him for something I could give his daughter as proof.

I could see Joe's lips moving in response, but I couldn't hear what he was saying. I asked him to repeat it so many times Joe became visibly exasperated.

Finally, as he mouthed the word, the image of a pumpkin popped into my mind and I heard someone say, "Punkin." (I don't mean I just *imagined* I heard it. It was like someone *said it,* out loud, and I heard it with my physical ears.) My mind suddenly raced back to the memory of my own father calling my little sister "Punkin" when she was a little girl, and I immediately concluded that Joe was giving me Rosalie's childhood pet name. But when I told Rosalie, she laughed and told me the word was his dog's name, "Punky." From the time she had arrived at her father's hospital bedside after the accident, until he died just two nights later, every time he was awake he made her promise to take care of his pet dog, Punky. And I thought, well, it was a pet name for Rosalie that validated the contact, just not a pet name in the way I'd interpreted it.

That experience greatly conflicted with beliefs I held about our afterlife's nonexistence—and about myself. Before this experience I wasn't certain our afterlife existed, and I strongly believed that even if it did it would take a special gift or talent that I did not possess to actually hear a dead person say anything. But I had directly experienced hearing the word, and was forced to accept that experience as real. My world crumbled and fell.

For the next two days I wandered around in a daze. I felt so disoriented that I literally swayed so much when I walked down the hall that I bounced off the walls. I felt disassociated from my physical body to the point that although I knew my body was sitting or walking, I was somewhere else. I didn't know who I was anymore, why I was still living, or what possible purpose my continued living could have. It felt like I might die soon, or had already died and didn't know it. It felt like I was grieving the loss of someone, but I didn't know whom. It felt like at any moment the scene around me would fade to black and I'd be left floating in some black formless void forever.

The worst part was that I could hear within my thoughts the voice of someone who appeared to have taken over my mind. It felt like he—whoever this was—was looking over events in my past and explaining aspects of those events I hadn't been aware of at the time. He was making all these associations back and forth to other experiences and sorting things out with profound insight. What I heard in my thoughts was making a lot of sense. Whoever was talking was doing a really good job of explaining things, but it felt like it wasn't me doing the talking. Very unnerving. We all have a sense of who we are. I couldn't feel those familiar feelings that identified me as me. I didn't know who I was any more.

Over a period of several days, I was pretty dysfunctional. If it hadn't been for my wife I doubt I would have remembered to eat or sleep. Very strange. Then, gradually the symptoms began to subside. I began to feel that, if the world around me did fade to black, some time later a new scene would materialize around me and I'd be living in a completely new world. I regained control over my body and didn't bounce off the walls any more. I began to realize that the voice I was hearing in my thoughts wasn't a stranger. It was a part of me that had always been there, previously blocked from my perception. I had become a different person. I was born again with a new identity.

What I've described I now call a *Belief-System Crash* and the *reintegration* that follows. If I'd visited a shrink describing those same symptoms he or she might have suggested I was experiencing an identity crisis and recovery. I'd agree with that diagnosis and here's my present understanding of what happened.

A list of every belief I hold, consciously or subconsciously, defines my identity. That list is who and what I believe myself to be. My Beliefs = My Identity. To illustrate what happened after *Punky* let's say I take each belief from my list and use it to label a little glass marble. Some of these beliefs are related to one another and as I use these marbles to assemble a model of my identity I'll put the related ones close to each other. For example, one marble that makes up my identity represents my belief in gravity. Other related beliefs might be: *what goes up must come down, I can't jump very high, gravity prevents me from flying around the room, I can't lift a car off the ground,* or *I can easily lift a feather.* As I assemble this model of my identity I'll draw lines between these interrelated, interconnected beliefs to show that they support each other.

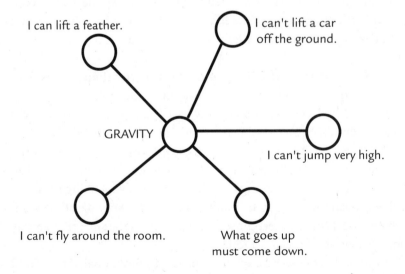

These interconnected, interrelated beliefs form a localized, self-supporting structure within my identity. They form a belief system. Let's say that I've formed a huge, solid sphere of interconnected marbles representing all of my beliefs and belief systems. This sphere represents the whole of my identity. As long as my experience does not conflict with any of my beliefs, they—and hence the portions of my identity they represent—survive. But what happens if I have an experience that conflicts with, say, my belief in gravity?

What if while I'm lecturing during a workshop I am suddenly floating up into the air? What if I begin to float out over the crowd, and I see everyone's eyes follow the movement that I feel? I'm having an experience that conflicts with my belief in gravity, and by the looks on everyone's faces, and their eyes following the movements I'm experiencing, I am forced to accept this experience as real. If I accept this experience as real, the marble representing my conflicting belief must disappear. Connections from that marble to others in its localized, self-supporting belief system also disappear. As this experience flows to other marbles within the belief system, acceptance of the experience as real may cause some of them to also disappear. This dissolution process will continue until my acceptance of the experience no longer conflicts with the marbles it encounters as it flows through my identity. When the process is complete, I will have lost some of my marbles, leaving a void in my identity. This is commonly experienced as the feeling of a big, gaping hole.

When I heard a dead man say Punkin and his daughter verified its meaning, I was forced to accept that our afterlife exists. I was forced to accept that an ungifted, no-talent person like me could actually hear the voice of a dead man. In a very short span of time all the beliefs and belief systems I held that conflicted with this experience—a huge portion of my identity—disappeared. I opened this chapter by saying that my world is built, as all worlds are, on beliefs. When I lost my afterlife-belief marbles, my world crumbled and crashed.

I now understand that the disassociation and disorientation I experienced were symptoms of a tenuous connection to what was left of my worldview. I had become disconnected from the reality surrounding me. The feeling of that black formless void was my awareness of the huge hole in my identity left behind by Punky. Feeling like I might die soon was my misinterpretation of something that had already happened. Part of me, the marbles that dissolved and disappeared, died as a result of that experience. As the *Punky* experience flowed through my identity, more would die. Feeling like I might die soon was my limited understanding of the ongoing process as that experience encountered other conflicting beliefs and caused more marbles to disappear. That voice I heard in my thoughts was part of that process, not an outsider. It was a new me, a portion of my identity whose perception was no longer blocked, colored, and distorted by those old, dead beliefs. As this new me looked back over its past experiences, gaining new insights into their meaning, those insights both dissolved more marbles and formed new interconnections between the parts of my identity that survived. That's the process of *reintegration*. New belief system structures were being formed. My identity was in the process of redefining itself. My feeling that I'd come out of that black, formless void into a scene in a new world was my limited understanding of the process of reintegration. As that reintegration process continued, I did indeed find myself living in a new world, a world that includes our afterlife as a real place populated by real people.

As my post-Punky reintegration continued, I noticed that it was much easier for me to make contact with the deceased, and to gather verifiable information from them. After a certain amount of reintegration such things became routine. Losing those old beliefs meant that information flowing into my awareness was no longer filtered, blocked, colored, distorted, or edited in the same way. You could think of those beliefs as little pieces of colored cellophane stuck in layers to the window of my perception. As the distortion of each one is removed, my perception becomes clearer and less obstructed. I might say I had a clearer picture of information flowing into my awareness, and a clearer understanding of its meaning. With my perception open wider and clearer, it was easier to have more experiences that conflicted with other beliefs. When these new experiences could be accepted as real, more of the old beliefs dissolved and disappeared, taking their distortion, blocks, and editing with them. I began to realize I was in a process that led to ever-widening, ever-clearing perception. That's the upside of Belief-System Crashes. Reintegration creates a new you with clearer perception and clearer understanding. The downside is the emotional upheaval we go through, the identity crisis and all the feelings that go with it. In my experience, once I caught on to this, the identity crisis feelings in future Belief-System Crashes were softer since I knew and understood they were just a part of a normal, natural process leading to clearer perception and understanding. Since Punky, my Belief-System Crashes have been little bumps in the road by comparison. Yet, I still have a couple of cautions to pass along and since I'm a storyteller I'll use another true story to illustrate the first caution.

A friend of a friend was having a problem. As we talked on the phone I recognized that she was describing the symptoms of a Belief-System Crash: feelings of disassociation and disorientation; feelings like she might die soon; feeling like she was grieving the death of someone, but not sure who; feeling like somebody else was using her mind to be thinking her thoughts; feeling like she really had no idea of the purpose of living. I shared my Punky experience and the feelings that followed, and said what I'd come to believe that experience meant.

More than a year later, I learned the rest of her story. Not long before the woman had called me, her boyfriend had died and a short time later had appeared to her. Things that happened during his visit, and things he said, made it impossible for her not to accept that our afterlife is real. When she began to feel that she might die soon, she misinterpreted those feelings to mean that she was *supposed* to die. When she called me that day she had a loaded 9mm pistol in her safe, waiting for the day she knew she was supposed to die. After our talk on the phone she realized those feelings didn't mean she was supposed to die, but rather, that part of her had already died. She realized she didn't need to use the pistol to end her life.

The reason I tell her story is that as you explore our afterlife you may experience the symptoms of a Belief-System Crash. If and when you do, *remember what you read here today.* Experiencing these feelings and symptoms is part of the normal, natural process of eliminating old beliefs and opening perception. As you reintegrate your identity these symptoms will fade away. Misinterpreting these feelings can get serious.

A second caution: Pace yourself.

Some of us are so driven to expand our perception that we refuse to give ourselves time to reintegrate. An experience causes a crash, opens perception, and we continue pushing too hard for more such experiences. A little of that is fine, but it can be carried too far. As perception opens further, the possibility increases that you will have a new experience that conflicts with even more of your beliefs. If you keep pushing for more experiences without giving yourself time to reintegrate your identity, you can start a chain reaction in which new experiences dissolve your identity faster than you can reintegrate it. In a sense you lose too many marbles at once. I call that a Chain Reaction Belief-Systems Crash and I do not recommend the experience. I'm certain that some people are locked up in mental institutions for no other reason than that things happened to them (not necessarily afterlife related) that caused this kind of chain reaction crash of their identity. They lost so many marbles they became dysfunctional.

To sum up my first and second cautions, here are feelings associated with what I call a Belief-System Crash:

Disorientation

Disassociation

Wondering if you're going insane

Feeling like you don't know who you are anymore

Feeling like you've lost your purpose in life

Feeling grief as if someone close to you has died, but you don't know who

Feeling like someone else is thinking within your mind

Feeling like your world is crashing down around you

Feeling like you might die soon

Feeling like you *should* die

Finding yourself thinking about suicide

If you begin to experience these symptoms, remember what you've read in this section on beliefs and identity.

Think about whether some of your recent experiences may have conflicted with your beliefs. Slow down! Give yourself time to reintegrate.

I don't mean to scare anyone. My experience indicates that our identity can take quite a thrashing as our perception opens, and it will do just fine. Knowing that what is going on is just part of the normal, natural process of opening perception softened future Belief-System Crash experiences for me. Know from my experience, and that of many others, that these feelings will pass as you reintegrate your identity. Be gentle with yourself and give yourself time to reintegrate before pushing for more conflicting experiences.

While we're on the subject of reintegration I'd like to pass along a few tips that I've found to help accelerate the reintegration process. And of course to explain what I mean, it's time for another story.

A friend e-mailed me to say that his mother had died and his dad seemed to have lost his will to live. He asked for advice to help his dad recover from the loss. I asked him to tell me about something his dad liked to do before he was married and stopped doing after he'd married. It turned out the man was a woodworker who built beautiful, handcrafted furniture before he married. When his new wife complained about the mess of sawdust and wood chips he tracked into the house, he'd given up woodworking. I advised my friend to ask his father to build him a piece of furniture (it didn't matter what it was) and if necessary gently force the issue. My friend asked his dad to build a small dresser for his granddaughter (my friend's daughter), which he did. Within a week or so the symptoms began to subside and the man's father began to recover from the death of his wife, and the loss of identity it represented.

When a spouse dies, that part of our identity that was that person dies with them. In essence that person has become some of our marbles. The symptoms the surviving spouse experiences are the same identity crisis symptoms as any other form of Belief-System Crash. By going back to wood-working, something he had enjoyed before marriage changed his identity, my friend's father reconnected with a part of his identity that existed before he married. This reconnection provided an anchor to that part of himself that survived the crash, and that anchor provided a sort of focal point from which the reintegration process could occur more smoothly and easily. ·

If you begin to experience the symptoms of a Belief-System Crash, first think back to your recent experiences, looking for the cause of the crash. Stop pushing so hard for more belief conflicting experiences. Then think about things you liked to do before the crash that are not connected to the experience that triggered it. Maybe you haven't been sailing on the ocean for a while, maybe you enjoy woodworking, perhaps you never find time to read a romance novel. Whatever it is, do it. In my experience the symptoms begin to subside more quickly, and the reintegration process is faster and easier using this technique. As you experience this reintegration you'll discover that your perception improves, too.

As I said earlier, our beliefs have a profound effect on our ability to *accurately* perceive within physical and nonphysical realities. Keep in mind as you continue that one of your major tasks is to eliminate the beliefs that block your perception, and that even the reality we call physical may not be as solid as it seems.

The ability of beliefs to color, block, distort, and alter our perception is at once subtle and powerful. My story about disappearing peanut butter jars illustrates this.

In the 1970s while taking a lunch break from building a house, I was standing at the kitchen counter trying to decide if I was going to make my peanut butter sandwich with organic peanut butter or Skippy. Staring at two slices of bread, already laid out on the counter, I decided on the fancy peanut butter. As I looked up into the open cupboard not a foot in front of my face I was thinking, *okay, where is the fancy peanut butter?*

I could see other things in the cupboard, a box of Rice-a-Roni, bottles of spices and such, but the peanut butter jar wasn't there. Looking back down at my bread I thought, *that's odd, the peanut butter is supposed to be there, guess I'll have to use the Skippy. Okay, where is the Skippy?* I shifted my gaze back to the cupboard: the Rice-a-Roni and spices were still plainly visible, but the Skippy was nowhere to be seen. Looking back down at my bread I thought, *this is ridiculous! That's where both jars of peanut butter always are!* When I looked back up into the cupboard, both jars of peanut butter were directly in front of my eyes, not ten inches away. Quickly shifting my gaze back down to the bread, I closed my eyes and remembered what I'd seen the two times the peanut butter jars were not there. (I pictured the Rice-a-Roni box, spices, boxes, jars, etc.) Looking back up, I moved the peanut butter jars out of the way and everything I'd seen was sitting exactly where I remembered it.

It took a while to come up with an explanation for how such a thing could happen.

Each time I'd looked for the peanut butter my *frame of mind*—my temporary belief—was, *where is the peanut butter*. Think about the logic of that belief. Perceiving the reality around me through the *filter* of wondering where the peanut butter jar is implies a belief that I don't (and can't) know where it is. Holding that implied belief caused my perception of the peanut butter jars to be blocked to avoid a conflict between belief and perception. So, they disappeared! I'm fond of saying that physical reality is not as solid as it seems.

Many years later my wife and I were watching television. She'd heard the story of the disappearing peanut butter jars, but I'm sure she didn't believe things could really disappear. I looked at the spot where the remote channel changer usually was, and it wasn't there. I asked, *where is the channel changer?* We both started looking for it. There was a narrow open space behind the sofa I was sitting on and my wife walked around behind the sofa to see if the channel changer had somehow fallen on the floor behind it.

I decided it was possible I was sitting on the channel changer, so I stood up to look. It wasn't where I was sitting. There was a short stack of newspapers on the sofa, next to where I'd been sitting, and I thought perhaps the changer was under them. My wife was looking at my hands as I scooped up the newspapers and looked under them. No channel changer. Looking at my wife I said, *well, it will probably show up at some point.* Before I sat back down on the sofa, there was the channel changer, sitting so close to the newspapers that my hand would have had to go through it in order to pick up the papers. When I looked at my wife she said, "Damn! Now you've got that peanut butter jar thing happening to me!"

As an aside, a friend taught me a technique to get around this problem. Instead of saying, *where is the channel changer?* say, *I need the channel changer.* Needing the channel changer is a different frame of mind, it is holding a different belief with different implications and expectations for the channel changer's whereabouts.

Here's a way for you to experiment with the subtle power of even implied, temporary beliefs. The next time you're scurrying around the house, trying to find your car keys or something, stop moving. Think about your frame of mind. Are you thinking something like, *where are my car keys?* Say to yourself, *I need my car keys.* Then, just start moving. It doesn't matter which direction you go, just start moving. Follow any impulse you have. You may even discover that you find your key cars in a spot you've looked several times in your scurrying!

At a recent workshop I told the story of the disappearing peanut butter jars and suggested the above experiment whenever the opportunity presented itself. That evening during dinner, the workshop hostess shared the story with her husband. The next evening her husband shared the results of his impromptu experiment.

There was a special pair of gloves he liked to wear when he was pheasant hunting. He wore them on other occasions also and it had been so long since he'd seen them he had no idea where the gloves were. Just as he was about to start searching for the gloves he remembered the disappearing peanut butter jar story. So, he stopped searching and said to himself, *I need my hunting gloves.* He said an image of a toolbox he hadn't been into for months suddenly popped into his mind's eye. He looked in that toolbox, and the gloves were there.

A woman from a Seattle workshop and her husband were trying to find a pair of his work boots he needed for a special job. They'd turned the house upside down, looked in every closet, on every shelf, and in every storage box in the house. No boots. She remembered the peanut butter jar story, stopped and said to herself, *I need my husband's boots.* Seconds later the phone rang. It was her husband's mother calling to say that he'd left a pair of boots at her house quite a while ago and if they needed them that's where the boots were.

So, next time you're trying to find something, stop and take a few moments to explore your frame of mind. Ask yourself what beliefs are implied and what effects they might have. You'll probably realize that you've gotten your frame of mind into a state of consciousness in which the thing you are searching for can't be. Say to yourself, *I need my . . .* and see what happens. You may begin to think, as I do, that this physical reality we live in is not as solid as it seems. Such a belief has some very interesting consequences for one's perception.

Changing and Eliminating Beliefs

When it comes to changing beliefs I'm a crash, burn, and recover kind of person. The surest way I know of to change beliefs is to intend to have experiences that conflict with them, have that experience, and then deal with the resulting Belief-System Crash and reintegration. While it's very effective and my personally preferred method, it relies on pursuing and waiting for such belief-conflicting experiences to arise. Another, more consciously directed way to change beliefs is a little gentler, and relies on a concept that may be new to you. It also relies on your becoming aware of the cues that indicate a belief is actively blocking your perception.

The new concept, which may conflict with your beliefs, is that we can create alternate selves, called Aspects of Self. If this strains credibility, that's okay, it's just a concept, a way for me to teach a technique for eliminating and changing beliefs. In this concept some of the Aspects of Self we create, consciously or subconsciously, function to hold and enforce a specific belief. They appear to operate automatically, and we may have little if any awareness of their existence. These Aspects act independently to apply the effects of the belief in situations the Aspect deems appropriate. That might be a lot of concept for you to swallow in one gulp, but my experience indicates that even if actual Aspects of Self don't exist, they are a useful way of illustrating something very real about how the effects of beliefs influence our consciousness and how to change or eliminate them.

An example to illustrate this concept of Aspects of Self might revolve around the belief that falling down can cause pain and injury to your body. Through experiences in the physical world in early childhood most of us came to believe this. I would say that most of us created an Aspect of Self to hold that belief and to function in a way that automatically attempts to prevent us from falling down. Whenever we embark on an experience that could lead to falling down, this Aspect of Self may decide the belief it holds must be enforced to prevent injuring ourselves. That Aspect will act in some way to resist our attempts to carry through with the experience. This is a useful belief-based limitation affecting where we ought to be willing to put our body. Try to get me to stand on a skinny little tightrope stretched between two poles 60 feet off the ground and I'm most likely going to feel some resistance to climbing that flimsy little rope ladder one uses to get up to the tightrope.

The Aspect of myself holding the belief that falling can cause pain and injury will do whatever it can to stop me from climbing that flimsy ladder to the tightrope. My arms and legs may suddenly feel too weak to climb. I may become frozen in fear, or I may suddenly remember that I've got an appointment at the dentist and don't have time to walk tightropes today. That Aspect I've entrusted to hold and enforce the belief will do whatever it can to stop my body from being put in a dangerous position.

Suppose I decide to learn tightrope walking. I'd have to change those "falling leads to pain and injury beliefs" as least as far as tightrope walking is concerned. To illustrate this gentler method of changing beliefs I'm suggesting, I'll use an imaginary conversation with the Aspect of myself holding the belief about pain and injury due to falling. We'll start with me standing at the bottom of that skinny little ladder I have to climb to get to the tightrope. As I reach for the ladder to begin my climb I realize I'm suddenly feeling weak in the knees and my feet feel glued to the floor by fear. I've just taken the first and most critical step in changing beliefs. *That is, I've become aware that I'm being prevented from doing something I desire to do.* My climb to the tightrope is being blocked, and that's my clue that an Aspect is enforcing a belief. Realizing this, I take the next step in changing beliefs: I take in 3DRB and 3EGB to prepare to explore this belief more consciously. That exploration is done by contacting and dialoguing with the Aspect holding the belief.

I know this might sound a little strange, but the next step in Changing Beliefs is to begin a conversation with that Aspect to learn what the belief is, why it is being enforced, and how it is being enforced. I'd suggest you begin learning this Changing Belief technique by pretending the conversation. I might open such a conversation by saying something like . . .

"I'd like to speak to the Aspect of myself preventing me from climbing this ladder."

"Yeah, what do you want?" a little boy's voice replies, in my thoughts.

"I want to climb this ladder. Why can't I?"

"Are you kidding! That sucker goes at least 60 feet up in the air! If I let you climb this ladder you might fall and wreck our body!"

"What is the belief you're holding and exercising, and where did this belief come from?"

"You took on beliefs about falling and getting hurt at a very early age," the little boy replies, within my mind. "I call the belief: 'little fall little injury, big fall big injury.'"

"Why are you exercising this belief right now?"

"You must be joking! Just climbing this ladder could lead to a really big fall, and furthermore, walking on that tightrope is totally out of the question!"

"How are you applying this belief in this case?"

"This belief seems to apply to this situation so I'm sending out signals of fear to paralyze our body so you can't move it up that ladder."

"But I really want to learn how to walk a tightrope!"

"Not if it's going to wreck our body, no way!"

In this conversation you have learned what the belief is, and why and how it is being enforced. The next step in Changing Beliefs is to thank the Aspect for holding and exercising the belief, and begin to define a new function for this Aspect. Continuing with the conversation I might say:

"I appreciate that you hold the 'little falls little injury, big falls big injury' belief for me. I'm thankful for all the times you've exercised that belief and prevented injury to our body, but in this instance, when I want to practice tightrope walking, that belief does not apply."

"Why not?"

"Because I desire to learn about tightrope walking!"

"So?"

"So I'm going to take responsibility for the safety of our body. I'm going to move very slowly up the ladder and be very careful to hang on and not fall off."

"But preventing that very thing is my function! That's why I hold and enforce this belief for you!" the little boy's voice screams.

"You can continue to act as I've come to believe about falling and injuring our body in every other case except this ladder climbing and tightrope walking right now. In this case we're going to change those beliefs. I take responsibility for this change."

"But, but . . ."

"It's what I desire."

"Okay. I'm still going to signal a little fear just so you don't forget to be careful but not enough to paralyze our body."

"Thank you."

You've just completed the next step in Changing Beliefs. You've stated that in this specific instance, while you are consciously taking responsibility for your actions, the belief is not to be applied or enforced. You created this Aspect and gave it its original function, and you can change it. At this point in the process of Changing Beliefs, I've met the Aspect of myself responsible, thanked it for performing its function and protecting me, and expressed my desire to change my beliefs to learn something I want to learn—tightrope walking. The Aspect has relinquished control of my body to the point I can now climb the ladder. Let's move to halfway up the ladder, where I again begin to feel fear and have difficulty continuing my climb. Taking in 3DRB and 3EGB, I focus my attention on the Aspect and hear . . . or pretend to hear . . .

"Are you sure you really desire to do this? We're up pretty far above the floor and if you slip and fall our body is going to get messed up bad."

Aspects can be very persistent in enforcing the beliefs they hold!

"Look! I desire it! Signals from that old belief are interfering with the concentration I need to safely climb this ladder. If you don't change it, your interference may be responsible for my losing concentration. If I slip and fall you'll be responsible! We both want to complete this climb without injury to our body, so be quiet unless you have something constructive to say."

"Okay," the little boy voice says, or I pretend it says. "Watch out for the third rung up. It's a little slipperier then the rest. Otherwise everything's okay."

"You're right. I can feel it's a little slick. I'll take special care on that rung. Thank you for your input."

So I keep climbing up the ladder toward the platform above. I get to the platform and I'm about to take my first steps onto the tightrope. My knees start to feel weak and wobbly and my hands feel glued to the platform railing. That I cannot do what I desire to do is again a clue that an Aspect is acting to enforce a belief. I again open a dialogue with the Aspect I suspect of being responsible.

"Hey, I told you I desire to learn about tightrope walking. Why can't I move?"

"You said you only wanted me to stop enforcing the belief in this specific instance and we were climbing the ladder when you said that. As I see it, walking on that skinny little tightrope is not the same specific instance so the belief I hold applies."

"Yes, thank you for holding that belief and exercising it, but in this instance the belief does not apply."

"Why not?"

"Because I desire to learn about tightrope walking."

"I don't know . . . it looks pretty easy to fall off that skinny little rope."

"You're right. I might fall off the rope."

"We might fall? From way up here?"

"Yes, we might, but if you'll look below us you'll see there's a safety net. We can safely fall without injury to our body."

"But . . . but . . . I'll have to experience falling? Everything about the belief I hold for us is based on never letting our body fall. Never, never, never!"

"Well, in this case it's safe to fall. So, in this specific instance, when there is a safety net below the tightrope I am walking on, I want you to hold the belief that it's okay to fall."

"You're sure that's what you want?"

"Yes."

Very often the process of Changing Beliefs has several steps. I force myself to take two steps out on the tightrope. I'm maintaining my concentration and balance just fine when I hear . . .

"But . . . but . . . but what if you lose your balance and we fall and get hurt even with the net? I can't let you do this! I'm going to freeze up every muscle in our body with fear to stop you from going any further . . ."

With every muscle in my body frozen I can't maintain my balance. After an uncontrollable lean to my left, I'm past the point of no return, and falling toward the net.

"Oops," I hear the little voice say.

The Aspect has just discovered that its old methods of controlling the body don't always work very well in new situations. I'm falling toward the net and I can hear the Aspect's little boy's voice screaming in terror all the way the down. After landing in it safely and bouncing a few times . . .

"That was absolutely terrifying! Body doesn't seem to be injured anywhere," I hear little boy's voice say. "Lucky for us the net was there."

"It wasn't lucky. I took responsibility and arranged for the net to be there. That's why you can change the belief in this specific case. We were doing fine until you tried to take over control."

"Yeah, guess the usual paralyze-with-fear method isn't going to be effective to protect our body in this situation. Maybe I should try something else? Wait a minute, you're climbing up the ladder again? Didn't you get enough the first time?"

"No, I didn't. I desire to learn more about tightrope walking and less about falling into a net!"

"Really?"

"Yes, and I suggest this time you put your efforts to control the body into something more useful than paralyzing fear."

"Like what for instance?"

I've made it to the platform and I'm ready to take my first steps onto the tightrope. I stop, take in 3DRBs and 3EGBs and ask for help to formulate a new belief, an Affirmation that will help me learn to walk the tightrope. The word "Balance" comes to mind. I'm ready to change the belief this Aspect holds in a way that will actually help me learn to walk the tightrope. I shift my awareness to placing intent consciousness and addressing that Aspect and I might say . . .

"I'd like you to focus all of your attention on the location of my body's center of gravity. I'd like you to do whatever is necessary to subconsciously control all the muscles in my body to keep my center of gravity directly, vertically, over the tightrope."

"Oh, okay. I'll put all my efforts into balancing body weight directly over the tightrope."

"You have correctly understood my intention and besides, that's how tightrope walking is done. The new belief you are to hold in this instance, when I desire to walk a tightrope is, 'Balance prevents falling and injury.'"

I can now test whether or not I've changed all the beliefs I had that were preventing me from doing what I desired to do. As I practice my tightrope walking I may discover other Aspects holding other beliefs, or other facets of the beliefs I've already found. The key is to recognize that I'm being prevented from doing what I desire to do, and then use the process of Changing Beliefs. While my example might have been a little silly, it contains all the elements of the Process of Changing Beliefs.

The Gentler Process of Changing Beliefs

Recognize you're being blocked from doing what you desire to do.

Ask to communicate with the Aspect of yourself responsible for the limiting belief.

Engage that Aspect of yourself in conversation, dialogue with it. Pretending this dialogue is a great way to start.

Understand what the belief is, its function, and how its enforcement limits you.

Express gratitude for the Aspect's functioning properly in the past.

Use what you've learned about Affirmations and placing intent. Express the desire to change the belief *in the situation you desire to learn about.*

Attempt to do what you desire to do again.

Continue to dialogue with that Aspect of yourself as more facets of the limitation of the belief come up.

Repeat this process until you know the Aspect has incorporated the desired change and is enforcing the new belief.

Changing Beliefs Exercise

As I mentioned earlier, my preferred method of changing beliefs is: to just place intent for an experience that conflicts with beliefs, accept as much of that experience as real as possible, work through any Belief-System Crash that follows, and reintegrate.

Some folks feel that they can think about and analyze beliefs they hold and make any changes at an intellectual level. While that might be true to some extent, no intellectual exercise really changes beliefs that block perception with the power and finality of direct, conflicting experience.

The tightrope-walking example above is a milder form of changing beliefs that can also lead to Belief-System Crashes. Since this method relies on your realizing you are being blocked from doing something you desire to do as it's happening, the real exercise is to be on the alert for such situations. While that makes it a little difficult to give a formal exercise to trigger awareness of a belief system conflict, realizing you're being blocked is the most critical first step in consciously changing beliefs. In reality any of the exercises contained in this *Afterlife Knowledge Guidebook*, or events in your everyday life, can trigger such a situation.

So, the exercise for Changing Beliefs is an ongoing one. From now on, each time you realize you're being blocked from doing something you desire to do, it's an opportunity to open your perception further. Practice, practice, practice, until realizing your efforts are being blocked and using the process of Changing Beliefs becomes your automatic response.

A Workshop Participant Example

Al attended my workshop near Brisbane, Australia, and after a retrieval exercise explained that he hadn't done the exercise that I had led but instead had visited a recently deceased friend. Al and his friend had grown up together and after high school graduation they'd each moved to different cities. It had been 20 years since Al had seen his friend, and a little before the workshop he'd heard his friend had died.

In the debriefing, Al explained that after he placed intent to visit his friend, a fuzzy, black-and-white image of his friend's face appeared a short distance away and began to move toward him. Then, the image began to move away and fade out. Al realized in that moment that he was being blocked from visiting his friend and decided to open a dialogue with the Aspect responsible. He said that after demanding to know what beliefs were preventing him from visiting his friend it was like several silent firecrackers went off in rapid succession. With the first little boom Al heard, *the Spirit World is a dangerous place*; the next boom was followed by, *demons wait to deceive you*; and the next, *Satan will steal your soul*, followed by several others.

Al explained that he realized right away these were beliefs from his religious upbringing. After all the little firecrackers exploded, disclosing all their beliefs, Al had with a wave of his nonphysical arm swept them all aside, mentally saying, *that's a lot of crap I no longer believe in*. According to Al, his friend's image then came back into view and they had a very nice visit during the rest of the exercise.

Dialoguing with an Aspect doesn't have to be a formal, long-drawn-out affair. As Al's experience demonstrates, once the realization is made that a blockage is occurring, changing beliefs can take no more than a sweep of the arm and the expression of the desired change.

From my own experience I know that both processes I've described work to change or eliminate beliefs and their blocking effects. If you use these processes, you should be aware that beliefs are the very bricks and mortar of your identity. Elimination of beliefs can cause a Belief-System Crash and a pattern of uncomfortable feelings. The crash may be so mild you hardly notice it or it may bring your world crashing down around you. I feel it's so important that you remember what I say about this pattern of uncomfortable feelings and how to deal with them I'm going to repeat it below. Remember the symptoms I described on page 56 as accompanying a Belief-System Crash.

If you begin to experience them, stop and remember what you've read in this section, think about your recent experiences, and whether or not some of them might have conflicted with your beliefs. Experiencing the above symptoms does not mean you are going to die, or need to die. They do not mean you are going insane. They mean it is time to slow down, to give yourself time to reintegrate your identity. These feelings are part of the natural process of opening and clearing your perception. As you integrate your new experience into your new identity, these feelings will dissipate. You'll discover you've become a new person with greatly expanded perception and abilities. Be gentle with yourself. Allow yourself time to reintegrate and get to know the new you.

5

Components of Consciousness

To explore the afterlife or any other nonphysical reality (There) you must be able to both observe and remember events that occur There. If you are unable to observe events There and then remember them in physical reality (Here), what you learn about afterlife exploration won't be of much use. You have already learned how to use State-Specific Memory and the Hemi-Sync Model of Consciousness to remember. To understand more about how we bring those events to conscious awareness Here it's helpful to understand the basic process by which our awareness operates. I use the concepts of the Perceiver and the Interpreter to describe it. In my jargon, the role of the Perceiver is observation, and the role of the Interpreter is bringing what is observed to conscious awareness. Each has a specific role to play, and understanding their strengths and weaknesses can greatly accelerate the pace of learning to explore the afterlife.

An Air Force study of bombardiers aboard aircraft points to the difference between the Perceiver and the Interpreter. Bombardiers who were connected to a brainwave-analyzing machine typically manifested a specific brainwave pattern (known to indicate recognition of the ground reference point) a full eight seconds before the bombardier recognized the reference point consciously. This suggests that the information first entered the bombardier's subconscious awareness (Perceiver), and then, after a short delay, his conscious awareness (Interpreter).

The role of the Perceiver is to bring new information into our awareness—at a *subconscious level*. This new information comes into our subconscious awareness as impressions, intuitions, thoughts, feelings, images, sounds, sensations, ideas, a sense of knowing, etc. But, what the Perceiver brings in does not come directly into our conscious awareness, and it appears that the Perceiver has no memory-building function. If *only* the Perceiver is functioning during your afterlife explorations, you'll have no conscious awareness or memory of the events you experience. You could be in a conversation with God, being told all the secrets of the Universe, but you would have no awareness or memory of the experience.

The role of the Interpreter is to bring information from the Perceiver into conscious awareness and in that process to create accessible memory of that information. This Interpreter function is *always done within the context of our beliefs, our language, and our preexisting memories*. In a sense the Interpreter acts as a translator continuously and automatically bringing the Perceiver's information into conscious awareness in an understandable, though not necessarily accurate, form. This translation always occurs within the context of our beliefs, language, and preexisting memories, which in my view is largely responsible for the *not necessarily accurate* statement in the previous sentence.

In my jargon the chatty little internal dialogue we hear in our mind, the one running a constant commentary on our experiences, is the *voice of the Interpreter*. It's through that chatty voice that we become consciously aware of information gathered by the Perceiver, and create accessible memory of that information. Memory of the information is created by building associative links between new information and the *nearest similar things* within preexisting memory.

In your conversation with God, if both the Perceiver and Interpreter are functioning properly, you will be aware of the conversation and get those secrets of the Universe, and you'll be able to remember it later, within the context of your beliefs, language, and preexisting memories. Perhaps sharing how I came to understand how our awareness operates will help you understand this critical issue of afterlife exploration.

I first became aware of the Perceiver and Interpreter during my first Lifeline program at The Monroe Institute. Early in the program's tape-guided experiences, I'd shift my awareness to the area of afterlife consciousness I was to explore, and would vaguely sense something in the empty blackness surrounding me, but any image that might begin to take vague form in my mind's eye would fade and disappear before it became clear. This became a frustrating pattern in my early exploration experiences. The key to understanding what caused these impressions to disappear came when I realized I was talking to myself about nonsense long after the impression faded. I decided that my internal dialogue was somehow responsible for losing contact with what I was observing, and I decided to try to shut that internal dialogue down as a way of maintaining awareness of the impressions.

My first approach was to try to argue the Interpreter's voice into submission. The Interpreter just took whatever argument I presented and started making associations between it and counterarguments in my memory. Its associations to associations to associations meant that arguing with it just gave the Interpreter fodder for rambling on and on and on. Eventually I learned that I could just intentionally relax, and the Interpreter's voice would gradually fade away. Even though this took quite a while to accomplish, it worked. As soon as I'd realize the voice of my internal dialogue was speaking, I'd intentionally relax and it would fade away. If I realized I was talking to myself early enough, the images that faded out as the dialogue started would fade back in as the dialogue's voice faded away. If the Interpreter's voice had run on too long before I realized it was doing so, I had to start the process of perceiving something in the empty darkness around me all over.

As I learned to shut down the Interpreter's voice earlier and earlier, I saw that the Interpreter takes whatever impression the Perceiver has brought into subconscious awareness and associates it with information previously stored in my memory. For example, suppose the impression of a big orange cat came into my awareness as my Perceiver examined one of the vague shapes in the surrounding blackness. The Interpreter would then bring into my awareness some image stored in my memory that is associated with cats, and would supply another image or bit of commentary from my preexisting memory associated with cats. If something about that previously stored memory was associated with dogs, the next image or bit of commentary might well be associated with preexisting dog memories. If one of those memories was associated with a trip to Texas, the next image or commentary could be associated with Texas. The Interpreter would continue supplying related, associated images or commentary to my awareness until it was consciously stopped or my awareness was diverted for some reason. So, in response to my seeing the image of a large orange cat in one of my exploration experiences the Interpreter might supply the following series of thoughts.

Hmmm . . . that looks like a big orange cat . . . I had a cat once that was accidentally locked in a sewing machine case overnight when I was about nine years old . . . We lived in a very small trailer house then . . . I built a house on a lake once, what a job . . . Job, oh yes, my job . . . I will soon be sharing my cubicle with that new guy from Brazil. Brazil . . . I wonder if they grow bananas in Brazil.

The problem with the Interpreter is that if it is allowed to ramble on, it begins making associations with its own associations to the point that what you're talking to yourself about can get so far away from what you originally perceived that you have no idea that it all started with seeing a big orange cat.

Figuring that shutting that voice down earlier and earlier would yield better results, I became extremely vigilant. With practice I got very good at shutting down the voice of my Interpreter's internal dialogue very soon after it started. As I managed to shut down that voice earlier in its running commentary, the images of my exploration experiences were faded out for shorter periods of time. I expected that if I could learn to relax that voice away at the first hint of its starting to talk, the images would remain in full view almost continuously. I expected I'd be utilizing the Perceiver full time, not realizing the implications of doing so.

You know how, if you're in a conversation with someone who refuses to let you get a word in edgewise, you begin to feel a kind of internal pressure to say something? It's almost like a pressure building up in your throat as what you want to say tries to push its way into voiced words. Well, I got so good at sensing when the voice of the Interpreter was about to say something that I experienced that *pressure-in-the-throat feeling* coming from the Interpreter. I got so good at shutting down the Interpreter's voice that I learned to relax away the first hint of that pressure feeling before the Interpreter was able to speak at all. That's when I discovered the limitation of the Perceiver. Not only did the images of my experiences *not* remain in full view continuously as I expected, but I completely lost consciousness.

Many esoteric disciplines teach various forms of meditation intended to help the practitioner to achieve something they call *dropping into the Void*. Monroe Institute jargon would label this a *click out*. Clicking out is a very strange experience. The very first hint you get that a click out has occurred is that you suddenly regain consciousness and it's not like you drifted off and fell asleep. When you wake up from falling asleep you usually have at least some vague memory of the process of drifting off and falling asleep. Clicking out is entirely different. When you regain consciousness after a click out you have absolutely no idea how or when you lost consciousness and no idea how long you were gone. When I come back from a click out there's a feeling like I could have been gone for five seconds or five hundred years, and

I have absolutely no idea which. What's worse, from an afterlife exploration point of view, there is absolutely no memory of anything you experienced during the click out. Clearly, if my desire was to consciously explore our afterlife, my experiments with shutting down the Interpreter's voice had gone too far. I began letting that voice make just a few comments about my experiences before relaxing it away to shut it up. That's when I discovered the real value of the Interpreter's function, creating accessible memory of my experiences.

I realized that when the Interpreter brings from preexisting memory into conscious awareness an image associated with a new image or information the Perceiver is observing, two vital things happen. First, the associated image the Interpreter brings to conscious awareness is its translation of what the Perceiver is observing into a form we can understand based on previous experience. The translation gives us a means to become consciously aware of the Perceiver's new information. Second, the Interpreter's associated images *are* the process of creating accessible memory of the Perceiver's new images and information.

As I learned more about how the Interpreter performs this translation, I realized that its first few comments were associations to the *nearest similar things* within preexisting memory. These *nearest similar things* give us a way to be aware, at all, of new information. For Perceiver images or information that are similar to familiar things this translation can be pretty accurate. Since most of us are familiar with seeing cats, most of us have many images of cats stored within preexisting memory. If the Perceiver is observing something that is emitting impressions, thoughts, feelings, ideas, etc., of cats, the Interpreter has a pretty easy time of finding and bringing to conscious awareness a close facsimile to what is actually being observed. So, if it's a big cat the Perceiver is observing, and the image of a big orange cat is the *nearest similar thing* stored within our preexisting memory, the first image we'll most likely see is a big orange cat. But, the big cat the Perceiver is actually observing isn't necessarily the big orange cat we see. It could just as easily be (for the sake of discussion) a never-before-seen big orange saber-toothed tiger from prehistoric times. The Interpreter can only bring to conscious awareness the *nearest similar thing* stored within our preexisting memory. Sam, a friend of mine from my engineering days at Coors, tells a story that perfectly illustrates this concept.

Sam's two-year-old nephew loved stuffed animals. Every time Sam visited his nephew he'd bring along a small stuffed animal as a gift. Sam, being the kind of person who enjoys educating kids, usually selected the toy with the intention to educate his nephew. On one of his visits Sam presented his nephew with a little stuffed walrus. The boy took it, looked at it, and by his facial expression it was obvious he'd didn't know what it was. The nephew pointed at the toy, and with a confused look on his face said, *Doggy?* As the nephew's Interpreter searched through his preexisting memory, *doggy* was the *nearest similar thing* it could find. When Sam said, *No, that's not a doggy, it's a walrus,* a new category of *nearest similar thing*s was formed within the boy's memory. The characteristics of that stuffed walrus are now associated with the sound of the word *walrus.* If Sam had later brought a stuffed sea lion the nephew probably would have looked at it and said, *walrus?* And that would illustrate the second vital function of the Interpreter's running commentary, creating accessible memory of new experiences.

When the Interpreter grabs the *nearest similar thing* and brings it to conscious awareness, a link is formed within memory between the new thing and the *nearest similar thing* it grabs. Once this link is formed, the associated image becomes a link within preexisting memory that leads back to the Perceiver's new image or other information. If Sam's nephew were later shown a photograph of a live walrus, the boy would first probably see, in his mind's eye, the toy stuffed walrus Sam gave him as a gift since that's the *nearest similar thing* in the boy's memory. He might then see himself pointing to the toy and saying, *doggy?* He might then hear, with his mind's ear, Sam saying, *No, that's not a doggy, it's a walrus.* The now-existing memory of the toy walrus has become a link within the boy's memory that he can follow to find the word *walrus* stored in his memory. Thus, the Interpreter's running commentary serves a useful purpose. It builds those associative links within preexisting memory that allow us to remember experiences. But it's important not to let the Interpreter ramble on too long.

If after my exploration experience with the saber-toothed tiger I can't remember much about the experience, I might suddenly find myself thinking about the time when I lived in a very small trailer house as a kid. I probably won't realize why I'm thinking about that, but if I just focus my attention on that memory I might find myself remembering my cat that was accidentally locked in a sewing machine case overnight when I was about nine years old. If I focus attention on that memory I might suddenly remember that during the exploration experience I was seeing a big orange cat. The associative links the Interpreter brought to conscious awareness during the exploration experience have become a pathway I can follow through preexisting memory back to the memory of that new experience. But if I'd let the Interpreter ramble on for too long, somewhere past *bananas in Brazil,* it could be extremely difficult to follow that path back to the big orange cat. There are just too many *nearest similar things* leading to too many different memory pathways.

As I continued to experiment with how long to allow the Interpreter to voice comments, I realized that I needed to find a Balance between the Interpreter and the Perceiver. Too much Perceiver led to clicking out. Too much Interpreter led to losing contact with the images and information of exploration experiences and not having easy access to memory of those experiences. In your explorations you'll probably have to find this Balance too, so I'll continue describing my experience of finding that Balance to illustrate how it can be done.

Whenever an image came into my awareness, I'd let the Interpreter make a few comments about that image, then relax its voice away. While the Interpreter was commenting, the image would have faded out. After I allowed just a few comments and relaxed that voice away, the image would fade back into view. As I got better and better at making the shift of my focus of attention between the Perceiver and the Interpreter I was able to make that shift more quickly. I discovered that when the image came back into view it wasn't exactly the same image. It was more like the new image was showing a progression of events. I discovered that if I could make the shift back and forth quickly enough, these still images related to each other in a way that told the story of what I was observing. Even though these still images were separated by periods of not seeing anything while the Interpreter was making comments, if I made the shift quickly enough, I could understand the story these single, separated, still images were telling. But if the Interpreter was allowed to continue its memory-building comments for too long, the next image I became aware of might appear to be totally unrelated to the previous series of images. Let's go back to the prehistoric saber-toothed cat to illustrate why it's important to find the proper Balance between the Interpreter and Perceiver.

Suppose the first image of the big orange cat has it sitting, just looking around. The next image might be a scene in which the cat changes into an orange lion, walking through tall grass. The next might be a scene in which this lion is stalking an elephant, and the next might be a close-up of the elephant turning toward the lion, trumpeting and threatening to charge. This series of still images tells a comprehensible story that the Perceiver is bringing into subconscious awareness. But suppose that after seeing the first image of the big orange cat I'd let the Interpreter ramble on so long that by the time I shut down its voice the Perceiver's story had progressed to seeing an elephant trumpeting. I don't have enough single still images to make sense of the story. By learning to make the shift between Perceiver and Interpreter more quickly, I began to become aware of enough of the Perceiver's input to make sense of the story it was observing.

Afterlife exploration is a process of observing nonphysical realities by allowing the Perceiver to bring information to your subconscious awareness, letting the Interpreter translate that information into conscious awareness and build a few associative links within memory, and then letting the process repeat. This process must cycle fast enough to bring enough of the story into conscious awareness for you to understand what that story is telling you. An example from a workshop participant's afterlife exploration experience illustrates the effects of an Interpreter's runaway associations, and the need for balance.

This participant—I'll call her Katie—placed her intent to make contact with a deceased person, and an image formed in her mind's eye of a black woman, standing near a curb. The woman reminded Katie of the comedian Whoopie Goldberg. Katie realized that the woman was at a bus stop, standing with her back to a busy city street, close to the curb. She was chatting with a young woman who was also waiting for the bus. The black woman absentmindedly stepped back, lost her balance, and fell over backward into the path of an oncoming car. She was struck by the car and killed instantly. It happened so fast that the woman didn't realize she'd been killed. Katie observed her nonphysically jump back up onto the curb and try to tell the young woman she'd been talking to about her fall. The young woman completely ignored her, acting like she couldn't see or hear her. The scene changed and now the black woman was standing alone, waiting for the bus.

Katie realized that the scenes in her experience were telling her that a woman had died very suddenly and unexpectedly, and was stuck because she didn't realize she had died. From this woman's perspective she was still in a body (it looked and felt to her like her physical body), and she was convinced that she was still physically alive and waiting for the bus. It was time for Katie to make contact with this woman and attempt to retrieve her, that is, assist the woman out of being stuck, and move her to a better afterlife environment. Katie played along with the woman's perspective on her situation (called *joining into her reality*) and pretended to walk up to her and ask her name. The woman told Katie her name was Charlotte. To further join into Charlotte's reality, Katie complained about how the buses in this city were never on time. In their ensuing conversation Katie learned Charlotte's address, the city they were in, and that Charlotte believed the year was 1954.

In her afterlife confusion Charlotte had been waiting for the bus for about 45 years. Katie gathered this information hoping she might later be able to verify that her contact and conversation with Charlotte were real.

Katie then took the next step by telling Charlotte there was someone she'd like her to meet. A man dressed in a bus company uniform stepped into the scene. He reminded Katie of the actor who played Amos, the cabdriver in the old *Amos 'n' Andy* television series. This bus driver was a Helper, someone others might call an angel or a guide, and he'd come to take Charlotte to a better place in our afterlife. The man apologized profusely for the late-running bus and explained that the bus company had sent him with a car to take Charlotte anywhere she'd like to go. Katie realized this was just a ruse the Helper was using to get Charlotte to leave the place she'd been stuck all those years. Charlotte agreed to go with him and Katie watched as both walked toward a 1950s vintage car with a bus company name painted on the door. The man opened the passenger-side door, and the woman got into the car. Katie pretended to open a rear door and get into the car too. She observed that the man engaged Charlotte in a conversation to hold her attention as the car pulled away from the curb and started driving down the city street. Charlotte was so distracted by the conversation that she didn't notice the scene outside the car change to a smooth gravel road through a beautiful park. Katie saw two people standing by the road up ahead, and as the man mentioned their presence to Charlotte she immediately recognized the two people as her deceased grandparents. The car stopped and Charlotte reunited with her grandparents. Her grandparents worked as Helpers too, and they'd come to help Charlotte understand that she had died, and welcome her into her new home, the afterlife.

If Katie had allowed her Interpreter to chat too long, here's how her experience might have gone. Katie might have heard herself think, *I'm seeing a black woman. She kind of reminds me of Whoopie Goldberg. Whoopie was so great in the movie* Ghost. The Ghost and Mrs. Muir *was one of my favorite old television series. We used to have that old black-and-white TV when we lived in Iowa,* and on and on and on. While Katie's Interpreter rattles on from one association to another, her Perceiver is bringing more impressions in at a subconscious level, like a movie telling the story of what happened to Charlotte. But Katie's attention is focused on the Interpreter's associations to associations, so her conscious awareness is too crowded to be aware of the progression of these scenes as they roll on. When she finally realizes what's happening, and relaxes away the voice of the Interpreter, Katie might see a black woman talking to a man in a bus company uniform. If she allows her Interpreter to rattle on too long again, more of the scenes go by unwatched and unremembered. When Katie comes back from her experience she hasn't seen enough scenes to make any sense out of what happened. She'll most likely report that she didn't get anything of value out of the experience, she just saw a woman who looked like Whoopie Goldberg, and a man in a bus company uniform. She wouldn't have remembered Charlotte's name or address, know what city Charlotte lived in, what year or how Charlotte died. Instead she might come away from her experience in this workshop exercise feeling like Bruce Moen's exploration techniques are totally bogus, or that she just doesn't have the ability to use them. Learning to maintain the Balance between one's Perceiver and Interpreter is an important aspect of learning to explore our afterlife.

But even if she had allowed that Interpreter's voice to divert her attention away from Charlotte's story, she could still use the Interpreter's associative links to help recover more memory of the experience. Suppose that immediately after Katie's experience she realizes she is having difficulty remembering what happened. Katie had shifted her awareness to the area of afterlife consciousness in which Charlotte was stuck during that experience, and then shifted back to physical reality after the experience. The memory of the experience is stored in the area of consciousness in which the events occurred. Remember State-Specific Memory? To clearly remember the experience Katie has to find a way to shift her awareness back to the area of consciousness in which it occurred. But let's say she can't even remember a single bit of information or a single feeling she experienced. The Interpreter's associative memory links make it easier for her to remember her experience with Charlotte. To remember the experience, Katie can just place her intent to remember.

For some reason unknown to Katie, she might start remembering watching an old black-and-white television during her childhood in Iowa. Next she might find herself remembering the old television series *The Ghost and Mrs. Muir*, without knowing why. She focuses her attention on any feelings she experiences and suddenly she's remembering the movie, *Ghost*, and how much she admired Whoopie Goldberg in her role in that movie. Katie still doesn't know why she's remembering any of these things, but she continues utilizing the Hemi-Sync Model of Consciousness, trusting that it will continue to shift her focus of attention back to the area of consciousness in which the experience occurred. As she focuses her attention on her feeling of admiration for Whoopie Goldberg's acting ability, Katie realizes that she's seeing a woman, who reminds her of Whoopie, standing at a bus stop waiting for the bus. Suddenly, memories of her experience come flooding into her conscious awareness.

In my view, when Katie placed her intent on remembering the experience, her Interpreter grabbed one of the associative links it made within its running dialogue. In this example the Interpreter started out with what it said about watching the old black-and-white television during Katie's childhood in Iowa. The next *nearest similar thing*, another associative link it created within Katie's memory, *The Ghost and Mrs. Muir*, popped up next. The Interpreter was using its own blabbering comments to lead Katie back to full memory of her experience.

If Katie can't remember much past talking to Charlotte, placing intent to remember more might cause her to remember the actor who played Amos the cabdriver in the *Amos 'n' Andy* television series. As she follows that associative memory link, created by the Interpreter's dialogue, she'll remember the Helper in the bus company uniform, the car, the change of scene from a city street to countryside, and Charlotte's reunion with her deceased grandparents. This whole process is why I recommend finding the Balance between the Perceiver and Interpreter functions rather than shutting down the Interpreter's internal dialogue completely.

Remembering Clicked-Out Experience

Many esoteric, meditative doctrines claim that one's chattering internal dialogue must be completely shut down to benefit from meditation. While I can see some wisdom in this *dropping into the void or quieting the mind* dogma, as an engineer I see it as a very inefficient way to explore beyond physical reality. In my view a quick, balanced shift back and forth across the edge between that chattering internal dialogue and clicking out serves that purpose far better. Without some measure of the Interpreter's incessant blabbering during an exploration experience, whatever the Perceiver observed during that experience will not be easily accessible. Tony's story illustrates what I mean.

Tony sat on the carpeted floor of the debriefing room after a tape exercise in an Exploration 27 program at The Monroe Institute. Most of the other participants had finished describing their exercise experiences, and I had just started describing mine. As I rambled on, in midsentence, Tony yelled, *stop!* so I stopped talking.

Tony explained that during a Lifeline program he attended at the Institute, a year earlier, he'd clicked out during one of the tape exercises. He'd yelled *stop!* because he had at just that moment, a year later, remembered what happened during that click out.

Tony explained that the first few people's experiences sounded oddly familiar. As more participants debriefed their tape exercise experiences, he started to feel like he knew what the next person was going to talk about before they spoke. He'd stopped me in midsentence because he was certain of the next words I was going to say.

During his click out a year earlier, Tony said he'd been in a nonphysical version of the same room he was now sitting in. All the people now physically sitting in the room were the same people he'd seen during the click out, all sitting in the same places. During his click out he'd heard exactly the same words being spoken by each person. Tony told me the next words I was going to say, and he was right!

I'd say that for some reason, during Tony's click out, his Interpreter could not find a *nearest similar thing* to use to translate into his conscious awareness the precognition of an experience that would not happen until a year later. What his Perceiver observed during that click out remained, stored at a subconscious level, until his Interpreter could find a *nearest similar thing*, the physical world event. As each person spoke, sitting in the same locations in the same room, using the same words, Tony's Interpreter finally had quite a number of *nearest similar things*. So, his Perceiver's observations were not forever lost and unrecoverable; it just took a rather amazing series of events to bring those observations to his conscious awareness. And, having such an amazing experience might conflict with beliefs Tony holds regarding precognition. Accepting that experience as real might eliminate some of those beliefs and their perceptual distortion and blockages. His perception will no doubt open further as a result.

When you experience a click out, don't worry that your Perceiver's observations are lost forever. I just chalk it up to having nothing within preexisting memory the Interpreter can use. You might think of click outs as gifted-wrapped presents that you'll get to open when something in your future experience gives the Interpreter a way to untie the bow and unwrap the gift. Click outs can be another *window of opportunity*, an experience that conflicting beliefs can't block because we are not conscious, yet, of conflicts wrapped up in that gift.

Techniques for Finding the Balance between the Perceiver and Interpreter

The way I found the Balance was first to just become aware of the Interpreter chatting away. You'd be surprised how long that can go on before it dawns on you. Once I got pretty good at catching me talking to myself I worked at shortening the amount of time I allowed my Interpreter to ramble on. You might try the same approach. Remember, we navigate consciousness by learning to recognize the feelings associated with areas of consciousness. The Balance can also be thought of as an area within consciousness that we can learn to navigate to by recognizing the feelings on either side of the center of the Balance.

This waiting-to-get-a-word-in-edgewise feeling, that *pressure-in-the-throat* feeling you get when there is something you really want to say but your friend keeps talking, is my best description of the feeling of being on the Interpreter's side of, and very close to, the Balance's center.

When your friend takes a breath, and you start to say your first word, only to be blocked when your friend starts to talk again, that *oops-my-friend-started-talking-again-so-I-can't* feeling is very close to what I'd describe as *relaxing that feeling away*.

This next exercise is intended to help you become aware of the feeling of being in the Balance. Once I found that Balance I discovered it was like simultaneously observing the experience and hearing the internal dialogue about that experience. Within that Balance, both functions—Perceiver and Interpreter—cooperate to bring our afterlife exploration experiences into conscious awareness, and create easily accessible memory.

The Balance Exercise: Description

If the Balance is a teeter-totter, most of us are sitting on the Interpreter's end, yammering away. For most of us, finding the Balance will be about learning to quickly recognize when we're talking to ourselves and shifting our weight back toward the center of the teeter-totter. This exercise is intended as a way to practice quickly recognizing the Interpreter's chatter and relaxing it away. With practice you may experience clicking out. If you do, you'll know you've shifted too far toward the Perceiver end of the teeter-totter.

Those of you who meditate and sometimes drop into the void pass over that Balance each time you do. Meditators who use a mantra will find the Balance point between losing your mantra and realizing you are experiencing thoughts. Completely shutting down those thoughts and dropping into the void is *not* the goal of this exercise. The goal is to experience the Balance between these two sides.

Once you learn to recognize these components of your consciousness in the exercise, and find that Balance, you'll be more likely to detect the subtle shift between them during your future explorations. It is during those explorations that the *real work* of this exercise is done. Learning to attain the Balance between these two functions is a key to observing and remembering. Though it can be done anywhere, this exercise benefits from being done in a darkened room, as it makes it easier to focus your attention into the surrounding blackness.

The Interpreter-Perceiver Balance Exercise: Script

This is the Interpreter-Perceiver Balance Exercise. (Wait 5 sec)

As you get ready to begin the exercise, adjust the volume of this recording so that you can comfortably and easily hear and understand my voice. You may do this exercise either sitting or lying down. (Wait 15 sec)

When you're ready to begin, please close your eyes. (Wait 15 sec)

To begin this exercise move your body into a comfortable, relaxed position in quiet place. (Wait 30 sec)

Remember the feeling of relaxation and take in Three Deep Relaxing Breaths, or as many as you need to feel some change in your level of relaxation. (Wait 45 sec)

Breathe normally as you focus your attention on the feeling of being relaxed. (Wait 15 sec)

Remember the image of establishing the flow of energy from below in the *Afterlife Knowledge Guidebook*. (Wait 15 sec)

Remember each of the individual steps and the feeling of establishing the flow of energy as you take in at least Three Energy Gathering Breaths to establish the flow from below. (Wait 45 sec)

Remember the image of Energy Gathering from Below you saw in the *Afterlife Knowledge Guidebook*. (Wait 20 sec)

Remember the image and feeling of a continuous, ever-increasing flow of energy through and around your body as you take in at least Three Energy Gathering Breaths from Below. (Wait 45 sec)

Remember the feeling of placing intent, or just imagine you are doing the Silly Little Finger Bending Exercise. (Wait 15 sec)

Remember the feeling of placing intent as you say in your mind, **I am placing my intent** (wait 5 sec) **to experience and to know** (wait 5 sec) **the Balance between the Interpreter and the Perceiver.** (Wait 10 sec)

Focus your attention into the blackness before your closed eyes. Quietly look into this blackness, paying specific attention to anything that stands out. (Wait 10 sec)

You might see only blackness. You might see shapes or images. You might see patches of color, or areas within this blackness that look darker or lighter. (Wait 20 sec)

Are you talking to yourself? If you are, listen to what you're saying within your thoughts. Is it about the blackness, or something else? (Wait 10 sec)

Again focus your attention into the blackness before your closed eyes. Quietly look into this blackness, paying specific attention to anything that stands out. (Wait 20 sec)

You might see only blackness. You might see shapes or images. You might see patches of color, or areas within this blackness that look darker or lighter. (Wait 20 sec)

Are you talking to yourself? If you are, do you recognize whose voice this is? Is it yours or someone else's? (Wait 20 sec)

Again focus your attention into the blackness before your closed eyes. Quietly look into this blackness, paying specific attention to anything that stands out. (Wait 45 sec)

Are you talking to yourself? If you are, try forcing the voice to stop and observe what happens. (Wait 60 sec)

Again focus your attention into the blackness before your closed eyes. Quietly look into this blackness, paying specific attention to anything that stands out. (Wait 20 sec)

You might see only blackness. You might see shapes or images. You might see patches of color, or areas within this blackness that look darker or lighter. (Wait 45 sec)

Are you talking to yourself? If you are, try arguing with that voice about why it should stop talking and observe what happens. (Wait 30 sec)

Again focus your attention into the blackness before your closed eyes. Quietly look into this blackness, paying specific attention to anything that stands out. (Wait 45 sec)

Are you talking to yourself? If you are, let that voice do what it will and observe what happens. (Wait 30 sec)

Do you see how what the voice says is related to what it previously said? (Wait 20 sec)

It's time to shift your focus of attention back toward the Perceiver. (Wait 5 sec)

Again focus your attention into the blackness before your closed eyes. Quietly look into this blackness, paying specific attention to anything that stands out. (Wait 10 sec)

When you realize you are listening to the voice of the Interpreter, talking to yourself, experiment with shutting down the voice of the Interpreter. Then focus your attention on silently observing the blackness before your closed eyes. (Wait 60 sec)

Did you start talking to yourself again? Experiment again with shutting down the voice of the Interpreter by just relaxing it away. (Wait 60 sec)

Did you catch the voice of the Interpreter earlier this time? (Wait 10 sec)

Begin taking in at least Three Deep Relaxing Breaths as you gaze into the blackness before your closed eyes, and feel yourself relax more deeply as you continue these Deep Relaxing Breaths. (Wait 30 sec)

Did the voice of the Interpreter stop while you were taking in Deep Relaxing Breaths? Do you remember something you saw in the blackness? (Wait 20 sec)

There is a FEELING that comes just before that voice begins talking. As you quietly peer into the blackness practice becoming aware of that feeling earlier and earlier in the process of the Interpreter beginning to speak. Then practice relaxing away the Interpreter's voice and repeat the process. (Wait 1 min)

I'm going to give you lots of time to practice. As soon as you realize the Interpreter's voice has started talking, relax and once again focus your attention into the blackness before your closed eyes. Take in Three Deep Relaxing Breaths as a way of learning to relax that voice away. I'll sit quietly while you practice. (Wait 3 min)

Did you click out? (Wait 10 sec)

When you're ready, open your eyes, and give yourself a few moments to fully return from the exercise. Then immediately begin to write about your experience and use the questions in the debriefing section for this exercise in the *Afterlife Knowledge Guidebook* as a starting point to record your experience in detail in your notebook.

Debrief

Take a few moments to record your experience in your notebook.

Did you experience that the Interpreter's voice had probably been rambling on for a while before you realized it?

Whose voice was it?

What was it talking about?

Did it start out talking about peering into the blackness and then change the subject?

Were the things it said related to what you saw in the blackness?
How long did it take for you to realize it was talking?
Did you find a way to quiet that voice?
Describe how you did that.
Did you experience the feeling that occurs just as that voice begins speaking?

This exercise bears repeating. You can do it with or without the exercise tape or CD once you've done it a few times. While it isn't necessary to fully master the Balance before you go on to later exercises in this guidebook, it's worthwhile to continue practicing during future exercises. The real work will begin as you begin the exercises that teach you how to consciously explore our afterlife.

Rosalie's Brilliant Method of Finding the Balance

When I was in the process of developing the exercises to be used in my Partnered Exploration of the Afterlife Workshop, I needed a volunteer to play the role of a student. My friend Rosalie volunteered and in the course of our work together she developed the most effective way I've ever seen of learning the Balance.

To make sure we had sufficient notes from our partnered exploration sessions I'd suggested that Rosalie describe her experiences during our sessions into a tape recorder. My preference is to use a voice-activated tape recorder and I suggested she purchase one also. Such tape recorders automatically turn themselves on when you start talking and off about five seconds after you stop talking. I found it a convenient way to save time when later transcribing the tapes by automatically eliminating the long blank spaces between my recorded comments.

But, there's a thing about using a voice-activated unit that Rosalie didn't like. If the tape recorder has shut itself off because you've stopped talking, when you start talking again it takes the unit a second to get the tape up to proper recording speed. It's recording your voice during this second but because the tape speed is still accelerating you can't understand what you said. What you hear when you play back the tape sounds like *burreeerruupp* just before you can understand what you said. Rosalie found that sound annoying. Her solution was to keep talking, so the recorder wouldn't automatically shut off. That turns out to be a perfect way of limiting the Interpreter's runaway blabbering and learning the Balance.

Because she was making comments during her exploration sessions, her physical voice became the voice of her Interpreter. Her comments were describing her experience as it unfolded, which limited how long she could talk about what had previously happened. Her Interpreter was forced to only make comments about what was happening instead of rambling on and on about what happened previously. I'd liken Rosalie's method to a good radio announcer describing a horse race. If the announcer spends too much time describing how the horses came out of the gate at the start of the race, the race will be over before he has time to describe anything else. A good horse race announcer has to keep up with the action, describing as best he can what's happening now, not dwelling on what happened ten seconds ago.

Rosalie's method is absolutely brilliant! After you've practiced the above exercise several times I'd suggest you give Rosalie's method a try. You don't have to actually use a tape recorder, just continuously describe your experience out loud, as if you were recording it. I'd suggest using short comments that describe your experience, with short spaces in which you are observing instead of talking. You'll be shifting your focus of attention back and forth between observing your experience and commenting about it. You'll be crossing over the center of Balance each time you make that shift. It's great practice not only for learning the Balance between the Perceiver and Interpreter, but for making verbal notes during your future afterlife exploration experiences.

Rosalie's Balance Exercise: Script

This is the Rosalie's Interpreter-Perceiver Balance Exercise. (Wait 5 sec)

As you get ready to begin the exercise, adjust the volume of this recording so that you can comfortably and easily hear and understand my voice. You may do this exercise either sitting or lying down. (Wait 15 sec)

When you're ready to begin, please close your eyes. (Wait 15 sec)

To begin this exercise move your body into a comfortable, relaxed position in your quiet place. (Wait 30 sec)

Remember the feeling of relaxation and take in Three Deep Relaxing Breaths, or as many as you need to feel some change in your level of relaxation. (Wait 45 sec)

Breathe normally as you focus your attention on the feeling of being relaxed. (Wait 20 sec)

Remember the image of establishing the flow of energy from below in the *Afterlife Knowledge Guidebook*. (Wait 20 sec)

Remember each of the individual steps and the feeling of establishing the flow of energy as you take in at least Three Energy Gathering Breaths to establish the flow from below. (Wait 45 sec)

Remember the image of Energy Gathering from Below you saw in the *Afterlife Knowledge Guidebook.* (Wait 20 sec)

Remember the image and feeling of a continuous, ever-increasing flow of energy through and around your body as you take in at least Three Energy Gathering Breaths from Below. (Wait 45 sec)

Remember the feeling of placing intent, or just imagine you are doing the Silly Little Finger Bending Exercise. (Wait 15 sec)

Reexperience the feeling of placing intent as you say in your mind, **I am placing my intent** (wait 5 sec) **to experience and to know** (wait 5 sec) **the Balance between the Interpreter and the Perceiver.** (Wait 10 sec)

Focus your attention into the blackness before your closed eyes. Quietly look into this blackness, paying specific attention to anything that stands out. (Wait 20 sec)

You might see only blackness. You might see shapes or images. You might see patches of color, or areas within this blackness that look darker or lighter. (Wait 20 sec)

As you quietly look into the blackness, we're going to experiment with the length of time between your verbal comments. When you hear me say the word "comment," make a short verbal statement describing what you've experienced or seen. (Wait 30 sec)

"Comment" (Wait 45 sec)
"Comment" (Wait 45 sec)
"Comment" (Wait 45 sec)
"Comment" (Wait 30 sec)
"Comment" (Wait 30 sec)
"Comment" (Wait 30 sec)
"Comment" (Wait 15 sec)
"Comment" (Wait 15 sec)
"Comment" (Wait 15 sec)

As you continue quietly looking into the blackness, we're going to experiment with the length of your verbal statements. When you hear me say the words "start comment," begin verbally describing what you've experienced or seen. When you hear me say the words "stop comment," stop talking and shift your focus of attention back to quietly peering into the blackness. (Wait 30 sec)

"Start comment" (Wait 5 sec)
"Stop comment" (Wait 20 sec)
"Start comment" (Wait 5 sec)
"Stop comment" (Wait 20 sec)

"Start comment" (Wait 5 sec)
"Stop comment" (Wait 20 sec)
"Start comment" (Wait 10 sec)
"Stop comment" (Wait 20 sec)
"Start comment" (Wait 10 sec)
"Stop comment" (Wait 20 sec)
"Start comment" (Wait 10 sec)
"Stop comment" (Wait 20 sec)

As you continue quietly peering into the blackness, on your own, experiment with the space between and the length of your verbal comments. As you do, find the shortest spaces and comments you're comfortable with. I'll be quiet now while you do this. (Wait 3 min)

When you're ready, please open your eyes, and give yourself a few moments to fully return from the exercise. Then immediately begin to write about your experience and use the questions in the debriefing section for this exercise in the *Afterlife Knowledge Guidebook* as a starting point to record your experience in detail in your notebook.

Debrief

Take a few moments to record your experience in your notebook.

What did you experience with shorter or longer times between your verbal comments?

What did you experience with shorter or longer verbal comments?

What happens if you talk about the same thing for a few seconds?

What happens if you talk about the same thing for 15 or 30 seconds?

Where's the best Balance for you that yields complete verbal notes versus missing new material because you were talking about one thing too long?

What happens if you talk continuously, pausing briefly to observe and then pausing briefly to make verbal comments?

Where's the best Balance between the Perceiver and Interpreter for you?

Is that Balance like the feeling of staying in one place, or is it like the feeling of moving back and forth across a place?

Perceiver and Interpreter Hints

Focusing your attention into the blackness with your eyes closed means, look around. It might help to get a better feel for this if you actually move your physical eyes around occasionally as you look around in the blackness. You're looking for anything that looks different from blackness.

The voice of my Interpreter sounds to me like my own voice. For you, the voice of your Interpreter might be a different voice from your own, or it may be the *sound of your thoughts.*

Stopping the voice of the Interpreter is sort of like stopping your thoughts. Meditators will recognize this state as a quieting of the mind.

People who are good at doing real-time, spoken, language translations of a lecturer, from the lecturer's language to another language, know all about the Balance between the Interpreter and Perceiver. As the woman who did the real-time voice translation at one of my workshops in Germany put it:

If I stop to try to figure out how I'm going to translate a certain word, I don't hear any more of the words that are said until I again focus my attention on listening to what is being said. That's like losing Balance on the side of the Interpreter, spending time analyzing a single thing and missing what is going on while I'm doing it. But if I just focus my attention on hearing your voice, to know what you are saying, the translation just comes out when I start speaking in German, and the troublesome word can be dealt with then.

Interpreter Overlay—The Root of Inaccuracy

The very nature of human perception leads to inaccuracy in the details of experience and information gathered when exploring nonphysical realities. What we consciously see and hear is never precisely what the Perceiver is observing. Instead, we are only consciously aware of the Interpreter's *nearest similar thing translations* that overlie the Perceiver's observations. Hence the term Interpreter Overlay, the concept I use to help understand the source of inaccuracy and to develop more accurate perception. At its most basic, the inaccuracy is a function of translating from the language of the Perceiver to the language of the Interpreter. It seems some things are always lost in a translation.

In our afterlife explorations we are always getting the *translation* (the Interpreter Overlay), never the actual *experience* (the Perceiver's observations). It is this *nearest similar thing* that comes into our conscious awareness. To illustrate how Interpreter Overlay affects the accuracy of our nonphysical perception, I'll use a workshop participant's retrieval experience.

As Tagashi described his experience after the first retrieval exercise of the workshop, it was apparent to me that he was having difficulty with Interpreter Overlay. I explained that sometimes the first *nearest similar thing* the Interpreter brings to conscious awareness isn't close enough to what the Perceiver is actually observing, and in such cases the information gathered could appear to be garbage. I suggested that, if what he perceived didn't make sense, or seemed too much like fantasy, he actively let go of whatever it was, and then place his intent to be open to reconnecting with the experience with more clarity, and begin again. If what he perceived next also didn't make sense or seemed too much like fantasy, he should repeat the process. If he let go of the image or experience and the same one came back, I suggested he should assume that was as close as his Interpreter's translation was going to get and to just continue the exercise from there. In an exercise designed to contact and retrieve a person who had become stuck after death, Tagashi's experience is one of the best examples of dealing with Interpreter Overlay I've ever witnessed.

After placing his intent to be of service to someone stuck after death, Tagashi said that the flat blackness transformed into the star-filled depths of outer space. Floating before Tagashi's eyes was a full-color, 3-D, holographic image from the television series *Star Trek*, of a Klingon warship known as a Bird of Prey. (Klingons were a warlike race of aliens.) This image confused him, making him wonder if he was to retrieve an alien, or perhaps someone from the television series. He decided this could be an Interpreter Overlay. Tagashi said that it was very difficult to allow that image to fade away as I'd suggested. It was the clearest 3-D, nonphysical image he'd ever seen and it was hard to intentionally cause it to disappear. The image of the Klingon warship faded into the blackness and Tagashi again placed his intent to connect with someone needing retrieval, this time being open to greater clarity.

A new image formed before Tagashi's closed eyes, once again in the star-filled blackness of deep space. Again the image was crystal clear, full-color, 3-D, and holographic. This new image was an X-Wing—a single seat, outer-space fighter craft from the *Star Wars* movies. *Star Wars* fans would recognize it as the fighter craft Luke Skywalker flew, with the R2D2 robot in the back, to launch the bomb that destroyed the Death Star. Again Tagashi felt confused, wondering if he was back to retrieving an alien, or perhaps a cast member from the *Star Wars* movie series. Realizing his confusion, Tagashi let go of the X-Wing image, allowing it to fade into the blackness. He again placed intent to reconnect with greater clarity with a person needing retrieval.

Tagashi suddenly realized he was flying high above the earth over a seemingly endless desert next to a French Mirage, a single-seat jet-fighter aircraft, in desert camouflage paint with Arabic markings. He then found himself in the cockpit of this aircraft, observing the jet's pilot, a dark-skinned man with thick black eyebrows and hair and a very prominent nose. Tagashi also noticed a shrapnel wound and hole the size of an apple in the right side of the pilot's chest. When he asked the pilot about his wound, the pilot expressed great pride in surviving this wound so he could continue to fly around looking for enemy aircraft to shoot down. Tagashi realized that the pilot had not survived his wound, and had the impression that the man had died in aerial combat during the Persian Gulf War. This man believed he was still on a mission to locate and shoot down enemy aircraft, ten years after the war had ended. Tagashi no longer felt the confusion he'd experienced with the previous images and experience. He retrieved the pilot, taking him to a better afterlife location.

Reflecting on Tagashi's experience, one can almost see a progression of *nearest similar things* unfolding. His first image was of a Klingon warship, a Bird of Prey. Fans of the *Star Trek* television series may see enough physical resemblance to understand how the Interpreter might have brought Klingons to conscious awareness as a *nearest similar thing* to an Arab. Dark olive skin tones, a prominent nose, and thick, dark hair and eyebrows come to mind for me. And, since the jet-fighter aircraft is a warship, it's not too far a stretch to understand how if the Interpreter grabbed Klingon in place of Arab, it could then grab the Klingon Bird of Prey in place of the jet fighter. See what I mean by the Interpreter making associations to its own associations?

By letting go of this first image and placing intent to reconnect with more clarity, Tagashi forced the Interpreter to select a new *nearest similar thing*. By the time Tagashi let go of that first image, the Interpreter had more information from the Perceiver's observations that could then be translated to his conscious awareness as a new *nearest similar thing*. So, when the Interpreter grabbed a new *nearest similar thing* from Tagashi's preexisting memory, it had more impressions to use in making that choice.

The next image was a little closer to the jet fighter he eventually found. Instead of a Klingon Bird of Prey, a warship that would contain a large crew, the Interpreter chose a single-seat X-Wing. See how this process of letting go of the image is allowing the Interpreter to get closer to the final image?

When Tagashi let go of this X-Wing image, the Interpreter was forced to choose again, this time bringing him into a scene in which he was flying alongside a modern jet fighter in desert paint with Arabic markings. Tagashi was willing to accept this image as possible and so continued from that point on to retrieve the pilot.

What do you suppose might have happened if Tagashi had let go of this image also? My feeling is that he'd have found himself flying alongside that same jet, in the same scene with the same pilot in need of retrieval. I suppose that some of the small details might have changed. For example, the Arabic markings on the jet might have been bogus gibberish that only looked like real Arabic markings. Perhaps in the next image those would have been more refined, perhaps the desert paint scheme would have been more accurate, or perhaps details of the pilot's uniform or the instrument panel would have been more accurate.

Letting the image go and placing intent to reconnect with more clarity is a way to work toward getting more accurate information, but that accuracy still has limitations. For example, if Tagashi does not have knowledge of the written Arabic language, getting the real Arabic markings on the aircraft might be difficult. Once again, we are only consciously aware of the Interpreter Overlay, not what the Perceiver is actually observing. Years of teaching my workshops shows that if you let go of the image and the same image comes back, that's about as close as your Interpreter is able to get to whenever is *really* there. My opinion about why this letting go process works is that the Perceiver is continually observing and feeding more new information into the subconscious for the Interpreter to translate. Each time you let go of the questionable image, the Interpreter seems to factor in any additional information in its selection of the next *nearest similar thing*. At some point in this updating process no amount of additional information seems to affect the Interpreter's translation. At that point the same image, impression, or Overlay begins to repeat. As you begin explorations beyond physical reality, it's important to remember the effects of Interpreter Overlay and allow yourself to let go of questionable Overlays. Tagashi's letting go of questionable images and impressions is a great demonstration of a way to improve upon our inherent perceptual inaccuracies.

Some of you might be wondering what would have happened if Tagashi had accepted the Klingon Bird of Prey image and gone ahead with the retrieval process. I expect that when he entered the warship he probably would have found a single Klingon in the ship, at the helm. This Klingon probably would have had a phaser blaster wound the size of an apple in his upper right chest. He probably would have been flying his ship around, proud to have survived his wound, looking for an enemy starship to blast to pieces. If Tagashi could have convinced the Klingon to leave, the Arab fighter pilot would have still been retrieved. In other words, I would expect that Tagashi's inaccurate perception of the details wouldn't have interfered with the process. Of course, when Tagashi related the details of this retrieval exercise he would have probably felt that the exercise—and perhaps the whole retrieval process—was just a fantasy.

A Few Words about Skeptics

Some of the most common comments heard from skeptics regarding any exploration beyond physical reality are that the results are vague, subjective, and inaccurate. Skeptics take the fact that results cannot be precisely replicated from experience to experience or from person to person as proof that no such thing as nonphysical reality exists. Most skeptics will attempt to explain away any positive results as merely lucky guesses, cold reading, random events, deception, collusion, etc. It's my feeling that if skeptics understood more about the nature of their own perception, they'd begin to understand why the lack of precise replication of results should be expected.

The totality of what becomes stored within an individual's memory is as unique as individual snowflakes. No two are exactly alike. Perception within nonphysical realities is always the result of the Interpreter's subjective *nearest similar thing* translation using the unique totality of an individual's stored memories. It will always yield subjective results.

PART II

Tools of Conscious Exploration

6

Guidance

Often, someone will ask me, "Bruce, how do I get in touch with my Guides?" Usually they want to have face-to-face conversations with a non-physical person they identify as a personal source of wisdom. When someone asks me that question, they are in for a long story about my own first recognition that there is such a thing as Guidance, and how that led me to contact in face-to-face conversations with Guides.

My first wife, Barbara, and I were eating dinner and talking about American Indians. After dinner, as I was standing at the kitchen sink washing dishes, I said out loud, to nobody in particular, *I wonder what the role of the medicine man was in American Indian culture?* It was an idle remark, quickly forgotten.

So, one Saturday morning, two weeks later, Barb wanted to go shopping for shoes in downtown Minneapolis, which was going to be an all-day experience. I was more than a little reluctant, but I was trying to learn to be a good husband. After the third shoe store, Barb spotted a bookstore and insisted we look around, although by this time my impatience was definitely showing.

Barb took off toward shelves of books, and I just stood by the front door with my arms folded over my chest, tapping my foot on the floor, hoping she would take pity on me and hurry up. This had no effect, so I started to wander down an aisle. I walked past a table piled with books. Something about the blue cover on one of them caught my eye. I absentmindedly picked it up and it sort of fell open.

I started reading at the top of the left-hand page and, honest to God, the first words I read were *the role of the medicine man in American Indian culture was* . . . It took a few moments for me to recognize that I was reading an answer to the question I had idly asked two weeks earlier.

I found the whole experience incredible. I'm an engineer and I began to think about how I could calculate the probability of such an obviously random event. I quickly realized that while I was standing at the sink I'd have calculated the odds as one-in-some-number-approaching-infinity. I kept moving the date of my intellectual, odds-calculating, mental exercise closer to the moment in time I'd starting reading the first words in that book. When I'd moved to the point at which I'd walked into the bookstore I thought the odds were at least somewhat less than one-in-some-number-approaching-infinity. After all, there were a finite number of pages in all the books in that bookstore. It was a big number, but at least it was finite. At least the odds were now one-in-the-number-of-pages-in-all-the-books-in-the-store. These were still incredibly long odds, but at least they were now definable as finite. In the end all my logical, rational, probabilistic analysis of the situation did was prove to me that I'd experienced a very long series of obviously random events, and somehow these completely random events had led to unexpectedly reading the answer to a two-week-old question in a randomly selected book on a randomly selected page.

A chain of decisions led me to that book. I could have asked Barb to call her sister and avoided going along on this shopping trip all together. We could have selected a different shoe store as our first visit and the pattern of one-way streets through Minneapolis might have prevented driving past the bookstore. Every decision we made had an effect, even the wrong turns we'd made going from one shoe store to the next had their influence. As I stood there I realized that despite what I believed, finding that book could not have been the result of a random series of events. The probability of finding it in the way that I did was less than infinitesimal. Good old, solid engineering logic led to the conclusion that there must have been some subtle, unrecognized influence upon each decision that led me to the book. As an engineer, who considered belief in such influence as a mark of borderline insanity, I was intrigued by the whole experience. I decided to do what any good scientist would do. I decided to run some experiments to see if I could replicate the results.

At first I tried asking lots of questions out loud, as I had done with my medicine man question at the kitchen sink. I had so many questions going at once it all got too confusing. I finally decided that the proper way to run my experiment was to ask one question and then not ask another until I'd gotten an answer. These first experiments demonstrated the phenomenon to be real and I began to see a pattern in the process. Once I asked the question, the answer usually popped up when I least expected it.

This chapter began with a question about how to get in touch with one's personal Guides. I now see my medicine man story as the first step I took toward answering that question. I now realize that my experiments eventually led to the more classic, face-to-face form of getting in touch with my Guides and led to my contact with Coach. Those of you who've read my previous books know about him.

Something else my experiments showed me is a way to know that this process is leading to face-to-face contact with Guides. As I continued my experiments I noticed that the time between asking the question and receiving the answer began to shorten. At first I'd ask my question and it might be a week, two weeks, or more before the answer would unexpectedly pop up. As I continued to gain confidence in this process, these time frames began to shorten. When the answer did pop up, often I'd realize there could have been other opportunities to receive it that I'd missed. Eventually it got to the point that I could be sitting in my cubicle at work and I'd ask my question related to something I was working on. Moments later my phone would ring and it would turn out to be an old buddy I hadn't talked to for months, who coincidently was an expert in the area of my question. He had picked that moment just to call and chew the fat. Sometimes really strange things would happen. I'd ask my question and realize that the answer was formulating itself within my thoughts. When I'd check out the answer I'd heard in my thoughts, it would turn out to be correct. When you see this beginning to happen in your own experience it's a clue you are getting very close to the more classic experience of getting in touch with your Guides.

No matter where people are in the process of getting in touch with their Guides, when they ask me how to do it, I tell them my medicine man story. I want to get across that it is a process. Each time I got an answer, beliefs that blocked more direct communication with Guidance were removed. With my improved perception of Guidance I was able to experience a new level of contact, which led to removal of more blocking beliefs, and better contact.

There's one more point: ask your questions out loud. It's a practical matter. In the course of a day I might mentally ask hundreds of questions, but a week from now how likely is it that I'll remember any of them? If I make a point of asking the question out loud, there's a much higher probability I'll remember having asked the question when the answer pops up in front of me.

Also, when I was standing at the sink, I asked my medicine man question out loud, out of real curiosity, and I asked it of *no one in particular*. The feeling of doing it that way is different from directing your question to a specific person. That feeling seems to open the possibility that the answer could come from any source, even sources presently unknown to you.

Learning to directly communicate with Guidance makes me think of what it must have been like for each of us, as infants, to learn to talk. For months after we were born, other beings made sounds that were intended to communicate with us. And for those first few months, those sounds were unintelligible. At some point we realized that within that gibberish were patterns that were becoming familiar. Later we realized that some of those patterns were associated with other experiences. Gradually we learned how to direct the attention of the beings around us, and we began to understand what language is and how to use it to get our needs met. Sometimes I think learning to directly communicate with Guidance is a similar process.

I have an exercise you can use to get information you desire, and to begin the process of getting in touch with your Guides.

Guidance Exercise

The exercise to begin learning how to communicate with Guidance takes patience and being alert to patterns in the "noise" around you. Not just noise as in sound, but noise as in everything that happens around you. To begin this exercise you're going to need a *burning question*, one you've been carrying around with you for a while. It's not just an ordinary question, it's one you really have a strong desire to know the answer to. Settle on one burning question to use and write it down in your notebook. Take some care in wording your question. Ambiguous questions get ambiguous answers. When you have carefully worded your burning question, and memorized it, this next exercise can teach you how to contact Guidance to receive an answer.

Guidance Exercise: Script

This is the exercise for Learning about Guidance. (Wait 5 sec)

As you get ready to begin the exercise, adjust the volume of this recording so that you can comfortably and easily hear and understand my voice. You may do this exercise either sitting or lying down. (Wait 10 sec)

When you're ready to begin, please close your eyes. (Wait 10 sec)

To begin this exercise move your body into a comfortable, relaxed position in your quiet place. (Wait 30 sec)

Remember the feeling of being relaxed. (Wait 20 sec)

At your own pace take in Three Deep Relaxing Breaths, or as many as you need to feel some change in your level of relaxation. (Wait 40 sec)

Remember the image of establishing the flow of energy from below in the *Afterlife Knowledge Guidebook*. (Wait 20 sec)

At your own pace, remembering each of the steps as you do this, take in Three Energy Gathering Breaths to establish the flow from below. (Wait 45 sec)

Remember the image of Energy Gathering from Below in the *Afterlife Knowledge Guidebook*. (Wait 20 sec)

At your own pace, remembering each of the steps as you do this, take in Three Energy Gathering Breaths from Below. (Wait 45 sec)

Remember the feeling of placing intent, or just imagine you are doing the Silly Little Finger Bending Exercise. (Wait 15 sec)

Reexperience the feeling of placing intent as you say in your mind, **I am learning to contact and communicate with Guidance.** (Wait 10 sec)

In the frame of mind that you are asking no one in particular, ask your question, out loud. (Wait 30 sec)

When you're ready, please open your eyes and give yourself a few moments to fully return from the exercise. Then immediately begin to write about your experience and use the questions in the debriefing section for this exercise in the *Afterlife Knowledge Guidebook* as a starting point to record your experience in detail in your notebook.

Debrief

Take a few moments to record your experience in your notebook. Write down the exact wording of your question, and any feelings you experienced as you placed your intent and asked your question.

From this day forward, you don't need to do anything more than be attentive to anything that reminds you of the question you just asked. When something reminds you of the question, follow through to see where it leads. Now, don't get carried away with this part. Sometimes people think you have to see everything that happens as a possible answer, and examine and analyze everything in great detail. That's not what I mean. Keep your eyes open for the synchronicities and coincidences that come along, and don't worry too much about missing the answer. In my experience if you miss the answer the first time, it will be presented over and over again until you get it.

That's all there is to it.

After you get an answer to your first burning question, do this exercise again with a new question.

A Workshop Participant's Experience

To show how easy this whole process can be I'd like to share a story from a workshop participant. The workshop host invited the participants to her home to socialize, the evening of the first day of the workshop. She had lots of snacks set out, including little dishes of peanuts. One participant picked up a peanut and wondered out loud what it is about peanuts that people are allergic to. Of course, somebody else jumped right on that one and said, well why don't you try using the Guidance exercise to get an answer. We all broke out laughing, and she said, "Ok, ok, I'll do it." She kind of looked at the peanut and said, "I wonder what it is about peanuts that people are allergic to." Everyone waited for a few moments for the answer to drop out of the sky and when nothing happened the whole group burst into laughter.

I got an e-mail from her several days after the workshop, and she said it was the strangest thing. She got back home to California and the next morning while paging through the newspaper she came across a double page article on peanuts. The article explained where peanuts are grown, how many tons are sold, and included a detailed explanation of what it is that people are allergic to. As if that weren't enough, two days later she was sitting in a doctor's office, picked up a magazine, and found an article with more information about peanuts and people's allergies to them. In her e-mail she said, "You know, we all had a good laugh about this at our Saturday night get-together, but this Guidance thing really works!"

Communicating with Guidance

In the beginning, limit the number of questions you ask to one, or perhaps two. If you have twenty questions going at once, it's more difficult to remember the questions and recognize when something reminds you of one of them. Limiting yourself to one and waiting until you have received an answer before asking the next one offers several benefits. First, you'll probably recognize the answers more quickly. Second, each time you receive an answer you'll learn more about how the process works. Third, you'll gain confidence in the process with each success.

As you practice this Guidance exercise and begin to gain some confidence, know that there is a progression to learning. There may come a time when you ask a question out loud and the answer comes immediately into your mind as a thought, impression, idea, etc. That's an indication you're progressing to a clearer connection with Guidance. There may come a time when you begin to communicate more directly with Guides using imagination as a means of perception, a topic that is coming up shortly.

Guides. Who are they? From my experience Guides are very often another one of our Selves. (Note: for more insight into what I mean by another one of our Selves, it might be worthwhile to reread the sections in my book *Voyages into the Unknown*, about the "Waking Vision of a Disk," "The Disk Vision's Meaning," and "The Flowers, Rebecca and Coach.")

7

Heart Intelligence

According to my old beliefs, my brain was the one and only location of my intelligence, so when Rebecca started talking about Heart Intelligence I thought it was a joke. The idea of intelligence residing anywhere but the brain was ridiculous.

When I began experimenting with Heart Intelligence my beliefs changed.

If our normal intelligence could be described as *rational*, Heart Intelligence could be described as *nonrational*. (Notice I didn't say *irrational*.) Rational intelligence could be described as sequential-logic, cause-and-effect, language-based thinking. Nonrational intelligence could be described as experiencing feelings, images, etc., that give a gestalt sense of knowing. Information we perceive via nonrational intelligence isn't understood by drawing logical, step-by-step conclusions. It's based on the sense of *knowing* that grows out of the feelings we experience while perceiving that information. Using Heart Intelligence requires learning how it communicates, which might best be described as nonverbal, not necessarily sequential, and often perceived as feelings or images. The best way I know to teach you about how to use Heart Intelligence is through your own direct experience.

First Heart Intelligence Exercise

In the first exercise you will locate the center of your awareness, or the center of your mental activity. Your center of mental activity could be anywhere, but let's at least assume it is in the same room you are sitting in. And let's assume it's probably near, if not within, your physical body. In this exercise I'll ask you to move your attention around, looking for your center of mental activity. Don't feel like I'm limiting that to inside your body. Feel free to move your attention anywhere.

First Heart Intelligence Exercise: Script

This is the First Heart Intelligence Exercise. (Wait 5 sec)

As you get ready to begin the exercise, adjust the volume of this recording so that you can comfortably and easily hear and understand my voice. You may do this exercise either sitting or lying down. (Wait 10 sec)

When you're ready to begin, please close your eyes. (Wait 10 sec)

To begin this exercise move your body into a comfortable, relaxed position in your quiet place. (Wait 30 sec)

Remember the feeling of being relaxed. (Wait 20 sec)

At your own pace take in Three Deep Relaxing Breaths, or as many as you need to feel some change in your level of relaxation. (Wait 40 sec)

Remember the image of establishing the flow of energy from below in the *Afterlife Knowledge Guidebook*. (Wait 20 sec)

At your own pace, remembering each of the steps as you do this, take in Three Energy Gathering Breaths to establish the flow from below. (Wait 45 sec)

Remember the image of Energy Gathering from Below in the *Afterlife Knowledge Guidebook*. (Wait 20 sec)

At your own pace, remembering each of the steps as you do this, take in Three Energy Gathering Breaths from Below. (Wait 45 sec)

Remember the feeling of placing intent, or just imagine you are doing the Silly Little Finger Bending Exercise. (Wait 15 sec)

Reexperience the feeling of placing intent as you say in your mind, **I am learning about the location of my center of mental activity.** (Wait 10 sec)

Begin moving your attention to various areas of your body. You are looking for the area that feels like the center of your mental activity. (Wait 30 sec)

This might be the place your thoughts about doing this exercise are coming from. (Wait 30 sec)

When you find that area, what does it feel like? (Wait 45 sec)

Is it large or small? (Wait 15 sec). Light or dark? (Wait 15 sec) Quiet or busy? (Wait 15 sec) Describe it to yourself in your thoughts. (Wait 20 sec)

Take in three more Deep Relaxing Breaths. (Wait 45 sec)

How would you describe the location and feel of your center of mental activity, in words, to someone else? (Wait 30 sec)

When you're ready, please open your eyes and give yourself a few moments to fully return from the exercise. Then immediately begin to write about your experience and use the questions in the debriefing section for this exercise in the *Afterlife Knowledge Guidebook* as a starting point to record your experience in detail in your notebook.

Debrief

Take a moment to record your experience in your notebook.

Describe your experience of moving your focus of attention around your body. Where was your center of mental activity located?

Would you say there are any sensations or feelings that describe what is going on in that area?

Tips to Read Only after Doing the First Exercise

When I first did this exercise I found my center of awareness to be in my head. If I drew one line from temple to temple, and another from the center of my forehead to the center of the back of my skull, my center of mental activity was at the intersection of those two lines. It felt like a sort of fuzzy ball, about the size of a golf ball, with a mildly electric stimulation, or like a small ball of tiny bees buzzing around. Others have described it as a similar sensation extending out into the air near their forehead, or at one side of the back of the head. Others describe it as a feeling of a void their thoughts seem to be coming from. Each of us apparently has our own experience of our center of mental activity, unique but sometimes sharing similarities with those of others.

If you feel like you didn't find anything you could describe as your center of mental activity, repeat this first exercise until you do experience something, even if you believe you are just pretending to know where yours is, or it is just a vague feeling.

Second Heart Intelligence Exercise

This second exercise is to help you distinguish between when you are using your normal intelligence center and when you are using Heart Intelligence. A feeling is associated with using Heart Intelligence, and once you can identity this feeling, remembering/reexperiencing this feeling will automatically shift your awareness to Heart Intelligence.

During this exercise you'll need to know what I mean by *the center of your chest.* With your fingers, press lightly, just below your neck, and find the top of your sternum, the center of your rib cage. Now move your fingers down your sternum, pressing lightly, until you locate the bottom of your sternum, the bottom of the center of your rib cage. For the purposes of this next exercise *the center of your chest* is about midway between these two points.

When I ask you to move your center of awareness to the center of your chest, you might try several different methods to see which is best for you. You might place your intent for it to be there. You might feel it moving from wherever it is to the center of your chest. You might focus your attention there. They may be other ways.

Second Heart Intelligence Exercise: Script

This is the Second Heart Intelligence Exercise. (Wait 5 sec)

As you get ready to begin the exercise, adjust the volume of this recording so that you can comfortably and easily hear and understand my voice. You may do this exercise either sitting or lying down. (Wait 10 sec)

When you're ready to begin, please close your eyes. (Wait 10 sec)

To begin this exercise move your body into a comfortable, relaxed position in your quiet place. (Wait 30 sec)

Remember the feeling of being relaxed. (Wait 20 sec)

At your own pace take in Three Deep Relaxing Breaths, or as many as you need to feel some change in your level of relaxation. (Wait 40 sec)

Remember the image of establishing the flow of energy from below in the *Afterlife Knowledge Guidebook.* (Wait 20 sec)

At your own pace, remembering each of the steps as you do this, take in Three Energy Gathering Breaths to establish the flow from below. (Wait 45 sec)

Remember the image of Energy Gathering from Below in the *Afterlife Knowledge Guidebook.* (Wait 20 sec)

At your own pace, remembering each of the steps as you do this, take in Three Energy Gathering Breaths from Below. (Wait 45 sec)

Remember the feeling of placing intent, or just imagine you are doing the Silly Little Finger Bending Exercise. (Wait 15 sec)

Reexperience the feeling of placing intent as you say in your mind, **I am moving my center of my awareness to the center of my chest.** (Wait 10 sec)

Once again locate your center of mental activity and focus your attention there. (Wait 30 sec)

Now move your center of mental activity to the center of your chest, and just let it be there. (Wait 30 sec)

If it moves back to where it was, that's okay; just once again move your center of mental activity back to the center of your chest, and just let it be there. (Wait 30 sec)

I will give you some time now to practice this on your own. (Wait 1 min 30 sec)

How would you describe to someone else any feelings or sensations you experience with your attention focused at the center of your chest? (Wait 30 sec)

How would you describe to someone else any feelings or sensations you experience with the movement of your center of mental activity to the center of your chest? (Wait 30 sec)

How would you describe to someone else any feelings or sensations you experience when your attention is at the center of your chest, and the feeling of just letting it be there? (Wait 30 sec)

When you're ready, please open your eyes and give yourself a few moments to fully return from the exercise. Then immediately begin to write about your experience and use the questions in the debriefing section for this exercise in the *Afterlife Knowledge Guidebook* as a starting point to record your experience in detail in your notebook.

Debrief of Second Heart Intelligence Exercise

Record your experience in your notebook.

Did you find the center of your mental activity again? Were you able to feel it move?

Describe how it moved. For example, did it move slowly or quickly?

Did it move all the way to the center of your chest?

Did it move part way and move back?

When your attention is at the center of your chest, how did you let it stay there?

How would you describe any feelings, sensations, etc., with your attention focused at the center of your chest?

Did you notice any difference in the level of mental activity with your attention focused at the center of your chest?

Second Heart Intelligence Exercise Hints

When I first learned to do this exercise, I'd locate my center of mental activity; I'd feel that fuzzy little ball in my head start to move, almost like the feeling of swallowing it down the back of my neck. I'd think, *Wow, it's moving toward my* . . . and with that thought, BANG, it would jump back to my head. I'd intend for it to move again, it would start moving, I'd think, *There it goes, it's moving* . . . and it would pop back into my head again. That gave me some clues about how to *let it be there.* Remember, the object of this exercise is to move the center of your awareness to the center of your chest and let it be there. If you start to think about the fact that it's moving, the act of thinking moves the center of awareness back to where those thoughts originate.

As you learn to place your intent for it to move, and then just experience that movement, you'll discover you can allow it to move to your chest. You'll be able to be aware of the feeling of its movement *without talking to yourself about it in your mind.*

Once you are able to move it to the center of your chest, and just allow it to be there, don't be concerned if it pops back to its original location. Just remember the feeling of it *being there* and repeat the exercise to move it back.

Some folks don't move it, they just focus their attention at the center of their chest. Try different ways to see which works best for you.

People using Heart Intelligence report a number of sensations or feelings at the center of the chest. A feeling of slight pressure or heat is fairly common, often accompanied by a sense of mild to strong euphoria. Some report the feeling of a funnel shape, a bubble, or a cloud of color extending outward from the center of their chest. Many report that their thoughts become very quiet with less internal dialogue. You may have a different feeling or sensation. And please remember the lesson of hearing sounds that first night you spent in a new house. If after lots of practice you don't always experience the same feeling in the same way, that doesn't mean you are not using Heart Intelligence.

With practice you'll be able to intend for your awareness to move and stay at the center of your chest and it just will. It takes practice, so practice often.

Using Heart Intelligence

In my experience Heart Intelligence is a tool of exploration that can be used to access information in a much faster, more direct way than other techniques. It can be used to get answers to burning questions. It can be used during afterlife explorations to get information or clear up confusion. In order to learn to use Heart Intelligence it's important to understand how this form of intelligence communicates with our awareness.

While it's easy for me to describe this as nonrational, feeling-based, or a sense of knowing, that won't mean much to anyone who hasn't experienced using Heart Intelligence. This next exercise is intended to guide you to that experience, and we can use a *burning question* again as a way of gaining that experience. Before you begin this next exercise take a few moments to remember one of those questions you've been carrying around that you really want to know the answer to. It could be as mundane as, should I take the promotion they're offering at my job, or as far out and esoteric as you like. Remember to word your question carefully, as ambiguous questions usually yield ambiguous answers. When you hear me say "state your question" during the exercise, repeat your question in your mind.

Using Heart Intelligence Exercise: Script

This exercise is about learning to use Heart Intelligence. (Wait 5 sec)

As you get ready to begin the exercise, adjust the volume of this recording so that you can comfortably and easily hear and understand my voice. You may do this exercise either sitting or lying down. (Wait 10 sec)

When you're ready to begin, please close your eyes. (Wait 10 sec)

To begin this exercise move your body into a comfortable, relaxed position in your quiet place. (Wait 30 sec)

Remember the feeling of being relaxed. (Wait 20 sec)

At your own pace take in Three Deep Relaxing Breaths, or as many as you need to feel some change in your level of relaxation. (Wait 40 sec)

Remember the image of establishing the flow of energy from below in the *Afterlife Knowledge Guidebook*. (Wait 20 sec)

At your own pace, remembering each of the steps as you do this, take in Three Energy Gathering Breaths to establish the flow from below. (Wait 45 sec)

Remember the image of Energy Gathering from Below in the *Afterlife Knowledge Guidebook*. (Wait 20 sec)

At your own pace, remembering each of the steps as you do this, take in Three Energy Gathering Breaths from Below. (Wait 45 sec)

Remember the feeling of placing intent, or just imagine you are doing the Silly Little Finger Bending Exercise. (Wait 15 sec)

Reexperience the feeling of placing intent as you say in your mind, **I am placing my intent to use Heart Intelligence to answer a burning question.** (Wait 10 sec)

Now, focus your attention at the center of your chest. When you can feel it there, just let it be there. (Wait 30 sec)

If it moves away that's okay; just move your focus of attention back to the Heart and let it be there again. (Wait 30 sec)

In a moment I'll ask you to state your question. After you do, focus your attention at the Heart. Then, observe and take note of anything that comes into your awareness, any thought, image, feeling, knowing, sound, itch, tickle, anything. State your question. (Wait 20 sec)

If you observed anything, or nothing, and don't understand it as an answer, use Heart Intelligence to gather more. Assume that Heart Intelligence has given an answer, but in a form that you didn't understand. Say in your mind, **I am willing to be receiving more in answer to my question.** Then focus your attention at the Heart and observe. (Wait 60 sec)

When you're ready, please open your eyes and give yourself a few moments to fully return from the exercise. Then immediately begin to write about your experience and use the questions in the debriefing section for this exercise in the *Afterlife Knowledge Guidebook* as a starting point to record your experience in detail in your notebook.

Heart Intelligence Debrief

Take a moment to record your experience in your notebook. Learning to use Heart Intelligence requires that you do not discard anything just because you don't know what to do with it. It is important to write it down. You don't have to try to understand it, explain it, or interpret it. Just record it no matter what it is.

At first, when using Heart Intelligence, there is a tendency to discard impressions, thoughts, feelings, or knowings as just idle thoughts or meaningless events. I'd advise that no matter what happens, assume it is an answer, although perhaps in a form you did not understand. As I said in the beginning, Heart Intelligence is different from the rational form of intelligence most of us are used to using.

If you didn't understand the answer(s) by the end of the exercise, you might consider reading your question again and reflecting on what you observed and experienced during the exercise. The answer may suddenly become clear.

Heart Intelligence Hints

Sometimes what is really part of receiving the answer to your question can seem to be a distraction that is causing you to have difficulty allowing your awareness to remain focused at the center of your chest. Thoughts, ideas, feelings, sensations, itches, tickles, or twitches can be part of the answer to your question. Here's an example.

Right after I asked my question, my nose began to itch something terrible. I didn't want to scratch it because I thought I had to keep my attention focused on my heart. But it was so distracting I finally had to reach up and scratch it. I then said in my mind, *Hey! Look guys. I've asked my question and all that happened was that my nose itched something terrible. If that was an answer to my question, all I got was an itchy nose and I don't understand this answer.*

As I refocused my attention on the feeling at the center of my chest I said in my mind, *I am willing to be receiving more in answer to my question.* The wording of that last statement is important!

With my attention focused at the center of my chest the next thing that might happen is that all of a sudden a muscle behind my left knee starts twitching like crazy. I'd then say in my mind, *Hey! Look guys. I've asked my question again and all that happened is a twitch behind my left knee. If that was an answer to my question, all I got was twitch and I don't understand this answer.* As I refocused my attention on the feeling at the center of my chest I said in my mind, *I am willing to be receiving more in answer to my question.*

It could just as easily have been an image of a red flaming ice cube, or the sound of a jelly bean hitting on the floor, or an emotion, or something else. Whatever it is, if you don't see that the *answer* you receive has any bearing on your question, acknowledge what you experienced as possibly being an answer that you couldn't understand. Say in your mind, *I am willing to be receiving more in answer to my question,* and again focus your attention at the Heart.

If you feel like nothing is happening, do exactly the same thing. Acknowledge that *nothing* might be an answer that you don't understand, say in your mind, *I am willing to be receiving more in answer to my question,* and again focus your attention at the Heart.

I know how ridiculous this might sound, but that's what it took for me to begin to learn to use Heart Intelligence. When I repeatedly expressed my willingness to receive more, the answer finally came in a form I could recognize. When it did, looking back, I could see how each thing I experienced had indeed been the answer, in a different form.

Sometimes Heart Intelligence's answer comes immediately, during the exercise. Sometimes the answer comes so fast I think I'm still formulating my question. Sometimes the answer comes after the exercise.

Practicing this exercise is a way to learn how to use Heart Intelligence. With practice it became easier for me to use Heart Intelligence to access information quickly and with a strong feeling of assurance—a knowing—that it was accurate. It can be especially useful during afterlife exploration sessions and retrievals as a way of quickly assessing a situation, eliminating confusion, or getting Guidance about what to do next in unfamiliar situations.

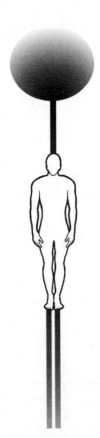

8

Gathering Energy from Above

In an earlier chapter you learned how to gather energy from below, establishing a flow of energy up through your body, and then building the level of that energy within and around your body. You've learned this as a way of putting your consciousness on the charger, so to speak, to give your awareness a boost.

Energy Gathering from Above, Establishing the Flow Exercise: Description

In this exercise you'll learn to use a new Energy Gathering technique, Gathering Energy from Above. The process is identical to gathering energy from below, except that the energy is from a source high above you and the flow is in the opposite direction. Once again there are two parts to this Energy Gathering Exercise: establishing the flow and building the level. These, done together, are Gathering Energy from Above. Imagination can play a role in both parts of the exercise.

Energy Gathering from Above, Establishing the Flow Exercise: Script

This exercise is for Gathering Energy to Establish the Flow from Above. (Wait 5 sec)

Before beginning this exercise look at the image in the Energy Gathering chapter in *Afterlife Knowledge Guidebook*. If you haven't done so, or if you can't clearly remember it from a previous viewing, please stop this recording and review that image to facilitate doing the exercise. (Wait 10 sec)

As you get ready to begin the exercise, adjust the volume of this recording so that you can comfortably and easily hear and understand my voice. You may do this exercise either sitting or lying down. (Wait 10 sec)

When you're ready to begin, please close your eyes. (Wait 10 sec)

To begin this exercise move your body into a comfortable, relaxed position in your quiet place. (Wait 30 sec)

Remember the feeling of being relaxed. (Wait 20 sec)

At your own pace take in Three Deep Relaxing Breaths, or as many as you need to feel some change in your level of relaxation. (Wait 40 sec)

Remember the image of establishing the flow of energy from below in the *Afterlife Knowledge Guidebook*. (Wait 20 sec)

At your own pace, remembering each of the steps as you do this, take in Three Energy Gathering Breaths to establish the flow from below. (Wait 45 sec)

Remember the image of Energy Gathering from Below in the *Afterlife Knowledge Guidebook*. (Wait 20 sec)

At your own pace, remembering each of the steps as you do this, take in Three Energy Gathering Breaths from Below. (Wait 45 sec)

Remember the feeling of placing intent, or just imagine you are doing the Silly Little Finger Bending Exercise. (Wait 15 sec)

Reexperience the feeling of placing intent as you say in your mind, **I am learning to establish the flow of energy from above.** (Wait 10 sec)

Remember the image of gathering energy to establish the flow from above in the *Afterlife Knowledge Guidebook*. (Wait 15 sec)

Now, begin thinking about a vast pool of clean, clear, bright, shiny, sparkling energy high above you. (Wait 20 sec)

Think about a column of that clean, clear, bright, shiny, sparkling energy flowing down from the pool toward the top of your head. (Wait 15 sec)

Focus your attention at the very top of your head. (Wait 10 sec)

Using the same no-stopping breathing pattern as for Deep Relaxing Breaths, as you begin a long, slow inhale, imagine energy flowing from the pool of clean, clear, bright, shiny, sparkling energy high above you, down into your body through the top of your head. (Wait 1 sec)

And as you begin to very slowly exhale, let this energy flow to wherever it wants to go. Notice any feelings that might indicate where it flows in your body. (Wait 15 sec)

Take in at least two more Energy Gathering Breaths to establish the flow from above. (Wait 20 sec)

Focus your attention on that pool of clean, clear, bright, shiny, sparkling energy high above you. (Wait 15 sec)

Imagine a column of this energy flowing downward from the pool toward the top of your head. (Wait 15 sec)

Once again, focus your attention at the very top of your head as you inhale this energy into your body through the top of your head. (Wait 2 sec)

Down through your body. (Wait 2 sec)

On your next exhale, breathe this energy out through the bottoms of your feet. (Wait 2 sec)

As you exhale imagine this column of energy continues flowing downward, out of sight. (Wait 10 sec)

Again, think about the pool of energy above you and a column of this energy flowing downward toward the top of your head. (Wait 2 sec)

Focus your attention at the very top of your head. (Wait 2 sec)

Breathe this energy down into your body through the top of your head, down through your body, and out through the bottoms of your feet. (Wait 2 sec)

As you exhale imagine the column of energy continuously flowing downward, out of sight. (Wait 10 sec)

At your own pace, using all the individual steps, take in more Energy Gathering Breaths to establish the flow from above. (Wait 45 sec)

As you continue establishing the flow of energy from above, taking in more Energy Gathering Breaths from Above, focus your attention on any feeling or sensation of a flow entering your body through the top of your head, flowing down through your body, and out the bottoms of your feet. (Wait 10 sec)

Be willing to imagine or pretend this flow. (Wait 30 sec)

Return to breathing normally and focus your attention on the feeling of establishing the flow of energy from above. (Wait 10 sec)

In future exercises, when I ask you to, take in Three Energy Gathering Breaths to establish the flow from above, remember the image and feeling of establishing the flow, and use the breathing pattern you have just learned to calmly and easily do this. (Wait 10 sec)

When you're ready, please open your eyes and give yourself a few moments to fully return from the exercise. Then immediately begin to write about your experience and use the questions in the debriefing section for this exercise in the *Afterlife Knowledge Guidebook* as a starting point to record your experience in detail in your notebook.

Debrief: Establishing the Flow of Energy from Above

In your notebook describe any feelings or sensations that indicated something flowing in through the top of your head during this exercise.

What did it feel like?

Describe any feelings that indicated where the energy went in your body as you let it go wherever it wanted to go. Where did it go and what did that feel like?

Describe any feelings or sensations you experienced as you exhaled this energy out through the bottoms of your feet and imagined it continuously flowing downward out of sight.

Describe any feelings or sensations you experienced that might have indicated establishing the flow of energy from above through your body.

Building the Level Exercise: Description

Once the flow of energy has been established, the next step is to build the level of energy, done by recirculating a portion of the energy flowing out the bottoms of your feet back up around the outside of your body as you exhale. With each succeeding inhale, both the recirculating energy and more from the pool above are inhaled in through the top of your head, and down through the body. With each exhale more of the established flow of energy is recirculated. Imagination again plays a role in this exercise.

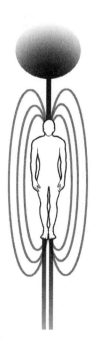

A way to help you imagine this recirculation is to think of the column of energy flowing downward as having a thin, outside layer. As you begin to exhale, imagine that this thin layer peels away from the column and its flow turns upward. As you continue to exhale imagine this thin layer of energy completely surrounds and showers up, outside your body, toward your head. Then inhale this showering energy and more from the pool into your body through the top of your head and repeat the cycle.

Building the Level Exercise: Script

This exercise to Build Up the Level of Energy from Above. (Wait 5 sec)

Before beginning this exercise look at the image in the Energy Gathering chapter in *Afterlife Knowledge Guidebook*. If you haven't done so, or if you can't clearly remember it from a previous viewing, please stop this recording and review that image to facilitate doing the exercise. (Wait 10 sec)

As you get ready to begin the exercise, adjust the volume of this recording so that you can comfortably and easily hear and understand my voice. You may do this exercise either sitting or lying down. (Wait 10 sec)

When you're ready to begin, please close your eyes. (Wait 10 sec)

To begin this exercise move your body into a comfortable, relaxed position in your quiet place. (Wait 30 sec)

Remember the feeling of being relaxed. (Wait 20 sec)

At your own pace take in Three Deep Relaxing Breaths, or as many as you need to feel some change in your level of relaxation. (Wait 40 sec)

Remember the image of establishing the flow of energy from below in the *Afterlife Knowledge Guidebook*. (Wait 20 sec)

At your own pace, remembering each of the steps as you do this, take in Three Energy Gathering Breaths to establish the flow from below. (Wait 45 sec)

Remember the image of Energy Gathering from Below in the *Afterlife Knowledge Guidebook*. (Wait 20 sec)

At your own pace, remembering each of the steps as you do this, take in Three Energy Gathering Breaths from Below. (Wait 45 sec)

Remember the feeling of placing intent, or just imagine you are doing the Silly Little Finger Bending Exercise. (Wait 15 sec)

Reexperience the feeling of placing intent as you say in your mind, **I am learning to build the level of energy from above.** (Wait 10 sec)

Remember the image of establishing the flow of energy from above in the *Afterlife Knowledge Guidebook*. (Wait 20 sec)

Begin thinking about the vast pool of clean, clear, bright, shiny, sparkling energy high above you. (Wait 20 sec)

Imagine a column of this energy flowing down from the pool toward the top of your head. (Wait 20 sec)

Focus your attention at the very top of your head. (Wait 10 sec)

At your own pace establish the flow of energy from above. Inhale it in through the very top of your head, down through your body, and exhale it out the bottoms of your feet as a column of energy flowing downward out of sight. (Wait 30 sec)

Repeat this and be willing to imagine or pretend this established flow. (Wait 30 sec)

Remember the image of Energy Gathering from Above in the *Afterlife Knowledge Guidebook.* (Wait 20 sec)

When the flow of energy is established, just as you begin to exhale, imagine that a thin layer of the column of energy below your feet peels away from the column, turns upward, and showers upward all around, outside your body, and continues flowing upward a little above the top of your head. (Wait 5 sec)

On the next inhale imagine breathing this showering energy and more from the pool into your body through the top of your head, down through your body, and out through the bottoms of your feet. (Wait 15 sec)

As you continue building the level, each time you begin to exhale imagine that another thin layer from the column peels off and showers up around your body, a little further out from your body each time. And as you inhale, inhale all the showering energy and more from the pool into your body through the top of your head. (Wait 30 sec)

Continue building the level of energy from above by imagining all the steps as you take in and recirculate at least six more of these Energy Gathering Breaths from Above. At your own pace. (Wait 60 sec)

Be willing to imagine or pretend this flow. (Wait 30 sec)

Begin breathing normally and focus your attention on the feeling of building the level of energy from above. (Wait 20 sec)

In future exercises when I ask you to take in Three Energy Gathering Breaths to build up the level of energy from above, remember the image and feeling of building the level and use the breathing pattern you have just learned to calmly and easily do this. (Wait 10 sec)

When you're ready, please open your eyes and give yourself a few moments to fully return from the exercise. Then immediately begin to write about your experience and use the questions in the debriefing section for this exercise in the *Afterlife Knowledge Guidebook* as a starting point to record your experience in detail in your notebook.

Debrief

Take a few moments to record your experience in your notebook.

What was your experience of imagining the pool of energy this time?
Did you notice any new sensations or feelings with your attention focused at the top of your head during the exercise?

Did you notice any sensations or feelings as you breathed this energy down through your body and out the bottoms of your feet to establish the flow?

Did you notice any sensations or feelings as you exhaled and imagined the column of energy continuing to flow downward out of sight?

Describe your experience of the showering and recirculating energy.

The Complete Energy Gathering from Above Exercise: Description

The two previous exercises have been in preparation for this one. When I began using this Energy Gathering exercise I tended to see it as alternating between bringing in energy during the inhale and recirculating it on the exhale. As with Energy Gathering from Below, gathering energy from above is actually a continuously flowing, ever-increasing level of energy.

There is a specific feeling, or set of feelings, associated with this continuously flowing, ever-increasing level of energy. Identifying the experience of that feeling is the object of this next exercise. As in other exercises, this set of feelings may include images or the impressions of images. In this exercise you'll again use two techniques to help you identify the feeling of a continuously flowing, ever-increasing level of energy. The first of these techniques will be for you to imagine that the flow of showering energy recirculates around and through your body three times with each inhale and each exhale. To do this you might pretend that as you inhale, your eyes follow a point in the flow of this energy as it flows in through the top of your head, down through your body, out the bottoms of your feet, showers up around you, and reenters through the top of your head three times as you inhale. Then imagine this again as you exhale. The second technique you will use in this exercise to help you experience the feeling of a continuous flow of energy will be to shift your focus of attention to various areas of your body at different points in the breathing pattern. This is how folks in my workshops learn to identify the feeling. Once you can identify this feeling and remember it, Energy Gathering from Above becomes a matter of remembering that feeling to begin gathering energy from above and boost the brightness of your conscious awareness.

By now you've become familiar with relaxation, establishing the flow, and building the level. Therefore, I'll begin saying less during the exercise to give you the opportunity to practice without the distraction of my voice.

The Complete Energy Gathering from Above Exercise: Script

This is the Complete Exercise to Gather Energy from Above. (Wait 5 sec)

Before beginning this exercise look at the image in the Energy Gathering chapter in *Afterlife Knowledge Guidebook*. If you haven't done so, or if you can't clearly remember it from a previous viewing, please stop this recording and review that image to facilitate doing the exercise. (Wait 10 sec)

As you get ready to begin the exercise, adjust the volume of this recording so that you can comfortably and easily hear and understand my voice. You may do this exercise either sitting or lying down. (Wait 10 sec)

When you're ready to begin, please close your eyes. (Wait 10 sec)

To begin this exercise move your body into a comfortable, relaxed position in your quiet place. (Wait 30 sec)

Remember the feeling of being relaxed. (Wait 20 sec)

At your own pace take in Three Deep Relaxing Breaths, or as many as you need to feel some change in your level of relaxation. (Wait 40 sec)

Remember the image of establishing the flow of energy from below in the *Afterlife Knowledge Guidebook*. (Wait 20 sec)

At your own pace, remembering each of the steps as you do this, take in Three Energy Gathering Breaths to establish the flow from below. (Wait 45 sec)

Remember the image of Energy Gathering from Below in the *Afterlife Knowledge Guidebook*. (Wait 20 sec)

At your own pace, remembering each of the steps as you do this, take in Three Energy Gathering Breaths from Below. (Wait 45 sec)

Remember the feeling of placing intent, or just imagine you are doing the Silly Little Finger Bending Exercise. (Wait 15 sec)

Reexperience the feeling of placing intent as you say in your mind, **I am learning to gather energy from above.** (Wait 10 sec)

Remember the image of establishing the flow of energy from above in the *Afterlife Knowledge Guidebook*. (Wait 15 sec)

At your own pace, take in Three Energy Gathering Breaths from Above to establish the flow. (Wait 45 sec)

When the flow of energy is established, remember the image of Energy Gathering from Above in the *Afterlife Knowledge Guidebook*. (Wait 15 sec)

At your own pace, build up the level of energy from above, imagining all the steps as you take in and recirculate at least six more of these Energy Gathering Breaths. (Wait 1 min)

As you continue building up the level of energy from above, imagine or pretend that your eyes follow a point in this flow as it circulates around and through your body three times with each inhale and three times with each exhale. (Wait 30 sec)

As you continue building the level, shift your focus of attention to the bottoms of your feet as you begin your inhale. (Wait 10 sec)

As you inhale, feel the energy flow out the bottoms of your feet and into the top of your head at the same time. (Wait 20 sec)

As you continue building the level, shift your focus of attention to the top of your head as you begin your exhale. (Wait 10 sec)

As you exhale, feel the energy flow out the bottoms of your feet and in the top of your head at the same time. (Wait 20 sec)

As you continue this Energy Gathering Exercise, imagine that you experience the flow of recirculating energy down through your body and showering up around your body at least three times per inhale and exhale. (Wait 1 min)

As you continue this Energy Gathering exercise, focus your attention on the feeling of a continuous, ever-increasing flow of energy through and around your body. (Wait 30 sec)

Be willing to imagine or pretend this flow. (Wait 30 sec)

In future exercises, when I ask you to, take in Three Energy Gathering Breaths from Above, remember the image and feeling of this complete Energy Gathering Exercise from Above, and use the breathing pattern you have just learned to calmly and easily do this. (Wait 10 sec)

When you're ready, please open your eyes and give yourself a few moments to fully return from the exercise. Then immediately begin to write about your experience and use the questions in the debriefing section for this exercise in the *Afterlife Knowledge Guidebook* as a starting point to record your experience in detail in your notebook.

Debrief

Take a few moments to record your experience in your notebook.

What was your experience of imagining the pool of energy this time?

Did you notice any new sensations or feelings with your attention focused on the top of your head during the exercise?

Did you notice any sensations or feelings as you breathed this energy down through your body and out the bottoms of your feet?

Did you notice any new sensations or feelings as you exhaled and imagined the column of energy continuing to flow downward out of sight?

Did you notice any new sensations or feelings as you recirculated energy upward, around your body, and back into your body at the top of your head?

Did you notice any images or impressions of images during the exercise?

Describe your experience of the continuous, ever-increasing flow of energy.

The object of moving the focus of your attention to the opposite end of your body was to have you experience any feelings that to you indicate a continuous flow of energy into, and recirculating around, your body during the exercise. The same purpose is intended for multiple passes of energy with each breath. As you practice the Complete Energy Gathering Exercise, there will come a point in which you will realize you can feel, or pretend to feel, both flows of energy, down through your body and showering up around you, simultaneously. That feeling is Energy Gathering from Above.

How Many Times?

As with gathering energy from below, many folks ask how long and how often they should do the Energy Gathering from Above exercise. When you first begin practicing, I recommend three- to four-minute sessions. As you continue practice sessions there may come a point, after you've experienced the feelings and sensations of the flow of energy, when you notice those feelings are not always present. That is an indication that gathering energy from above is becoming an easy, natural shift of your focus of attention to gathering energy consciousness.

Energy Gathering from Above, Tips

Many report a tingling feeling, or a feeling like air passing through open nostrils, at the top of the head during this exercise.

Many report that with the first few breaths the energy seems to flow to various and very specific areas of the body with each breath. Some report the feeling that this flow is filling the body with this energy.

Some report that once the body feels full, continuing to breathe energy in from above seems to fill space surrounding the body.

Some report the occurrence of spontaneous images, visions, voices, etc., during this exercise. If this is your experience you might consider using Heart Intelligence for further exploration of these on your own. My suggestion would be to remember the image, etc., focus your attention at the center of your chest, and say in your mind, *I am willing to be receiving more about the meaning of this image, etc.* This can lead to some very interesting experiences.

Many report the energy has color: golden-white, blue, green, and other colors are reported.

In terms of the Hemi-Sync Model of Consciousness, *color* is considered a *feeling*. For some people the act of remembering the color at the beginning of the exercise shifts awareness to Gathering Energy from Above Consciousness, and gathering this energy automatically begins.

Using Energy Gathering from Above in Future Exercises

From now on when you hear the instruction, "Take in Three Energy Gathering Breaths from Above" or read "Take in 3EGBA" it means:

Begin thinking about that vast pool of clean, clear, bright, shiny, sparkling energy high above you.

Remember the feeling/image of establishing the flow of energy.

Establish the flow.

Remember the feeling/image of letting energy shower up around you.

Begin recirculating energy.

Remember the feeling of gathering energy from above.

Gather energy from above.

9

Love

I agree with Robert Monroe: Fear is the greatest barrier to human progress, especially in the field of afterlife exploration. All of us begin exploration of the afterlife carrying beliefs we've taken on from many sources, many based in fear.

The church I grew up in taught that the nonphysical world (the Spirit World, as they call it) is inhabited exclusively by demons, devils, and Satan, and taught that venturing into the Spirit World risked attack and/or deception by demons whose intent was to steal my soul and lead me to an eternity in Hell.

Hollywood's horror movies are another source of fear-inducing beliefs. So often, nonphysical beings like ghosts are portrayed as violent, malevolent creatures we are powerless to defend against. Watching such movies can subtly slip fearful expectations into our consciousness. (And yet, Hollywood has also given us movies with some fine depictions of what the afterlife is really like. *Ghost*, *What Dreams May Come*, and *The Sixth Sense* are three of the best that come to mind. I highly recommend that you watch them. While none of these movies is 100 percent accurate, my quibbles are only about small details.)

Wouldn't it be nice to have a tool to deal with the effects of fear? Well, that's exactly what this chapter is about. Let me tell you a story.

Bill (not his real name), after attempting for quite some time to have an out-of-body experience (OBE), finally succeeded. But he hadn't moved very far from his physical body before he encountered a horrible beast. Before he could get back to his physical body, he and the beast fought two horrendous battles. After Bill finally got back into his physical body, he lay there in heart-pounding terror. In an e-mail he told me that if going out of body meant encountering that half man, half dragon beast again, he didn't want to do it.

I wrote Bill that I don't use OBEs as a means of exploration, but that perhaps my experience of dealing with fear within nonphysical realities would help. I explained that nonphysical realities are so easily molded that thoughts can be things. In a nonphysical reality if I begin thinking about a hot fudge sundae, I can make one appear. And this hot fudge sundae can be so real in a nonphysical reality that if you were there with me you'd see it, smell it, and taste it (if I were willing to let you have some).

But creation within nonphysical reality is not limited to what I *consciously* think about. Subconscious expectations and fears can be projected into nonphysical reality as well, without our realizing we're doing it. Thus I may create some horrible half man, half dragon beast who can then terrorize me by reflecting the image of my own fear back to me. If I don't realize what's happening I can mistakenly believe that the beast is real, and once my fear gets my attention all sorts of idiotic, unnecessary mischief is possible. Fortunately, in the nonphysical world there is something as all-pervasive as the physical world's Law of Gravity called the Law of Love and Fear, which states:

Love and Fear Cannot Coexist

I told Bill the story of the banshee from my second book, *Voyage Beyond Doubt*.

A friend's terminally ill father was screaming in terror every night from the moment he fell asleep at night until he awoke in the morning. My friend called to see if there was anything we could do. My friend Rebecca and I went nonphysically to find out what the screaming was about, and found my friend's father confronting a huge, stereotypical banshee, a green, vaporous apparition with a hideous face and the shape of fluttering, flowing robes trailing behind it, that kept attacking him. Rebecca resolved the problem by demonstrating, and then teaching him, to extend love to the banshee. Each time he was able to do it, the banshee disappeared.

The banshee was his own creation, fabricated out of his fear of death. It terrorized him whenever he slept and could see it. But the power of love can eliminate objects created out of fear. Love and fear cannot coexist.

So I suggested to Bill that he use the Law of Love and Fear: remember a time in his life when he was feeling loved or loving and let remembering that feeling cause him to *reexperience* it. Then project that love directly at the dragon man. I also suggested that Bill ask for the assistance of a Helper if need be. These Helpers are everywhere, and they are loving beings who will assist you.

A few days later Bill reported that he'd gotten out of his body again, and that dragon man was right there waiting for him. His first thought had been to attack, but instead he did what I had suggested. He was a little surprised that remembering a time he was feeling loved actually made him feel love. When the feeling had built up a little, he took a great big ball of love and threw it at the dragon man. Damnedest thing happened! The dragon part of the man started shimmering and shaking, and then it disappeared. Then there was just an ordinary man standing where the dragon man had been, who said something like *Thank God you can see me!*

Bill went on to have an interesting learning experience adventure that would not have happened if he'd continued battling his own fear-generated dragon man. His experience demonstrates one way that fear can appear when it is projected and takes form within a nonphysical reality. His fear formed what I call a Fear Mask over something that was actually there. When he projected love, the fear masking the man disappeared, because, again, love and fear cannot coexist.

The other way fear acts when projected within a nonphysical reality is to create an apparently autonomous being like the banshee. In either case projecting love eliminates the fear's manifestation. It just disappears. In your own explorations beyond physical reality, when you encounter anything that causes you to feel fearful, remember to utilize the Law of Love and Fear.

More Uses for Love Energy

Love Energy has other powerful uses. Feeling love seems to throw open windows of opportunity, opening perception beyond our beliefs, limitations, and expectations. It's no accident that Heart Intelligence and love are centered in the same area of our consciousness.

As you begin to explore our afterlife, sometimes you will be faced with seemingly impossible situations. Whenever you are, remember the power of love. If you just stop and feel love you may discover that the confusion or ignorance is no barrier. If you project love to, say, a hopelessly trapped person, it may provide a moment of clarity in which they can—perhaps for the first time in centuries—see and understand their true situation. Projecting love may be the one and only thing capable of helping that person.

The most important exercise I teach is this next one, Feeling and Building Love Energy. I say that because I so firmly believe that just the act of feeling love removes and eliminates all blocks to knowledge of who and what we really are.

Feeling and Building Love Energy Exercise: Description

This exercise is intended to facilitate the experience of feeling love. I want to stress that I don't mean that you should *think about* love, or *analyze* love, or try to *understand* what love is, or why it happens. This is *not* an intellectual exercise. The intent of this exercise is to learn to *feel* love.

For me love is like any other area of consciousness, in that it has a feeling, and remembering the feeling of a state of consciousness automatically focuses our attention There. Learning to shift your awareness to love consciousness can be learned by remembering the feeling.

I was present when both of my children were born, and if I close my eyes and remember when I first held my newborn babies, I reexperience the feeling of love I felt then. If I want to intensify that feeling, I remember bouncing my infant daughter on my knee. I remember her smiles and giggles, the feel of her tiny hands holding on to my fingers, talking baby talk to her. Not just *remembering* doing those things, but *reexperiencing the feeling* of doing those things—the longer I do this, the more the feeling of love grows and builds up within me.

In this exercise it doesn't matter what event you remember. It could be the memory of holding your newborn baby, the last time you petted your cat, or a really memorable first kiss. The event doesn't matter as long as it helps you remember and reexperience the feeling of love, and helps you let that feeling grow and expand until it fills your entire being. As you practice this exercise you may experience the feeling of love for a short time and then lose it. That's okay. Just remember another time you were feeling loved or loving. One goal of this exercise is that you learn to reexperience the feeling of love continuously for half a minute or longer. This is one of those cases in which more is better and so the longer you reexperience that feeling the better.

If I could get you to do only one exercise daily, it would be this one.

Feeling and Building Love Energy Exercise: Script

This is the Feeling and Building Love Energy Exercise. (Wait 5 sec)

As you get ready to begin the exercise, adjust the volume of this recording so that you can comfortably and easily hear and understand my voice. You may do this exercise either sitting or lying down. (Wait 10 sec)

When you're ready to begin, please close your eyes. (Wait 10 sec)

To begin this exercise move your body into a comfortable, relaxed position in your quiet place. (Wait 30 sec)

Remember the feeling of being relaxed and at your own pace take in Three Deep Relaxing Breaths, or as many as you need to feel some change in your level of relaxation. (Wait 45 sec)

Remember the image of establishing the flow of energy from below in the *Afterlife Knowledge Guidebook*, and take in Three Energy Gathering Breaths to establish the flow from below. (Wait 45 sec)

Remember the image of Energy Gathering from Below in the *Afterlife Knowledge Guidebook*, and take in Three Energy Gathering Breaths from Below. (Wait 45 sec)

Remember the image of establishing the flow of energy from above in the *Afterlife Knowledge Guidebook*, and take in Three Energy Gathering Breaths to establish the flow from above. (Wait 45 sec)

Remember the image of Energy Gathering from Above in the *Afterlife Knowledge Guidebook*, and take in Three Energy Gathering Breaths from Above. (Wait 45 sec)

Remember the feeling of placing intent, or just imagine you are doing the Silly Little Finger Bending Exercise. (Wait 15 sec)

Reexperience the feeling of placing intent as you say in your mind, **I am learning to experience the feeling of love and building Love Energy.** (Wait 10 sec)

Remember a time in your life when you were feeling loved or loving, or a time you were feeling great gratitude and appreciation for the beauty of nature. (Wait 30 sec)

Let this memory help you to remember and reexperience the feeling of love. (Wait 20 sec)

If the feeling fades that's okay; just remember another time you were feeling loved or loving, and let that feeling build. (Wait 20 sec)

Let that feeling into you and feel it. (Wait 20 sec)

Let the feeling build and expand to fill your entire being. Let it bring that inner smile. (Wait 20 sec)

If the feeling fades that's okay; just remember another time you were feeling loved or loving, and let that feeling build again. (Wait 20 sec)

Let that feeling of love expand into the air around you. Let it fill and surround you. (Wait 20 sec)

When you reexperience the feeling of love, just let yourself be in it, feel it, experience it. (Wait 60 sec)

When you're ready, please open your eyes and give yourself a few moments to fully return from the exercise. Then immediately begin to write about your experience and use the questions in the debriefing section for this exercise in the *Afterlife Knowledge Guidebook* as a starting point to record your experience in detail in your notebook.

Debrief: Feeling Love Energy Exercise

Were you able to reexperience the feeling of love? If not, repeat this exercise until you do. In your notebook describe what love feels like.

Were you able to allow that feeling to build up within you? If not, repeat this exercise until you can.

Did you feel it more in some places in your body than others? If so, where?

Did you have any impressions, visual, auditory, or other during the exercise?

Repeat this Feeling and Building Love Exercise often. It's the most valuable tool I know to teach you. Practice until you can feel it for at least half a minute. Then, practice some more. Ideally, this exercise will become a daily meditation you'll do for at least five minutes every day.

Tips for Feeling and Building Love Energy

Many people report a sense of pressure, warmth, or heat at the heart during this exercise.

Many people report a strong sense of well-being, mild euphoria, a sense of being nurtured and cared for, a sense of being completely accepted without judgment.

Some people describe impressions of a conelike shape emanating from the center of the chest. Some describe a spiraling motion within this cone shape and a sense of energy moving into or out of this cone shape. Others describe various shapes of clouds of light in various colors.

Some people report experiencing strong emotions during this exercise, often associated with a painful memory. We sometimes carry around unresolved issues and feeling love automatically opens awareness, often bringing these suppressed memories out into the open. If that happens I'd suggest that you allow yourself to feel whatever the emotion is, remember whatever life event or events the emotion is associated with, and then project love to the emotion, the life events, and to anything or anyone involved.

Often these strong emotions are accompanied by memories of life experiences. When such unexpected, strong feelings come into awareness during this exercise, my inclination is to express them freely in whatever form seems appropriate. For me crying often feels appropriate. Releasing such emotion-filled feelings by expressing them can have a healing quality.

Experiment with remembering different experiences when you felt loved or loving. You may find some that work better than others.

Some would say that they use the memory of a feeling closer to gratitude or appreciation in this exercise. One participant explained he was getting nowhere using memories of feeling love or loving, but loved the feeling he felt when walking along an ocean beach. In this exercise he remembered walking along the shore and reexperiencing the feeling it gave him. This or other feelings like it are completely acceptable for this feeling love exercise.

Do this exercise often, no matter what your results. In my view learning to reexperience the feeling of love continuously for at least half a minute is just the beginning. I encourage you to continue practicing this exercise until you can allow yourself to reexperience love for several minutes.

As you learn to reexperience the feeling of love using this exercise, I encourage you to do it in combination with the Heart Intelligence Exercise. Many report some incredibly powerful healing experiences, insights, understandings, and other information-gathering experiences using this combination.

Some people report having difficulty continuing the exercise due to experiencing painful memories of life experiences. If you have this kind of experience, as I do from time to time, I strongly suggest that you use the Heart Intelligence Exercise in combination with the Feeling and Building Love Exercise to explore the source, effects, and resolution of these feelings. As I described in the More Uses for Love Energy section, feeling Love may automatically bring to awareness unresolved, painful emotions, memories, or feelings. I personally see this as an opportunity to resolve them. That's why I recommend using the Heart Intelligence and Feeling Love Exercises in combination to explore these issues. Doing this can be as simple as saying in your mind, *I am willing to be receiving more about the source and resolution of this feeling.* Then use the Heart Intelligence Exercise technique to observe, ask again, and continue the resolution process. This process has led to life-changing, healing experiences for some people, myself included. Remember what you learned about Belief-System Crashes and reintegration, as such life-changing, healing experiences may be a challenge to your present beliefs and identity.

Some people report an achy feeling, bordering on pain, at the center of the chest during this exercise. When this happened to me I learned it was an indication of my own resistance to allowing myself to experience the feeling and flow of Love Energy. If you experience pain during this exercise I urge you to avoid letting your fear of a heart attack take over. I discovered that this pain *felt* physical but actually *was* nonphysical. When you focus your attention within nonphysical realities, these two are easily confused. Robert Monroe claimed that pain experienced during exploration of nonphysical realities, if it subsided with full return to physical reality consciousness, was a beacon pointing to an issue requiring resolution. My experience supports his statement. Those who have read *Voyages into the Unknown* might recall that my retrieval of Joshua led to resolution of a disease called sarcoidosis.

If you experience strong pain during this exercise I suggest that you begin taking in Deep Relaxing Breaths, then stop the exercise and get up and walk around, to help bring yourself back to full, physical reality consciousness. If the pain subsides as you do this, it's a beacon pointing to an issue that requires resolution, and I again strongly suggest you use the Heart Intelligence Exercise in combination with feeling love to explore the source of this pain. Doing this can be as simple as saying in your mind, *I am willing to be receiving more about the source and resolution of this pain*; then use the Heart Intelligence Exercise technique to observe and continue the resolution process. In my case I discovered that chest pain during this exercise indicated I was carrying beliefs about what love is, and what it is not, beliefs about when it is appropriate to allow myself to experience it, and when it is not, that caused me to resist experiencing the feeling of love. That resistance was the cause of the pain. As I resolved these issues I found that I was able to experience feeling love not only without pain, but also accompanied by some other, rather pleasant feelings.

Projecting Love Energy

In the previous section you learned to feel and build Love Energy as a way of automatically opening your awareness beyond its normal limits and as a way of dealing with fear. In this section you will learn to Project Love Energy, which can be used to automatically open the awareness and shift the focus of attention of others. We'll begin by using Energy Gathering from Above as a new way of building Love Energy.

In this exercise you'll Gather Energy from Above, and this time after several breaths in which *you let the energy go where it will go, establish the flow, and begin recirculating,* as you exhale you'll gather the energy at the center of your chest. To do this, begin gathering energy from above in the usual way, and as you exhale, focus your attention at the center of your chest, intending that a portion of this energy gather and build up, or collect there.

Gathering from Above at the Heart Exercise: Script

This is the Gathering Love Energy from Above at the Heart Exercise. (Wait 5 sec)

As you get ready to begin the exercise, adjust the volume of this recording so that you can comfortably and easily hear and understand my voice. You may do this exercise either sitting or lying down. (Wait 10 sec)

When you're ready to begin, please close your eyes. (Wait 10 sec)

To begin this exercise move your body into a comfortable, relaxed position in your quiet place. (Wait 30 sec)

Remember the feeling of being relaxed and at your own pace take in Three Deep Relaxing Breaths, or as many as you need to feel some change in your level of relaxation. (Wait 45 sec)

Remember the image of establishing the flow of energy from below in the *Afterlife Knowledge Guidebook,* and take in Three Energy Gathering Breaths to establish the flow from below. (Wait 45 sec)

Remember the image of Energy Gathering from Below in the *Afterlife Knowledge Guidebook,* and take in Three Energy Gathering Breaths from Below. (Wait 45 sec)

Remember the image of establishing the flow of energy from above in the *Afterlife Knowledge Guidebook,* and take in Three Energy Gathering Breaths to establish the flow from above. (Wait 45 sec)

Remember the image of Energy Gathering from Above in the *Afterlife Knowledge Guidebook,* and take in Three Energy Gathering Breaths from Above. (Wait 45 sec)

Remember the feeling of placing intent, or just imagine you are doing the Silly Little Finger Bending Exercise. (Wait 15 sec)

Reexperience the feeling of placing intent as you say in your mind, **I am learning a new way of gathering Love Energy at the heart.** (Wait 10 sec)

Remember a time in your life when you were feeling loved or loving. (Wait 20 sec)

Let this memory help you to remember and reexperience the feeling of love. (Wait 20 sec)

If the feeling fades that's okay; just remember another time you were feeling loved or loving, and let that feeling build. (Wait 20 sec)

As you continue gathering energy from above, as you slowly exhale, allow some of this energy to gather, mix with the energy of love, and build at the heart. (Wait 30 sec)

It may be helpful to alternate between feeling love and Energy Gathering Breaths from Above to help you build up the level of Love Energy at the heart. (Wait 20 sec)

Again, remember a time in your life when you were feeling loved or loving. (Wait 20 sec)

Let this memory help you to remember and reexperience the feeling of love. (Wait 20 sec)

If the feeling fades that's okay; just remember another time you were feeling loved or loving, and let that feeling build. (Wait 20 sec)

Again as you continue gathering energy from above, as you slowly exhale, allow some of this energy to gather and build at the heart, and mix with the feeling of love. (Wait 30 sec)

When you're ready, please open your eyes and give yourself a few moments to fully return from the exercise. Then immediately begin to write about your experience and use the questions in the debriefing section for this exercise in the *Afterlife Knowledge Guidebook* as a starting point to record your experience in detail in your notebook.

Debrief

Describe in your notebook any feelings associated with movement of the energy through your body or gathering at the heart.

What impressions did you have of the energy after it gathered at the heart?
Describe any feelings at the center of your chest that might indicate a buildup of energy there.

Tips

Many describe an intense sense of mild pressure building, warmth, or heat at the center of the chest during this exercise.

Some have a sense of color in a cloud or funnel shape, which expands outward from the center of the chest.

Some report a feeling like their whole body is heating up.

Some report a mild achy feeling at the center of the chest.

Many report that the sensation of mild pressure, warmth, or heat persists for some time after the exercise.

Projecting Love Energy Exercise: Description

One of the more powerful tools of afterlife exploration is Projecting Love Energy. In the previous section I described some of the kinds of situations you may encounter in your afterlife explorations where Love Energy may be a very useful tool. (In my experience, too, this tool can be used in many situations within physical reality.)

It is useful to know how to project Love Energy in situations such as dealing with nonphysical manifestations of fears, opening your own or someone else's awareness beyond its normal limits, bringing clarity and insight into a situation, and for other purposes. In this exercise, we're going to again combine Gathering Energy from Above at the Heart and Feeling Love as a way of building up the level of Love Energy. You can think of this like charging up a battery, or, for you electronics types, like charging up a huge capacitor. And you're going to learn how to send this built-up charge of Love Energy to someone else.

You'll need a target or object to practice on. That target can be any person, place, relationship, situation, animal, automobile, or any other thing you can think of. Often workshop participants use a person close to them. And often, after the workshop, participants report changes in their relationship with that person.

Before beginning this next exercise, take a few moments to consider who or what you might like to project Love Energy to. It's okay to add others during the exercise, but have at least one in mind before you start.

Projecting Love Energy Exercise: Script

This is the Projecting Love Energy Exercise. (Wait 5 sec)

As you get ready to begin the exercise, adjust the volume of this recording so that you can comfortably and easily hear and understand my voice. You may do this exercise either sitting or lying down. (Wait 10 sec)

When you're ready to begin, please close your eyes. (Wait 10 sec)

To begin this exercise move your body into a comfortable, relaxed position in your quiet place. (Wait 30 sec)

Remember the feeling of being relaxed and at your own pace take in

133

Three Deep Relaxing Breaths, or as many as you need to feel some change in your level of relaxation. (Wait 45 sec)

Remember the image of establishing the flow of energy from below in the *Afterlife Knowledge Guidebook,* and take in Three Energy Gathering Breaths to establish the flow from below. (Wait 45 sec)

Remember the image of Energy Gathering from Below in the *Afterlife Knowledge Guidebook,* and take in Three Energy Gathering Breaths from Below. (Wait 45 sec)

Remember the image of establishing the flow of energy from above in the *Afterlife Knowledge Guidebook,* and take in Three Energy Gathering Breaths to establish the flow from above. (Wait 45 sec)

Remember the image of Energy Gathering from Above in the *Afterlife Knowledge Guidebook,* and take in Three Energy Gathering Breaths from Above. (Wait 45 sec)

Remember the feeling of placing intent, or just imagine you are doing the Silly Little Finger Bending Exercise. (Wait 15 sec)

Reexperience the feeling of placing intent as you say in your mind, **I am learning to Project Love Energy.** (Wait 10 sec)

Remember a time in your life when you were feeling loved or loving. (Wait 20 sec)

Let this memory help you to remember and reexperience the feeling of love. (Wait 20 sec)

If the feeling fades that's okay; just remember another time you were feeling loved or loving, and let that feeling build. (Wait 20 sec)

As you continue gathering energy from above, let a portion of it build and mix with the feeling of love at the heart. (Wait 30 sec)

It may be helpful to alternate between feeling love and Energy Gathering Breaths from Above to help you build up the level of Love Energy at the Heart. (Wait 20 sec)

Remember another time when you were feeling loved or loving. Let that feeling build and grow within you. (Wait 20 sec)

Let it bring that warm inner smile. (Wait 20 sec)

As you feel Love Energy building, bring the person, situation, or other target you've chosen to mind. (Wait 10 sec)

When you feel ready, send the Love Energy at your heart to the target you have chosen in whatever way feels appropriate to you. (Wait 15 sec)

Notice any impressions you may have of the recipient as they receive your Love Energy. (Wait 15 sec)

You may wish to repeat this exercise using a different person, situation, or other target. Feel free to continue this exercise in that way. (Wait 30 sec)

When you're ready, please open your eyes and give yourself a few moments to fully return from the exercise. Then immediately begin to write about your experience and use the questions in the debriefing section for this exercise in the *Afterlife Knowledge Guidebook* as a starting point to record your experience in detail in your notebook.

Debrief: Projecting Love Energy Exercise

Describe your experience in your notebook.

Did you notice any differences in the level or intensity of feeling love by using Gathering Energy at the Center of your Chest and Feeling Love together?

When you projected Love Energy, describe how you did it.

Did you have any impressions of a response by the person, situation, or other target to your Projecting Love Energy?

Tips on Projecting Love Energy

Workshop participants report several different ways of Projecting Love Energy. Some pretend (or observe) that it emerges like a laser beam from the center of their chest and travels to the target.

Some report that a ball of Love Energy forms at the heart, often perceived as a ball of colored light that then travels to the target.

Others describe throwing it or just thinking about it going to the target.

One participant was surprised to observe what looked like a toy squirt gun that spontaneously appeared in her hand. A tube connected this squirt gun to the center of her chest. She used this toy to squirt Love Energy at various targets during the exercise. In later exercises she used this squirt gun to effectively deal with her own fear-manifested demons. When they appeared, she just squirted them and they disappeared.

Some folks report that they were concerned because they only felt a pretty low intensity level of Love Energy, too low in their opinion to have any effect. I urge you not to worry about having enough to be worth projecting. Project any amount you sense, even if you sense none. Love Energy is powerful stuff, and even what you perceive as a small amount can have strong effects. In your continuing practice of this Projecting Love Exercise, you may begin to notice effects that indicate the process is working. You may be carrying beliefs about Projecting Love that will be changed or eliminated through repeated experience. I did.

An Interesting Participant Experience

As I mentioned previously, feeling love has a way of automatically opening perception beyond its normal limits. It can add a clarity of mind and thought that boosts understanding and insight.

One workshop participant meditates regularly, and often intends to send love to various people for various reasons. The workshop she attended took place during an increase in tension and violence in the Middle East. During the Projecting Love Energy Exercise she decided to Project Love to Yasser Arafat and others around him. After building the intensity of Love Energy she projected it, first to Arafat, and then to a few younger men who appeared, to her perception, around him. As she did this she had the distinct impression that Arafat became aware of the love she was sending and gladly received it. The other younger men around Arafat also appeared to sense the love she was sending, but acted immediately to deflect it so as not to receive it. In all the times she had sent love during her previous meditations she had never before had any sense of response on the part of the person receiving it. I'll leave it to you to experiment with Projecting Love and come up with your own stories.

Again, I urge you to do the Feeling and Projecting Love Exercises often, perhaps as part of a daily meditation. Become so familiar with feeling Love and projecting it that it becomes part of your normal, automatic response to things that come into your awareness. In my experience the benefits are many and far-reaching.

10

The Preparatory Process

It is time to assemble your practice of relaxation, placing intent, Energy Gathering, and feeling Love into a single exercise.

While you are still in the early phases of learning to explore beyond physical reality it's important to go through this Preparatory Process step by step. I recommend that you imagine and complete each step in detail. Some folks have a tendency to rush through preparation for exploration as if it's not really all that important. I urge you not to skimp. With sufficient practice you'll be able to complete the Preparatory Process in a very short time by remembering the feeling of each step. Until then, please do it by the numbers, step by step, imagining and completing all the details.

The following script is given in detail. I recommend that you do this exercise at this level of detail to receive the full benefit of the Preparatory Process.

Preparatory Process for All Future Exercises: Script

This is the Preparatory Process Exercise. (Wait 5 sec)

As you get ready to begin the exercise, adjust the volume of this recording so that you can comfortably and easily hear and understand my voice. You may do this exercise either sitting or lying down. (Wait 10 sec)

When you're ready to begin, please close your eyes. (Wait 10 sec)

To begin this exercise move your body into a comfortable, relaxed position in your quiet place. (Wait 30 sec)

For each of the activities in the remainder of this Preparatory Process Exercise take your time. Remember and imagine each of the individual feelings, images, impressions, and details as you do of each step in the process. (Wait 10 sec)

Remember the feeling of being relaxed. (Wait 15 sec)

Take in Three Deep Relaxing Breaths. (Wait 45 sec)

Take in Three Energy Gathering Breaths to establish the flow from below. (Wait 45 sec)

Take in Three Energy Gathering Breaths from Below. (Wait 45 sec)

Take in Three Energy Gathering Breaths to establish the flow from above. (Wait 45 sec)

Take in Three Energy Gathering Breaths from Above. (Wait 45 sec)

Remember a time when you were feeling loved or loving. (Wait 30 sec)

Let this memory help you to remember and reexperience the feeling of love. (Wait 20 sec)

If the feeling fades that's okay; just remember another time you were feeling love and then let that feeling build. (Wait 20 sec)

In future exercises, when I ask you to, complete your Preparatory Process, remember and imagine each of the individual feelings, images, impressions, and details as you do each step in the process. (Wait 10 sec)

When you're ready, please open your eyes and give yourself a few moments to fully return from the exercise. Then immediately begin to write about your experience and use the questions in the debriefing section for this exercise in the *Afterlife Knowledge Guidebook* as a starting point to record your experience in detail in your notebook.

Debrief: Preparatory Process Exercise

Describe your experience in your notebook.

PART III

Afterlife Exploration Techniques

11

A Map of the Afterlife Territory

Our religions call nonphysical reality the Spirit World, and many of them claim it's inhabited by demons or Satan's minions. They claim that anyone venturing beyond the edge of physical reality will be tricked by the Great Deceiver into losing his or her soul. Our science tells us that nothing exists beyond the edge of physical reality and claims that exploration beyond that edge is only for the delusional.

But throughout history some explorers have claimed to visit a new world beyond physical reality and beyond death. The Egyptians, Tibetans, and many others drew maps of that territory. In modern times a few among us claim to have explored beyond physical reality, either as a result of a near-death experience, via dreams, waking visions, or driven by curiosity.

Perhaps the landmarks on my maps will help you to explore the territory. No doubt my map has inaccuracies. I hope that you as a new explorer will bring back more pieces of the jigsaw puzzle that is an image of this New World, so that a clearer and more accurate understanding will emerge.

I was curious to know what lies beyond physical reality. After reading books by authors like Ruth Montgomery, Judy Boss, Edgar Cayce, and many others I came to the conclusion that if an afterlife exists it is in the same neighborhood as we go when we dream. Carlos Castaneda's writings gave me a clue as to how to explore that neighborhood. He described a technique called *finding your hands in your dreams* that he claimed led to lucid dreaming, a dream state in which one can become conscious and make choices about activities during dreaming. That meant I could be awake and aware within the same neighborhood as our afterlife. Practicing his technique led to the discovery of another method.

During my first lucid dream I encountered a being with an odd combination of facial features who was dressed in a robe. Two weeks later I found myself reading a description of this being in a book entitled *Journeys Out of the Body*, by Robert A. Monroe, who described his explorations beyond physical reality using a technique he called out-of-body-experience (OBE). I learned that Monroe had developed a weeklong program called Lifeline, taught at The Monroe Institute he founded, in which participants were taught how to explore our afterlife. The afterlife map used in this Lifeline program was drawn by Monroe based upon his OBE explorations of human existence beyond physical reality. The lines, boundaries, and labels Monroe uses to define different areas of afterlife consciousness were drawn based on the kinds of people he found within these areas.

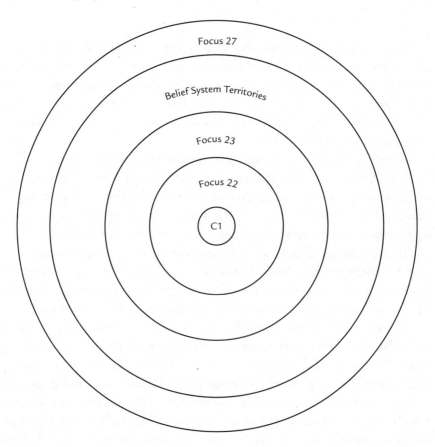

Physical Reality: C1 on the Map

Monroe defined the area at his map's center as physical reality and labeled it C1 Consciousness, or just C1. All the inhabitants of this area of consciousness are physically alive human beings.

Focus 22: Not Quite Afterlife Territory

Just beyond the edge of physical reality, conceptualized as a concentric sphere surrounding C1, Monroe described an area of consciousness he labeled Focus 22, an area of consciousness inhabited by humans who were physically alive, but whose awareness was not entirely focused within physical reality. Thus Focus 22 might include someone who is under anesthesia or in a coma, or is passed-out drunk or under the influence of drugs. They are still physically alive, but their focus of attention is not fully within physical reality. Some categories of the mentally ill—psychotics, catatonics, and schizophrenics—could be found in Focus 22. Those in delusional states of mind, perhaps from high fever or the effects of disease, may be among the kinds of people Monroe used to define the area of nonphysical consciousness he labeled Focus 22.

Focus 23: The Nearest Afterlife Territory

The next shell on Monroe's map he labeled Focus 23. Those who inhabit Focus 23 are no longer physically alive, but they are stuck within their own self-created, isolated version of reality. Remember when I said that in nonphysical reality, thoughts can be things? Beliefs about what comes after death can create a new area of consciousness within Focus 23 that is constructed around that belief. Within Focus 23 are untold numbers of individual realities created by, and solely inhabited by, the individuals who created them.

A sudden unexpected death can lead to people not knowing that they have died. They experience a short period of confusion between physical and nonphysical awareness and, since they can still see and hear activities within physical reality, believe they are still physically alive. These are what we call ghosts. You'd think these ghosts would realize their mistake as they try to continue to interact within physical reality with little or no success, but it appears that their existence is very much like being trapped in a dream. In the movie *What Dreams May Come*, Robin Williams's portrayal of being trapped in this dreamlike state is very accurate.

Other Focus 23 inhabitants get stuck by carrying the habit of a disease, such as dementia or Alzheimer's, into their afterlife experience. *Voyage Beyond Doubt* contains the story of one such person, who had become so habituated to totally fragmented thinking over the years of her Alzheimer's disease that her death probably occurred without her awareness. For her there was no apparent change, just continuation of the habit of fragmented thinking within her nonphysical body after death.

I need to emphasize that not all people who die under these circumstances get stuck after death. Those who do not get stuck, and those who are retrieved, move to a place in which they can be completely healed by unlearning their habit. Those who do get stuck always have someone who knows how to contact and communicate with them, who will be able to escort them to that place of healing.

Some of the most heartbreaking stories of people stuck after death involve children. One of my workshop participants encountered a young boy in a hospital room, a dark-haired, frail boy of perhaps eight or nine, on a bed with the curtain pulled around it. Jamie had gotten sick and had no longer been allowed go outside to play with his friends. He'd then gotten sicker and couldn't go to school, then sicker still and put in the hospital. Jamie's parents were distraught at the impending death of their young son. Every time his mother visited she told Jamie to *stay here, don't leave me.* He pointed at all the machines surrounding his bed and explained that the doctors had turned them off and pulled the curtain around his bed. Jamie's mother and father had walked out of the room with the doctor. *I've stayed here just as mum told me to,* Jamie explained, *but she hasn't come back to visit me since then.* Jamie didn't understand that he'd died and even if he did, he was going to obey his mum. Jamie was stuck, a frightened little boy waiting in the hospital bed where he died for his mother and father to return.

In my experience most of the children who become trapped in Focus 23 do so in response to rules they've accepted and obeyed. In *Voyages into the Unknown*, there's a story of a little boy named Benjie who refused my attempts to retrieve him because he'd been taught to never go anywhere with a stranger. I had to leave him standing on a sidewalk where I'd found him, waiting for his parents to find him.

Focus 24, 25, and 26: The Belief System Territories

While inhabitants in Focus 23 are stuck in isolated, individual, self-created realities, the next area of human afterlife consciousness is one in which the deceased are stuck within group-created realities. These are the Belief System Territories (BST) that Monroe labeled Focus 24, 25, and 26. Just as the thoughts or beliefs of individuals can manifest their own non-physical reality, the thoughts and beliefs held by a group can create a group reality.

One clear illustration of a BST is created by a religion. If a religion can convince a group of people to accept a set of beliefs regarding the afterlife, all those believers project the same, specific set of beliefs into nonphysical reality. If the believers have an image of heaven as a place where no one has to work, a paradise where food, clothing, and housing are all free and you live like you're on a perpetual paid vacation, that heaven is created as a nonphysical reality. Thoughts are things. Group-held beliefs create a nonphysical reality that perfectly embodies and supports those beliefs. A BST created by group-held beliefs is the area of afterlife consciousness those holding the beliefs may enter at death. I say *may* because under some circumstances they may bypass that heaven and go to a better place. The beliefs that create this heaven act to prevent nonbelievers from entering. So, the only inhabitants within a specific BST heaven are those sharing that same, specific set of beliefs. A short way to say this is that there are no Catholics in Lutheran heaven, or Baptists in Buddhist heaven. Each religion has its own BST heaven. The BST contains the heavens and hells of all religions as well as other realities created out of the beliefs held by other groups, such as thieves.

Focus 27: The Last Area of Human Afterlife Consciousness

In the area conceptualized as a shell surrounding the BSTs is an area of human afterlife consciousness Monroe labeled Focus 27. Within this area, the inhabitants never force their own beliefs or will on other people. People are in free association with all others living there, free to exist in pretty much any way they can imagine. If there is another way to live that they would like to experience but can't imagine, others in this area of consciousness are willing to show them how to imagine, manifest, and experience it. Focus 27 has many interesting facets to explore, and some are described in my third book, *Voyages into the Afterlife*. Some of the places within Focus 27 can be valuable tools and sources of information that can have profound, positive effects on our physical lives. I strongly suggest that as you learn to explore our afterlife, you visit and explore Focus 27. The exercises later in this book will teach you how.

Focus 34/35: Beyond Human Consciousness

Monroe claimed that beyond Focus 27 one found areas of nonhuman consciousness. One such area Monroe visited in his early OBE explorations he called the Gathering. In more recent times the label for this area has been changed to Focus 34/35. Here we can communicate with intelligences from other planets, other universes, and other dimensions.

With all these fascinating places to explore, it's time to teach you how to perceive within realities beyond physical reality.

12

A Review of Exploration Techniques

First I'd like to briefly review some of the more common methods others describe using. Each of these categories of exploration techniques has certain strengths and weaknesses.

Ordinary Dreaming

In ordinary dreams, you don't realize you were dreaming until you wake up into physical reality. During ordinary dreaming we react to what we perceive (the elements of the dream) as if they are real. During the dream there is no recognition that you are dreaming, and even if the content of the dream is ridiculous, you continue reacting to the elements of the dream as if they are real.

It's entirely possible that what you are experiencing in a dream as a tiger chasing you is actually a nonphysical person trying to communicate with you. During ordinary dreaming the Interpreter operates without any restrictions that I am aware of. There's just no telling where your Interpreter Overlays will take you. From that nonphysical person's perspective, s/he might be calling your name and moving toward you, trying to get your attention, not realizing that you are seeing a tiger. Each time s/he calls your name, you may perceive a tiger's growl.

Ordinary dreaming is similar to being trapped in Focus 23. Everything you perceive is perceived through the context of the reality you have created.

Your Interpreter grabs a *nearest similar thing,* then makes an association to its own association and grabs the *nearest similar thing,* etc. From that point onward you've lost your Balance on the side of the Interpreter, and its unchecked associations to its own associations can lead to some bizarre dream experiences. When you awake (shift your awareness to physical reality) you might remember the bizarre chain of events of your ordinary dream, and you might spend hours trying to analyze the symbols and elements of this dream. But it's quite possible that all that happened was that some nonphysical person tried to make contact with you, and you went on an Interpreter Overlay joyride.

As a tool of afterlife exploration, ordinary dreaming has some potential, but the lack of ability to become aware of (let alone control) the influence of Interpreter Overlay is its major weakness.

Lucid Dreaming

In a lucid dream, you are aware that you are asleep and dreaming. This awareness can add a level of conscious volition to the dream experience. Often something in an ordinary dream triggers us to shift toward a lucid dream. Perhaps you are running up the outside of the Empire State Building and you realize that what you are doing is physically impossible, causing you to question the reality of the experience. That questioning could be thought of as recognizing that you are dealing with an Interpreter Overlay. That recognition might cause you to stop running and question the validity of the whole experience. You might let go of the image, while standing on the outside of the Empire State Building, with the intent to gain clearer understanding of what's going on. You might suddenly see a person, the one who has been trying to contact you all along, standing in front of you. Depending on your ability to maintain your Balance between the Perceiver and Interpreter, you might be able to enter into a conversation with this person. You might be able to be in full, conscious control and make decisions about your activities within this dream as you would within physical reality. The length of time you're lucid in a lucid dream probably depends on how well you deal with further Interpreter Overlays in the dream. We probably drop out of lucidity when we take the bait of an Interpreter Overlay and once again begin following the Interpreter's associations to its own associations.

The strength of lucid dreaming is the level of conscious decision-making it affords. It's quite possible that in a lucid dream one could decide to visit a deceased friend to gather verifiable information or explore some facet of our afterlife existence. Its primary weakness is that one must fall asleep, lose consciousness, and then find a way to regain consciousness within the dream. Typically it can take considerable time and effort to learn the technique.

As a side note, those who begin practicing various forms of meditation often report an increase in the incidence of lucid dreams. Meditation techniques that are intended to *quiet the mind* are teaching how to recognize and Balance the effects of the Interpreter, and in my view an increasing incidence of lucid dreaming is a natural result. Developing the ability to extend the lucid dream state is probably about learning to shift one's perspective to within the nonphysical body they are using. Often lucid dreams are experienced from the perspective of watching yourself, your nonphysical body, as you participate in the activities of the lucid dream. Learning to experience a lucid dream from the perspective of being inside that nonphysical body may lead to a classic out-of-body-experience.

Out-of-Body Experience (OBE)

The classic OBE contains elements like a feeling of floating upward and looking down to see your physical body asleep on the bed. Other OBE indications can be strong, buzzing, vibrations and loud roaring noises. If there is a difference between lucid dreaming and OBE it probably revolves around the OBE sensation of being in a body, as opposed to being a mere *viewpoint*. Those unfamiliar with OBE would do well to read Robert Monroe's first book, *Journeys Out of the Body*. Often, physical reality can be perceived to some level while out of body (OB) and interaction within physical reality appears to be one of the characteristics of the OBE state. In his first book Monroe described experiments he did with such interactions. As I recall, one of his pinching experiments left a bruise on the physical body of the woman he nonphysically pinched.

The allure of the OBE for me was that, within that state, perception is remarkably similar to perception within physical reality. I naturally assumed that if perception was more like the physical world variety, what I perceived OB was more *real* than what I perceived in ordinary or lucid dreams. Believing that OBE was the only means of true and accurate nonphysical perception led me to spend about six years trying, unsuccessfully, to learn to have OBEs at will. I would now say that I wasted six years trying to learn a completely unnecessary, exotic technique. There are far simpler ways to explore beyond physical reality.

The advantage of OBE is its perceptual familiarity. It is so similar to

149

physical reality perception that it is perhaps easier to bring the Perceiver/Interpreter Balance learned in physical reality into one's nonphysical experience. The full set of physical senses seems to be replicated and useful within this nonphysical environment. The weakness of OBE is in the extreme difficulty most people have in learning to do it at will. Many of those considered very good at OBE still report difficulty with this aspect of using the technique.

13

Focused Attention for Exploration

Ideally a technique for afterlife exploration should not require losing consciousness—i.e., falling asleep—before the technique can be used. It should be something simple that utilizes natural abilities that all humans have. Focused Attention is the name I've given to the simple system of techniques I've developed that incorporates these characteristics. In developing this system I strove to follow the engineer's Keep It Simple, Stupid (KISS) principle.

If I asked you to explore your present physical surroundings, you would probably use your sense of sight to look around and observe whatever you can see. You might use your sense of hearing to listen for any sounds in your physical environment. You might sniff the air to gather any odors or scents to add to your perception of your physical surroundings. You might reach out and touch some nearby object to gather more information about what it is. You might even use your sense of taste to sample anything in the vicinity that appears to be edible. In essence you would focus your attention through your physical senses upon anything you could observe within your present physical surroundings. Change *physical* to *nonphysical* in the previous sentences and you'll begin to understand what I mean by using Focused Attention to explore beyond physical reality. It's just a matter of focusing your attention through your nonphysical senses to explore your nonphysical surroundings. All of us have both physical and nonphysical senses, yet most of us have become so accustomed to using our physical senses that we're seldom even aware of using our nonphysical senses.

Only two basic skills are necessary for you to begin exploring our afterlife and other nonphysical realities. The first is to learn to use your natural nonphysical senses. The second is to learn to shift your awareness to any nonphysical reality within which you can use those senses. In the next two chapters you'll begin learning what your nonphysical senses are and how to use them; then you'll learn how to shift your focus of attention to any nonphysical reality you desire to explore.

14

Imagination as a Means of Perception

It is said that someone told St. Joan of Arc that the voices she heard were only in her imagination, to which she replied, *Of course, that is where you hear them!* Of all that is contained in this guidebook, understanding what St. Joan meant by her statement is the most important concept to grasp. This was the most difficult issue I faced. My father once told me that the best mistakes to learn from are those made by other people. You will cut years off your efforts to perceive, communicate, interact within, and explore beyond physical reality if you can learn from my mistakes.

My first big mistake was the belief that because a thing is only perceived within one's imagination it is, by definition, not real. I believed that *imagination* and *fantasy* are two different words for the same thing. That belief is probably responsible for the vast majority of failures to perceive, communicate, interact, and explore beyond physical reality. It is common for someone to say their experience was *only their imagination*, thereby implying that it was not real. It means nothing of the sort.

My second mistake was to believe that if I allowed myself to pretend any portion of an exploration experience, the entire experience was a fantasy. I have since come to understand that pretending can be the beginning of the process of shifting one's focus of attention from the physical senses to the nonphysical senses. An experience that begins with pretending—with active fantasizing—can progress to an experience that is real. Pretending also helps deal with the perceptual blockages of beliefs by opening one of those *windows*

153

of opportunity. If I know I am actively pretending an experience, my beliefs are less threatened and less likely to interfere. If my experience shifts from fantasy to real, the window of opportunity can remain open long enough for me to have an experience that is verifiably real and only later realize conflicts with my beliefs. *Pretending can serve to hold the window of opportunity open*. You will hear me say, over and over, that it's okay to pretend and when you hear me say that, I really mean it.

The third and biggest mistake I made was to discard any information about nonphysical reality gathered using pretending and imagination before attempting to test that information's validity. A dictionary defines imagination as *the power of reproducing images stored in the memory under the suggestion of associated images or of recombining former experience to create new images*. That might remind you of how the Interpreter function translates into conscious awareness what the Perceiver brings in at a subconscious level. The dictionary also says that imagination's root word "imagine" means, *to form a mental image of something not actually present to the senses*. Personally, from a nonphysical exploration point of view, I feel it would be more accurate to rewrite the last part of that definition to, *not actually present to the physical senses*. My own exploration beyond physical reality was stymied until the experience of verifying information gathered using imagination forced me to change my beliefs about pretending, imagination, and fantasy. I would now say that pretending can be the beginning of the process of using imagination as the sense we can use to perceive our fantasies, or, to perceive something that is real. I now understand imagination to be a means of perceiving information along a continuum defined by pretending and fantasy on one end and verifiably real information on the other.

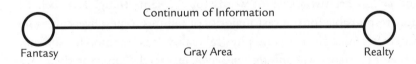

Continuum of Information

Fantasy   Gray Area   Realty

Using Imagination to Explore—An Illustration

Most of us are familiar with using imagination as the means of perceiving our fantasies. You're at work, bored out of your mind. You put your feet up on the desk, close your eyes, and wish you were at the beach. You might see an image of the sea in your mind's eye, you might smell the salt air or suntan lotion. You are using imagination as a means of perceiving within a nonphysical environment your fantasy. So, how do we use these same senses to perceive something nonphysical that's real? And, how do we know that what we are perceiving is not just a fantasy, but real? In my workshops I use the following fictional story to answer both of these questions.

Let's suppose I decide to attempt communication with my grandfather, who we'll further suppose died ten years before I was born. I begin by actively pretending. I might imagine I am sitting on a back porch on a hot, humid, Minnesota summer day. I'd pretend to be seeing the backyard, trees, the lawn, perhaps a picnic table. I might pretend I could feel an ice cold, wet bottle of beer in my hand. I might pretend that Gramps is in the house and that I call out to him, inviting him to join me on the back porch for a beer. I might pretend to hear his footsteps as he walks toward the squeaky old wooden screen door that leads out of the house to the back porch. As I pretend this, I might hear that screen door creak open and slam shut as Gramps steps out onto the porch. I might imagine I hand Gramps a cold bottle of beer as he sits down beside me. Then I'd begin to actively pretend a fantasy conversation with the old man. I'd be making up, fantasizing, both sides of this conversation, perhaps even pretending to use a different voice for Gramps in my mind. That conversation might go like . . .

"Hey, Gramps, I'm Bruce."

"Yeah, I know," I pretend he replies.

"I never got a chance to meet you in real life; you died ten years before I was born."

"Yeah, I know."

This not-very-creative fantasy conversation might go on for some time before Gramps says, "Hey, bet you didn't know I was a bank robber."

I'm certain I'm still fantasizing this whole conversation, but using the technique of Focused Attention I begin to play along with this unexpected turn in the conversation . . .

"Really, Gramps? What banks did you rob?"

"Last job I pulled was the First National Bank of Eau Claire, Wisconsin. Got away with $12,000 dollars," I imagine he says. "Never got to spend a penny of it."

"Why not?" I wonder, still playing along to see where this goes.

"I put the canvas bank bag full of money in an old fishing tackle box and buried it ten paces north of the old oak tree, in the backyard of the house on Elm Street. The cops arrested me two days later for another bank job I pulled," Gramps replies. "They sent me to prison and I died there."

"Really, Gramps?"

"Yeah, I told Arny, my cell mate in Stillwater Prison, all about it."

This fantasy conversation might continue. Sometimes I know for certain I'm making up both sides, and sometimes it might take an unexpected turn that I play along with. I strongly suggest that if you record nothing else in your notebook after an exercise, *write down everything that happened unexpectedly*. If your experience is anything like mine, one of the biggest mistakes you will make will be to not write down some details because you think they are small, useless, fantasized information, or because you don't see how the information fits with what is previously known, could possibly be true, or has any relevance. You will tell yourself, *it was just my imagination*. My advice is to write it down. That doesn't mean you have to understand it, see its significance, or interpret what it means, it just means, *write it down* for future reference.

My list of Gray Area events after my fantasy conversation with my deceased grandfather would include:

1. Gramps was a bank robber
2. Last robbery, First National Bank in Eau Claire, Wisconsin
3. $12,000
4. Canvas bag, may have the bank's name on it
5. In a tackle box
6. Buried, ten paces north of an oak tree, backyard, house on Elm Street
7. Gramps died in Stillwater Prison
8. Cell mate's name in prison, Arny

So far this fictional story illustrates a simple beginner's technique of using imagination as a means of perceiving beyond physical reality. This nonphysical experience may be a complete fantasy, or some of it may be real. Willingness to allow yourself to actively pretend is one of the keys to using imagination as a means of perception. But—how can you know if any of this contact with Gramps was real or fantasy? Let's say my father, Gramps's son, is still physically alive. My attempt to verify any part of the imagined experience might begin as a telephone conversation with Dad. After a little small talk, I might work up the courage to say, "Hey Dad, is it true your father was a bank robber?"

Knowing my dad, I would expect his gruff-voiced response to be, "Who told you? That's a family secret that no one is supposed to talk about."

"Is it true he died in Stillwater Prison?"

"Who have you been talking to?"

"Nobody, Dad, it was kind of like a dream I had," I say, to keep my relatives out of trouble. "Say, did you ever live in a house on an Elm Street?"

"Yeah, why?"

"Think you could find that house again?"

"Yeah, it's in North Minneapolis. I drive by it sometimes."

"Was there an oak tree in the backyard when you lived there?"

"Yeah, when I was a kid I had a tire swing in that tree."

"Dad, I'm going to throw a shovel in the car and I'll be right over."

Suppose we drive to the house on Elm Street, get permission from the owners and dig up a tackle box containing $12,000 in a canvas bag. If that bag is labeled First National Bank of Eau Claire, Wisconsin, that's pretty good evidence that what started out as a fantasy conversation has elements within it that are validated. If I needed more verification, a search of prison records might reveal that Gramps did have a cell mate named Arny Swenson.

The first major step in learning to explore our afterlife is to prove to yourself through your own direct experience that our afterlife exists. That will remove belief-based perceptual blocks and open perception. The key to proving to yourself that our afterlife exists is to *obtain and verify previously unknown information* during contact with someone known to be deceased. The way to know if the information you gather using imagination is real is to find a way to verify its accuracy, within physical reality. If an experience like my fantasy conversation with Gramps actually happened to you, you'd be faced with having had an experience that might conflict with your beliefs. Verifying the information may force you to accept the afterlife as real, and conflict with beliefs you might hold to the contrary. Those beliefs and their blocking, distorting effects on your perception will be removed. Your perception will be opened further; it will become easier for you to perceive beyond physical reality and gather more verifiable information.

15

Focusing Attention through Your Nonphysical Senses

I am old enough to remember using a hand pump to get water. Mom would hand me a bucket and send me outside to fill it at the pump. After hanging the bucket on the spigot I'd start pumping the handle up and down but nothing would happen. Then Mom would remind me there was a little water in the bucket for a reason. Eventually I caught on. To get the hand pump to work I had to pour a little water into the top of it. I had to prime the pump. Pretending and fantasy can be that little bit of water that primes the pump of imagination to begin the flow of information, as in the story of visiting Gramps in the previous chapter. Here are some exercises to "prime the pump."

Imagination as the Means of Perception: Exercise #1 Script

This is the Imagination as a Means of Perception: Exercise Number 1. (Wait 5 sec)

As you get ready to begin the exercise, adjust the volume of this recording so that you can comfortably and easily hear and understand my voice. You may do this exercise either sitting or lying down. (Wait 10 sec)

When you're ready to begin, please close your eyes. (Wait 10 sec)

To begin this exercise move your body into a comfortable, relaxed position in your quiet place. (Wait 30 sec)

Complete your Preparatory Process, remembering and imagining each of the individual steps.

Take in Three Deep Relaxing Breaths. (Wait 45 sec)

Take in Three Energy Gathering Breaths to establish the flow from below. (Wait 45 sec)

Take in Three Energy Gathering Breaths from below. (Wait 45 sec).

Take in Three Energy Gathering Breaths to establish the flow from above. (Wait 45 sec)

Take in Three Energy Gathering Breaths from above. (Wait 45 sec)

Remember a time when you were feeling loved or loving. (Wait 20 sec)

Let this memory help you to remember and reexperience the feeling of love. (Wait 20 sec)

If the feeling fades that's okay; just remember another time you were feeling loved or loving, and let that feeling build. (Wait 20 sec)

Remember the feeling of placing intent, or just imagine you are doing the Silly Little Finger Bending Exercise. (Wait 20 sec)

Reexperience the feeling of placing intent as you say in your mind, **I am learning how to use imagination as a means of perception.** (Wait 10 sec)

Remember, it is okay to pretend during this exercise. (Wait 5 sec)

Take in at least two more Deep Relaxing Breaths. (Wait 20 sec)

Remember one of your parents. (Wait 10 sec) Just remember a parent. (Wait 45 sec)

Take in at least two more Deep Relaxing Breaths. (Wait 20 sec)

Remember a pet. (Wait 10 sec) Just remember one of your pets. (Wait 45 sec)

Take in at least two more Deep Relaxing Breaths. (Wait 20 sec)

Remember a friend. (Wait 10 sec) Just remember one of your friends. (Wait 45 sec)

When you're ready, please open your eyes and give yourself a few moments to fully return from the exercise. Then immediately begin to write about your experience and use the questions in the debriefing section for this exercise in the *Afterlife Knowledge Guidebook* as a starting point to record your experience in detail in your notebook.

Debrief of Exercise #1

Take a few moments to record your experience in your notebook.

Would you say that at any time during this exercise you saw something? In your notebook describe what you saw and how it looked.

Did you see images that were in color or black and white?

Were they 3-D, full color, and holographic images, or more like flat 2D images?

Were they clear or fuzzy?

Did you see a single still image, a series of still images, or something more like a movie?

Did what you saw appear as a grainy, barely discernable black-and-white image? Or would you describe what you saw as nothing but blackness? If so, would you say you knew which parent, pet, or friend you were remembering?

Would you say you knew what scene your parent, pet, or friend was in and perhaps what they were doing?

Describe it in detail.

Tips for Using Nonphysical Sight

No matter how you've described seeing a parent, pet, or friend, you have just experienced what I mean when I write in one of my books that I saw something. Any of those ways of *seeing* is a form of using imagination as a nonphysical sense of sight.

One big mistake I made as I began learning to perceive beyond physical reality was to believe that the *quality* of the images I saw was a measure of the accuracy or reality of what I was *seeing*. I expected to see within nonphysical reality in exactly the same way I normally see within physical reality, and I automatically discarded as useless and unreal any images that weren't 3-D, holographic, and in full color. It took a long time to realize that nonphysical sight can best be described as a continuum, and that **the quality of the images has absolutely nothing to do with the quality of information that can be obtained from those images.**

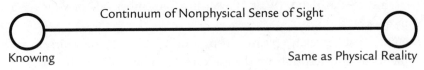

Continuum of Nonphysical Sense of Sight

Knowing   Same as Physical Reality

On one end of the continuum, what we see is almost indistinguishable from what we see by using our physical eyes. On the other end of this continuum I might be tempted to say I didn't *see* anything, but I *knew* that I was looking at a little boy riding his bike down a driveway toward a street. Visually, I'm *seeing* total blackness, yet I *know* the little boy had his head turned away from the street, looking at his mother, who was standing by the open front door of the house. He was waving at her and didn't see there was a truck coming. I never really *saw* any of this—just blackness—but I *know* that truck ran over and killed the little boy. I didn't see a thing, yet I knew what it would have looked like if I could have seen it, right down to the style and color of the mother's housedress. That's why I label the other end of the Continuum of Nonphysical Sight as *Knowing*.

Sometimes for a brief instant you see one image, like a picture of your mother or your father, and then nothing but blackness. This is fairly common. When it happens to me, I take it as an indication that I can now proceed using the Knowing end of the Continuum of Nonphysical Sight. From that point on in the experience I may *see* other flash images, or I may not. I may *see* short movie clips, or I may not. But experience has proven that I can continue to gather accurate, verifiable information no matter where along the continuum I am.

Where our perception is along the Continuum of Nonphysical Sight can vary from one exercise or experience to the next. Sometimes it can be like watching a movie; sometimes all you're *seeing* is blackness.

It's probably normal to expect progress toward the 3-D end of the Continuum over time. In my experience either that's not true, or you can't develop that ability and be as lazy about practicing as I am. Perhaps exercises in visualization might lead to an increase in using perception at that end of the Continuum, but it is not at all necessary to succeed in having experiences in which you gather accurate, verifiable information. Developing nonphysical sight is more about learning to be aware of what your Perceiver is observing than about developing the ability to see as you do with your physical eyes.

Practice. Close your eyes and listen to a really good novel being read by someone. Books on tape are a great way to do this. Use your Preparatory Process as you relax and begin to listen. Focus your attention on how you perceive visual *images* as you listen to the novel. Are you seeing exactly as you do with your physical eyes? Keep at it until you understand what I mean by saying, "I wasn't seeing anything, but I know exactly what it looked like." Then continue practicing with your books on tape.

Before beginning a retrieval exercise, or other nonphysical reality exploration, do a prime-the-pump-of-imagination exercise as a way of stimulating your nonphysical sense of sight.

Imagination as a Means of Perception: Exercise #2 Script

This is the Imagination as a Means of Perception: Exercise Number 2. (Wait 5 sec)

As you get ready to begin the exercise, adjust the volume of this recording so that you can comfortably and easily hear and understand my voice. You may do this exercise either sitting or lying down. (Wait 10 sec)

When you're ready to begin, please close your eyes. (Wait 10 sec)

To begin this exercise move your body into a comfortable, relaxed position in your quiet place. (Wait 30 sec)

Complete your Preparatory Process, remembering and imagining each of the individual steps.

Take in Three Deep Relaxing Breaths. (Wait 45 sec)

Take in Three Energy Gathering Breaths to establish the flow from below. (Wait 45 sec)

Take in Three Energy Gathering Breaths from Below. (Wait 45 sec)

Take in Three Energy Gathering Breaths to establish the flow from above. (Wait 45 sec)

Take in Three Energy Gathering Breaths from Above. (Wait 45 sec)

Remember a time when you were feeling loved or loving. (Wait 20 sec)

Let this memory help you to remember and reexperience the feeling of love. (Wait 20 sec)

If the feeling fades that's okay; just remember another time you were feeling loved or loving, and let that feeling build. (Wait 20 sec)

Remember the feeling of placing intent, or just imagine you are doing the Silly Little Finger Bending Exercise. (Wait 20 sec)

Reexperience the feeling of placing intent as you say in your mind, **I am learning how to use imagination as a means of perception.** (Wait 10 sec)

Remember, it is okay to pretend during this exercise. (Wait 5 sec)

Take in at least two more Deep Relaxing Breaths. (Wait 20 sec)

Remember a radio. (Wait 10 sec) Just remember . . . a radio. (Wait 20 sec)

Remember a time you were hearing a favorite song or program playing on the radio. (Wait 20 sec)

You might remember the sound of the lyrics or voices. (Wait 20 sec)

You might remember the sound of the announcer's voice. (Wait 20 sec)

You might remember the sound of instruments, or the rhythm. (Wait 20 sec)

Remember how you change the station on this radio? (Wait 5 sec)

Pretend to reach up and change the station until you remember hearing another favorite song or program on the radio. (Wait 20 sec)

You might remember the words of the song or the voice of the commentator. (Wait 30 sec)

When you're ready, please open your eyes and give yourself a few moments to fully return from the exercise. Then immediately begin to write about your experience and use the questions in the debriefing section for this exercise in the *Afterlife Knowledge Guidebook* as a starting point to record your experience in detail in your notebook.

Debrief of Exercise #2

Describe your experience of this exercise in your notebook.

What did your radio look like and how did you see it?

Where was this radio, inside or outside, in a car, at a friend's house, or somewhere else? Describe the scene your radio was in.

Would you say that at any point during this exercise you heard something?

Did you feel the need to change to a different radio for some reason during the exercise?

If you heard a song, what was it?

Did you hear the words of the song, perhaps in the lead singer's voice?

Did you hear the instruments? Which ones and what did they sound like?

As you heard the song did you remember some of the words you'd forgotten?

Did you notice you could actually hear the song?

If you were hearing a program, what program was it and what did you hear? What were the voices saying?

What happened when you changed the radio station? Did you unexpectedly hear that static sound as you changed the station?

What song or program was playing on the radio after your changed the station?

Tips for Using Nonphysical Hearing

Just as in nonphysical sight, the experience of nonphysical hearing is a continuum. The end I've labeled Knowing might also be described as absolute silence in which you know what is being said by someone, the accent that person speaks with, and that there was the sound of traffic in the background, even though you didn't actually *hear* anything. The Physical Reality end of the continuum could be described as just like hearing with your physical ears. No matter which end of this continuum (or anywhere in between) describes your experience of nonphysical hearing, you have just experienced what I mean when I write in one of my books that I heard the old woman in the chair say, "Maggie? Maggie! What are you doing here?" Just as with nonphysical sight, the similarity to physical reality experience has absolutely nothing to do with the reality or accuracy of information you can gather.

Some participants compare their experience during this exercise to hearing a song running through their head that won't quit. In fact, actively pretending that you are hearing a song to the point that it starts doing that is a great way to practice using your nonphysical sense of hearing. (Then you're just stuck with learning how to stop the music.)

Some participants report that the first radio they saw was too old for the song they heard playing on it, sort of like seeing a 1930s vintage radio in the house you lived in as a kid, but hearing a song by the Beatles. If you had a similar experience during this exercise, how you responded to it might be worth reflecting on. Did your experience conflict with your beliefs? Did you spend so much time trying to *see* a different, more appropriate radio that you lost your focus of attention? Was this a window of opportunity to learn about the Interpreter function, or perhaps how beliefs can act to interfere with or block experience?

Some participants report that the song they heard felt like it was selected because it carried a special message for them and they wondered who selected that specific song.

Did you *hear* static as you changed to a different radio station? Did that surprise you? Since I didn't make any suggestions about hearing static, could the Interpreter have had a hand in bringing that into your awareness?

Before beginning a retrieval exercise, or other nonphysical reality exploration, do a prime-the-pump exercise as a way of stimulating your nonphysical sense of hearing.

Imagination as a Means of Perception: Exercise #3 Script

This is the Imagination as a Means of Perception: Exercise Number 3. (Wait 5 sec)

As you get ready to begin the exercise, adjust the volume of this recording so that you can comfortably and easily hear and understand my voice. You may do this exercise either sitting or lying down. (Wait 10 sec)

When you're ready to begin, please close your eyes. (Wait 10 sec)

To begin this exercise move your body into a comfortable, relaxed position in your quiet place. (Wait 30 sec)

Complete your Preparatory Process, remembering and imagining each of the individual steps.

Take in Three Deep Relaxing Breaths. (Wait 45 sec)

Take in Three Energy Gathering Breaths to establish the flow from below. (Wait 45 sec)

Take in Three Energy Gathering Breaths from Below. (Wait 45 sec)

Take in Three Energy Gathering Breaths to establish the flow from above. (Wait 45 sec)

Take in Three Energy Gathering Breaths from Above. (Wait 45 sec)

Remember a time when you were feeling loved or loving. (Wait 20 sec)

Let this memory help you to remember and reexperience the feeling of love. (Wait 20 sec)

If the feeling fades that's okay; just remember another time you were feeling loved or loving, and let that feeling build. (Wait 20 sec)

Remember the feeling of placing intent, or just imagine you are doing the Silly Little Finger Bending Exercise. (Wait 20 sec)

Reexperience the feeling of placing intent as you say in your mind, **I am learning how to use imagination as a means of perception.** (Wait 10 sec)

Remember, it is okay to pretend during this exercise. (Wait 5 sec)

Take in at least two more Deep Relaxing Breaths. (Wait 20 sec)

Remember an orange, the fruit. (Wait 10 sec) Just remember an orange. (Wait 20 sec)

Remember a time you were holding an orange in your hand. (Wait 20 sec)

Remember its color, the texture of its skin, and the feel of the weight of it in your hand. (Wait 20 sec)

Remember it's okay to pretend. (Wait 10 sec)

Remember digging your fingernails into the skin of the orange and peeling it. (Wait 20 sec)

Remember peeling back the skin of the orange. (Wait 10 sec)

Remember the scent of the orange. (Wait 10 sec)

Imagine peeling the entire orange and pulling out a section of it. (Wait 20 sec)

Bring the section to your lips and tongue, remembering how that feels. (Wait 15 sec)

Remember eating the orange. (Wait 20 sec)

Remember, it is okay to pretend during this exercise. (Wait 10 sec)

Take in at least two more Deep Relaxing Breaths. (Wait 20 sec)

Remember a favorite flower (wait 10 sec), its shape and color (wait 10 sec), the feel of its stalk and texture of its petals. (Wait 30 sec)

Remember the scent of this flower. (Wait 20 sec)

When you're ready, please open your eyes and give yourself a few moments to fully return from the exercise. Then immediately begin to write about your experience and use the questions in the debriefing section for this exercise in the *Afterlife Knowledge Guidebook* as a starting point to record your experience in detail in your notebook.

Debrief of Exercise #3

Record your experience in your notebook.

What kind of orange did you remember?
Did you get sprayed when you first peeled back the skin of the orange?
Did you get a burst of the scent of the orange?
Did you feel like some of the inside of the orange peel got stuck under your fingernails?
Did your orange have seeds?
Does it still feel like you've got sticky orange juice on your fingers?
What flower did you remember?
Describe what your flower looked like.
Did you remember the scent of this flower to the point that you smelled it?

Tips for Using Nonphysical Smell and Taste

Just as in using nonphysical sight and hearing, the experience of nonphysical smell and taste are continuums. On the Knowing end you might describe that you didn't smell or taste a thing, but you know what it tasted or smelled like. And as with other nonphysical senses, no matter which end of the continuum describes your experience, or anywhere in between, you have just experienced what I mean when I write "the smell of skunk was so strong my eyes started watering."

Just as with nonphysical sight and hearing, the similarity to physical reality experience has absolutely nothing to do with the reality or accuracy of information you can gather from the way you smelled or tasted it.

Some participants report surprise at the variety of oranges that appear during the exercise. Some who prefer tangerines had that fruit spontaneously appear. Some discovered their orange was dried out and bitter, so they decided to change to a different orange. For those who changed to a different orange, bravo! You may be learning more about how your perception responds to pretending.

166

Some participants report their orange unexpectedly had seeds. Another opportunity to observe how the Interpreter grabs the *nearest similar thing* and adds details that were not suggested during the exercise?

Many participants didn't expect to have that white stringy stuff under their fingernails, or the sensation of drying sticky orange juice on their fingers after the end of the exercise. The Interpreter strikes again.

Some participants report strong visual images of the flower, but realize the variety they picked doesn't have a strong scent. Bravo again to those who had this experience and changed flowers.

Odors can trigger shifts of one's focus of attention to various nonphysical places. The more interesting ones are odors that have only been experienced a few times within physical reality. This seems to limit the number of *nearest similar things* the Interpreter has to choose from. Interpreter Overlay is perhaps more easily observed since it is the odor that shifts awareness to the activity in the stored memory, and is less likely to be connected to what the Perceiver is bringing into subconscious awareness.

Before beginning a retrieval exercise, or other nonphysical reality exploration, do a prime-the-pump exercise as a way of stimulating your nonphysical sense of smell and taste.

Imagination as a Means of Perception: Exercise #4 Script

This is the Imagination as a Means of Perception: Exercise Number 4. (Wait 5 sec)

As you get ready to begin the exercise, adjust the volume of this recording so that you can comfortably and easily hear and understand my voice. You may do this exercise either sitting or lying down. (Wait 10 sec)

When you're ready to begin, please close your eyes. (Wait 10 sec)

To begin this exercise move your body into a comfortable, relaxed position in your quiet place. (Wait 30 sec)

Complete your Preparatory Process, remembering and imagining each of the individual steps.

Take in Three Deep Relaxing Breaths. (Wait 45 sec)

Take in Three Energy Gathering Breaths to establish the flow from below. (Wait 45 sec)

Take in Three Energy Gathering Breaths from Below. (Wait 45 sec)

Take in Three Energy Gathering Breaths to establish the flow from above. (Wait 45 sec)

Take in Three Energy Gathering Breaths from Above. (Wait 45 sec)

Remember a time when you were feeling loved or loving. (Wait 20 sec)

Let this memory help you to remember and reexperience the feeling of love. (Wait 20 sec)

If the feeling fades that's okay; just remember another time you were feeling loved or loving, and let that feeling build. (Wait 20 sec)

Remember the feeling of placing intent, or just imagine you are doing the Silly Little Finger Bending Exercise. (Wait 20 sec)

Reexperience the feeling of placing intent as you say in your mind, **I am learning how to use imagination as a means of perception.** (Wait 10 sec)

Remember, it is okay to pretend during this exercise. (Wait 5 sec)

Take in at least two more Deep Relaxing Breaths. (Wait 30 sec)

With your physical fingers touch your nose. (Wait 10 sec)

Feel your nose; is it warm or cool, moist or dry, smooth or rough? (Wait 20 sec)

Feel the contours and shape of your nose. (Wait 20 sec)

Move your physical fingers away from your nose and remember feeling your nose. (Wait 20 sec)

Remember it from the perspective of your fingers feeling your nose. (Wait 20 sec)

Remember it from the perspective of your nose feeling your fingers. (Wait 20 sec)

Remember the feeling of relaxation as you take in at least three more Deep Relaxing Breaths. (Wait 30 sec)

Again with your physical finger, feel your ear lobe. (Wait 15 sec)

Is it warm or cool, moist or dry, soft or rough? (Wait 15 sec)

Feel the contours and shape of your ear lobe. (Wait 15 sec)

Move your physical fingers away from your ear lobe and remember feeling it. (Wait 15 sec)

Remember it from the perspective of your fingers feeling your ear lobe. (Wait 15 sec)

Remember it from the perspective of your ear lobe feeling your fingers. (Wait 15 sec)

When you're ready, please open your eyes and give yourself a few moments to fully return from the exercise. Then immediately begin to write about your experience and use the questions in the debriefing section for this exercise in the *Afterlife Knowledge Guidebook* as a starting point to record your experience in detail in your notebook.

Debrief of Exercise #4

Record your experience in your notebook.

When you remembered feeling your nose and ear lobe, describe how you experienced it.

Describe your experience of shifting the perspective from which you remembered the experience, from that of your fingers feeling your nose, to your nose being touched by your fingers.

Tips for Using Nonphysical Touch

Just as with other nonphysical senses, the experience of nonphysical touch is a continuum. The end I've labeled Knowing might also be described as not *feeling* the touch of anything, but *knowing* you are petting a longhaired dog with a clean shiny coat. On the other end of the continuum you might describe the experience as so real that while petting the dog you felt the sting of a cocklebur poke your finger that made your hand jump. No matter which end of this continuum, or anywhere in between, describes your experience of nonphysical touch, you have just experienced what I mean when I write something in one of my books like, "the nearby craft felt hard, shiny, smooth, and curved," even though I didn't at all feel like my fingers were touching anything. Just as with other nonphysical senses, the level of similarity to physical world experience has absolutely nothing to do with the reality or accuracy of information you can gather from the way you touched something.

Shifting the perspective from which you remembered the experience points to a useful tool of exploration. There have been times in my own explorations where I've been observing from one perspective and only realized I was getting a very narrow view after I shifted to a different perspective. This shift can be as simple as deciding to observe from a different nonphysical location, sort of like choosing a different camera angle, or by deciding to observe from a different set of assumptions. Either of these can suddenly add a wealth of information about what you are observing.

Some participants report that remembering feeling their nose or ear lobe was as if they had nonphysical fingers feeling their nose and ear lobe while they remembered doing it.

Before beginning a retrieval exercise, or other nonphysical reality exploration, do a prime-the-pump exercise as a way of stimulating your nonphysical sense of touch.

16

Shifting Your Focus of
Attention to Other Realities

I have said that only two basic skills are necessary for you to begin exploring our afterlife and other nonphysical realities. In the previous two chapters you've learned about using imagination to focus your attention through your nonphysical senses. This chapter teaches the second basic skill, shifting your focus of attention to any nonphysical reality you desire to explore.

As I began developing Focused Attention as a simple system of exploration techniques, I was faced with what seemed an insurmountable problem. I'd learned to explore our afterlife in The Monroe Institute's Lifeline program using special, proprietary Hemi-Sync audiotapes with sound patterns that provided the means of learning to shift one's focus of attention from one area of consciousness to another. Exploring Focus 27, for example, was facilitated by special Hemi-Sync sounds that precisely shifted my focus of attention from C1 to Focus 27. Once I'd learned the feeling of Focus 27, I could use State-Specific Memory and the Hemi-Sync Model of Consciousness to return to Focus 27 without the tapes. But in developing a simpler system of exploration, I could not provide students with the proprietary audiotapes. I could teach folks how to use imagination as a means of perceiving within an area of consciousness like Focus 27, but I had to find a way to teach people to shift their focus of attention to Focus 27 in the first place.

As I pondered this, I realized that in every exploration I had ever done there were always nonphysical people nearby who were willing to provide assistance. Through my years of exploring I'd developed relationships with some of these folks in much the same way I develop friendships with people within physical reality. In fact, I'd come to rely on their assistance in many situations. This was the solution. I wouldn't need to teach folks how to shift their focus of attention. All I'd need to do would be to teach folks how to become aware of and work with nonphysical friends, the ones I call Helpers. To explore Focus 27, all they'd need to do would be to make contact with a Helper and let that Helper guide them to Focus 27. And if someone wanted to explore beyond Focus 27 or any other area of consciousness, Helpers could guide them there too. Learning to shift your focus of attention to other realities or areas of consciousness is just a matter of learning to work with Helpers.

17

Helpers

You might call them Angels, Guides, Masters, Light Beings, Archangels, Seraphs, Guardian Angels, Spirit Guides, or something else. I prefer the more generic name Helpers. These nonphysical people play several vital roles in afterlife exploration.

Who are these people? Where do they come from? What do these Helpers do? How do we make contact with them and how do we recognize them? Is there a way to know if a nonphysical person is not a Helper? How can contact with Helpers assist in our afterlife explorations? How do we recognize a Helper's assistance? Why do Helpers do what they do? How do I begin working with Helpers? This chapter will provide some answers from my experience and the experience of workshop participants. Your own experience will provide more answers.

Helpers have usually lived physical lifetimes on the Earth. From first-hand experience they are familiar with the kinds of experiences we go through. They understand the perceptual limitations of physical existence, how physical life experience can lead to erroneous beliefs and expectations, and how to work around these difficulties. They intimately understand how beliefs can distort and block perception, and how to move past these limitations. After death these people, for a variety of reasons, chose to provide assistance to others in any way they can. They are willing to provide assistance to the physically living as well as the nonphysically living.

If I had to guess I'd say most of the Helpers I've worked with are inhabitants of Focus 27, and some most likely reside beyond Focus 27. The ones I've met and worked with don't *ever* force their will or beliefs on anyone else. They are willing to provide assistance to anyone, for anything, but to get their assistance you have to remember to ask. That seems to be a function of the kind of people they are. From their perspective as Helpers, providing uninvited assistance looks like forcing their will or beliefs on another person. In essence they need permission to be of assistance to avoid what they see as uninvited interference in our experience. If you want their help, you have to ask. This gives them permission to provide it. This might sound like a nit-picky detail but many times when I couldn't figure out what to do next, things would have gone much better if I had remembered to ask for assistance. There may also be another factor working here. It may be that the act of asking for their help serves to focus our attention on them in order to bring them into our awareness. In any case, if you want the assistance of a Helper, you have to remember to ask for it.

Is There a Way to Know If a Nonphysical Person Is Not a Helper?

Yes. There are two guidelines or rules I use and they are based on the most fundamental thing I know about Helpers.

Rule #1: If a nonphysical person ever attempts to force, coerce, manipulate, deceive, or intimidate you into *doing* something you feel any resistance to do, that person is not a Helper.

Rule#2: If a nonphysical person ever attempts to force, coerce, manipulate, deceive, or intimidate you into *believing* something you do not already believe, that person is not a Helper.

You might be thinking, well, if the person I'm dealing with is not a Helper, then who else could it be? I would answer by saying that within physical reality there are many different kinds of people. Some I'd cross a street to meet; some I'd cross a street to avoid. I'd say that the same goes for people in nonphysical reality.

How Can Contact with Helpers Assist Our Afterlife Explorations?

In the context of learning to explore our afterlife, Helpers provide Guidance.

If you need to find a specific deceased person to make contact and communicate, Helpers know where this person is and can guide you into contact with that person.

If you can't seem to get a person's attention, ask for a suggestion from a Helper.

If you can't seem to make any progress in convincing some stuck person to come with you to a better place, ask for the Helper's assistance.

If there is some specific afterlife place you'd like to visit and explore, but you have no idea where it is or how to get there, ask a Helper.

If there is an area of consciousness beyond our afterlife you'd like to visit and explore, ask a Helper.

If you are seeking specific Afterlife Knowledge and don't know how or where to find it, ask a Helper.

In my experience Helpers are, metaphorically, like old-school master carpenters. There isn't anything in the field of carpentry that they haven't done many times. There isn't any trick of the trade they don't know. They are willing to share anything they know with anyone who asks. Think of Helpers as Albert Einstein, Nikola Tesla, William Shakespeare, Mother Teresa, Albert Schweitzer, and Robin Williams all rolled into one.

How Do We Recognize a Helper's Assistance?

Making contact with Helpers is as simple as asking for their assistance. Learning to recognize their presence comes through experience. The first few times I attempted to make contact with a Helper I would have said nothing happened. The next few times, I would have said that I didn't see anyone, but felt something—a presence—approach me. That progressed to a sense that this something felt male or female. At some point I would have said that I perceived a small, dim ball of light that moved toward me and was accompanied by the feeling of a male or female approaching me. Continued attempts led to a perception of a larger light, sometimes white, sometimes multicolored, and eventually to perception of a human form. Sometimes I'd get an impression of the Helper at a distance and be able to follow its approach to me. Sometimes it was more like they'd been standing next to me the whole time, and I'd just become aware of their presence.

Helpers take many forms, not all of them human. One workshop participant reported that when she asked for a Helper to come, no one came, but when I asked her to describe what happened after she asked for a Helper, she said that a multipaned, multicolored stained glass window had appeared, floating next to her. I had to explain that sometimes Helpers might look like a stained glass window. Another workshop participant described that when she asked for a Helper a wolf sauntered up next to her. Sometimes Helpers appear as animals.

Helpers sometimes arrive in a costume that seems out of place. A woman doing her first retrieval exercise said that when she asked for a Helper to come, a clown stepped out of the darkness and stood beside her, dressed in baggy pants, a polka dot shirt, and big boots, with a big red nose, bright bow tie, and a bowler hat. The Helper's appearance in a clown costume was completely unexpected and seemed odd until she realized that the stuck person she was to retrieve was a little boy who had died in a hospital. The clown outfit worked to make the boy's retrieval easier.

The assistance Helpers give also covers a wide range. They may guide us to a stuck person we are to retrieve, or to a specific person in the afterlife we'd like to visit. They may provide suggestions about how to handle situations in retrievals. They may guide us to places in nonphysical realities that we'd like to explore. As an example, a workshop participant explained to the Helper at the beginning of a retrieval exercise that she wanted to get the retrieval done in a hurry and then be taken to a place where she could study the history of her sect of Buddhism. She was taken to a place she described as having bookshelves filled with books, each labeled with the name of her sect of Buddhism and a year. She spent the rest of the retrieval exercise time reading one of those books.

Recognizing the Helpers' assistance isn't always straightforward. Sometimes it is provided in a conversational form, much like you'd expect a teacher to explain something to a student. Sometimes a thought occurs to us that answers the request but seems like one of our own thoughts. That one has happened to me more times than I care to admit.

Why Do Helpers Do What They Do?

People who become Helpers after physical death appear to decide to do it for a number of reasons. Many are people who were themselves stuck after death and choose to assist others out of gratitude for the assistance they received. I suspect that some Helpers did the same sort of thing in physical reality, and just continue to do so in their new afterlives. All of them seem to do it out of compassion. In my view, whether Helpers realize it or not, the work they do for the benefit of others is part of a much larger picture of the purpose of humankind's existence.

Some Helpers may even have taken on this work out of boredom. If I lived in a place where I could have anything I desired merely by imagining it into being, eventually I'd probably get bored. Focus 27 is such a place. I love sailing on the ocean. But after I sailed in every conceivable wind condition, on every conceivable type of sailboat, to every destination I could imagine, such experiences might become a little stale. And after exhausting my list of every other conceivable desire by fulfilling them all, ad nauseam, I might be interested in doing something new.

How Do We Begin Working with Helpers?

Focused Attention begins teaching you afterlife exploration by teaching the Art of Retrieval. Learning to contact and communicate with our fellow human beings who have become stuck after death is just the beginning of learning to explore our afterlife. Your interactions with these stuck people can teach you through your own direct (sometimes verifiable) experience that our afterlife indeed exists. The pace of removing the distorting influences of your beliefs, and thereby opening clearer perception, can be greatly accelerated. Metaphorically, the Art of Retrieval is like becoming Christopher Columbus at the point that he first set foot in the New World.

As you'll soon discover, we physically living human beings have an advantage over Helpers in retrieving some of those stuck people. We can use our advantage to assist Helpers in their work, and that's where we begin working with Helpers.

18

Cautions and Shortcuts, Advanced Tools, and Places to Explore

As I assembled this *Afterlife Knowledge Guidebook* I had some difficulty deciding where to put the information in this next section. On the one hand, this information would be very useful as you are learning the Art of Retrieval and afterlife exploration. On the other hand, disclosing it before you have had the opportunity to discover it on your own risks front-loading that can detract from your confidence in its use. If you read about this prior to your own experience, it is easy for you to dismiss the experience as having happened only because you had previously read about it. As you read the information in this section, you may recognize that you have gathered this information or experienced the use of these tools or discovered some of these places. Or they may be something you have yet to experience. Either way, these cautions, shortcuts, and advanced tools warrant investigation, exploration, and use.

Seeing It Not There and Black Stuff

As I mentioned earlier, I give few cautions to those interested in learning to explore our afterlife, because I've found nothing that really warrants any fear. However, while hot stoves are nothing to fear, children do need to learn not to touch them. One such hot stove is what I call *Black Stuff*, as I described in *Voyage Beyond Doubt*. I'd like to pass on what I've discovered about *Black Stuff* and how to deal with it using an advanced tool called Seeing It Not There.

A woman who was concerned that she might be developing ovarian cancer asked my friend Rebecca to examine her nonphysically to determine the source of her symptoms. Rebecca invited me to tag along, nonphysically, as part of a partnered exploration training session.

Shortly after we arrived, I saw what appeared to be a puddle of some kind of black, tarry material in the area of one of her ovaries. I had the sense that this spot was the source of the symptoms and needed to be removed. Being a jump-in-with-both-feet kind of guy, I flew over to the woman and began pulling this Black Stuff out of her body with my hands.

Ouch! This Black Stuff on my nonphysical fingers began to burn intensely, like boiling hot, sticky tar, and my fingers felt like I'd stuck them in a light socket. When I tried to get the goo off the fingers of my left hand, I transferred some of this Black Stuff to the fingers of my right hand. If it hadn't been so painful, the experience would have been comical. After maybe ten or fifteen seconds, Rebecca flew between the woman and me to put a stop to it.

We both stepped back a few feet from the woman, and Rebecca motioned for me to watch. I couldn't see exactly what she did, but in a few seconds the Black Stuff over the woman's ovary disappeared. Rebecca then made some odd motions with her hands and the hole where the Black Stuff had been was filled with bright, pink light. During our debriefing after this experience Rebecca explained what the Black Stuff was and what she'd done to make it disappear.

Rebecca's first words on the subject were, *I couldn't believe my eyes when I saw you go in and start pulling at that Black Stuff with your fingers! I've never met anyone dumb enough to touch that stuff, much less keep pulling at it after they experience the intense burning/electrocuting sensation it has!* (I wanted to ask how she knew what it felt like to touch the Black Stuff, but thought better of it.) Rebecca explained that the Black Stuff was not cancer, but the woman's *fear* of cancer. When I asked what she had done to make it disappear, she explained that she had not made it disappear, she instead had *seen it not there.*

According to Rebecca, trying to *force* the Black Stuff to disappear automatically carries the belief or expectation that it can in some way prevent you from succeeding. Since in nonphysical reality thoughts can be subconsciously projected to become things, the expectation of resistance can *cause* that resistance, foiling attempts to remove the Black Stuff. The harder you feel you have to try to force it to disappear, the more your action implies, and creates, stronger resistance to your efforts. Seeing It Not There sidesteps implied resistance. Think of it like this: if you had Black Stuff on your fingers, seeing it there and trying to make it disappear is trying to force it to be gone. Seeing your fingers as they normally appear (without Black Stuff on them) is more like "Seeing It Not There." When you encounter this Black Stuff, if you touch it with your fingers, please remember that I suggested that you see your fingers with the Black Stuff not there—in other words, as they normally appear. In my view this Black Stuff is not a danger as long as you treat it like a hot stove. When you see this stuff, don't touch it.

Seeing It Not There can also be particularly useful in some retrieval situations. Those of you who have read *Voyages into the Unknown* may recall the woman who died in the Oklahoma City bombing who was convinced she was still alive and trapped by fallen debris. After failing to convince her that she'd died and wasn't really trapped by fallen debris, I used Seeing It Not There on the space surrounding her. As I focused my attention on the debris pile and began to see it not there, a spherical shape perhaps two of her body lengths in diameter took form around her, and replaced the debris with a dim, whitish, gray light. In a few moments she was floating freely inside the ball. From her floating position it was a simple matter for her to move toward me. A Helper who stepped out from behind where I was standing greeted her. With a somewhat puzzled look on her face she left with the Helper heading for the Reception Center. With the bright light people still at my sides illuminating the darkness, we began moving quickly through the debris pile scanning for other trapped victims of the blast. The same Seeing It Not There technique worked repeatedly for every person we found.

This is a very effective, multiuse tool. I've encountered folks, nonphysically, whose bodies appear to be totally encased in thick, gooey plates of Black Stuff, the embodiment of some strongly felt fear. Moments after they remember the feeling of Seeing It Not There, all the Black Stuff is gone. My advice to you, should you encounter this Black Stuff on a person during your explorations, is to deal with that Black Stuff before you continue whatever you intend to do with this person. It helps reduce or eliminate their feelings of fear, and if you touch them you won't burn your nonphysical fingers. I trust that in your own explorations you will discover new uses for Seeing It Not There.

Releasing Picked-Up-Emotion Energies

Within physical reality the people and things around us can affect our emotional state. People's feelings of great joy, sadness, anger, etc., can *rub off on us*. Just being in the company of people experiencing such feelings can

179

cause us to experience them also. While our attention is focused within a nonphysical reality, this effect can be magnified. On occasion you may return from one of your explorations sessions in a different emotional state than you were in before the session. Sometimes you may experience feelings of great joy, happiness, or gratitude, sometimes a darker emotional state. This chapter teaches you how to recover your emotional Balance. I have needed this only a very few times, but when you need a special wrench, no ordinary pair of pliers will do.

My experiences in April 1995, when I was retrieving people who had died in the Oklahoma City bombing, illustrate what I mean by *picked-up energies* and how to use this tool to release them. I want to emphasize that this is a very extreme example and not something I would expect you might encounter very often, if ever. In fact since following Rebecca's advice given toward the end of this excerpt, I have not experienced anything even approaching the extreme described here. The following is an excerpt from *Voyages into the Unknown,* edited for length.

As I searched I became aware of a feeling that had been there all along. It must be something like a firefighter going into a burning building. At first he is so busy that he is barely aware of the surrounding maelstrom. If he stops to think about his surroundings, all of a sudden he can see the flames and feel the heat. Firefighters probably know better than to stop and do such a thing. I'm not a firefighter. I didn't know.

I naively opened up my awareness to the now strong feeling, and realized that it was emotional energy of incredible power. All of a sudden, the burning, searing power and intensity of these emotional energies was incredible. I felt my awareness quiver, wavering toward unconsciousness. Unbelievably horrendous levels of grief, fear, anger, frustration, and rage surged through me.

I was not prepared in the least. Instants passed like years as I struggled to push the door of my awareness closed against the tremendous pressure of these emotions! Finally, after I was able to move my attention away from the emotional energies of the blast site, I could stop and catch my breath. It took me several moments to regain my composure.

As I hovered in the blackness, resting, I realized that those powerful emotions were coming not from the people I was assisting but from physically alive people at the site and throughout the country and the world. The bombing had focused the emotional energies of millions into the blast site. Rescue workers, victims' family members, and people around the world were all feeling frustration, anger, grief, and more as they worked, waited, and watched. Those emotions were being projected into the blast site area because people's attention was focused there while they were feeling them.

I had begun the retrieval while eating dinner at a Bennigan's restaurant. I left the restaurant and went home to my apartment. Soon I began to feel as if I had radiation burns from exposure to the emotional energies at the blast site. These burns didn't show on the outside. These were emotional burns, on the inside. Like sunburn, they burned more and more as time went by. Grief, rage, and anger engulfed me. Anxiety, sadness, and frustration rolled over me like twenty-foot breakers. I phoned Rebecca to tell her what had happened and compare notes. I also wanted her advice about the emotional energy burns.

Her first words were, "Oh, Bruce, the babies." I felt a crest of grief rise up through and above me, and then crash down through me.

As we talked, the emotional waves were less like a giant surf pounding the beach and became more like gigantic swells out at sea, with high crests and deep troughs. I would feel anger, rage, or frustration below me rising upward with great power. A wave of emotion would pass upward through my body until I was completely submerged and overwhelmed by the feeling.

This was not a pleasant experience!

At the peak of intensity, with the crest of a wave high above my head, I'd lose almost all emotional control. Grief and rage were the most powerful and difficult to deal with. Through my confusion and disorientation Rebecca and I continued to talk about our experiences. After ten minutes or so I calmed down some and began to feel physically exhausted. After hanging up the phone I spent fifteen minutes doing Tai Chi, and then I collapsed into bed to rest. Lying there, I felt the continual rise and fall of the strong emotions I'd felt at the blast site in Oklahoma City. Those energies had stuck to my nonphysical body like hot black tar and I had carried them into my physical world awareness.

Too strong a dose of this stuff, left in place too long, can make a person physically ill. Luckily I had previous experience with this hot black tar and knew how to remove it. I relaxed into Focus 10 and envisioned many small, hollow balls floating in the air above my body. Mentally, I directed anything within my energy field that was not mine into an appropriate ball. When it felt like everything had been transferred from my field into the balls, I sent each one back to its rightful owner. I felt great relief as the envisioned balls carried it all away. The waves of emotion that moved through me after that were still strong but manageable. I was no longer in any danger of totally losing emotional control.

Most of Thursday, Friday, and portions of Saturday were emotionally rough seas. Waves of grief would bring tears to my eyes. During waves of anger I'd stomp around my apartment wanting to strike out and hurt the bastards who had set off the bomb. Over those three days the waves gradually came fewer and further between. It was Sunday before their intensity began to diminish.

My exposure in Oklahoma City had stirred up every bit of my own unresolved emotional baggage. To release what they had stirred up in me I had to welcome my feelings and give them expression. As I cried and raged and talked and fretted, the strength of the waves gradually subsided.

I awoke Monday morning to a suggestion from Coach to form a rebal (Resonant Energy Balloon) before getting out of bed. Think of it as visualizing a large balloon of energy surrounding your entire body. Within this balloon, visualize currents and flows of energy passing through your body, cleaning and recharging the energy field that surrounds and permeates you. This particular rebal turned out to have a rather intricate appearance, a pair of counter-rotating helixes. One carried energy from below my feet, inside my body, to above my head. The other helix shape rotated in the opposite direction outside my body. It carried energy from above my head to back down below my feet. Each helix fed the other, circulating fresh, clean, clear energy throughout my body. Within three or four minutes the last of the emotional goo I'd stirred up in me in Oklahoma City was cleared away. After thirty-five minutes of Tai Chi I felt fully energized and back to what is normal for me. Monday was the first day I felt really good again.

My mother always said that experience is the best teacher and a hard master. Oklahoma City made her point again. There was much to learn from the experience of this voyage into the afterlife.

- I learned how to prepare for such emotionally charged encounters in the future. Pushing the door of my awareness closed against the pressure of those emotions had been a mistake. My preparation for trips to places like Oklahoma City now begins with Rebecca's affirmation. *All my energy channels are clean, clear, open, and functioning perfectly. Any energies I encounter pass through me easily with no effect.* I try to remember to use this one all the time.

- Starting my assistance in a busy, noisy public place like Bennigan's restaurant had not been a wise choice either. The whole experience would have been better done in the quiet and privacy of my apartment. A better choice yet would have been to work together in the company of someone else with experience. I'd approached it entirely too lightly without respect for the potential power of the experience.

I again want to emphasize that this example is an extreme. Since learning to use Rebecca's affirmation, I have never again experienced anything even approaching that level of emotional turbulence. (You might consider utilizing such an affirmation as part of your Preparatory Process.) I now utilize the message of Rebecca's affirmation more on an as-needed basis. When I encounter strong emotional energies during an exploration experience, I restate her affirmation to remind myself that they can pass through me with no effect. When I forget to do this—usually because I'm following my knee-jerk habit of resistance—I sometimes return from an exploration feeling some emotional imbalance. I use the *back to the rightful owner* tool. I suggest that you remember this tool, and use it should the need arise.

The 3-D Blackness

The 3-D (three-dimensional) Blackness is unique. It is both an area of consciousness and a powerful tool for use in the exploration of consciousness. While I don't have a specific exercise to help guide you into the 3-D Blackness, you may stumble into it during your explorations, as I did. Hopefully my description will be clear enough that you will recognize when this happens. The 3-D Blackness can be used as a sort of a shortcut to

other areas of consciousness,
specific individuals,
specific nonphysical locations, and
places as yet to be discovered.

My first encounters with this 3-D Blackness occurred very early in my explorations. These early encounters were infrequent and random. My first clue that 3-D Blackness existed came when I noticed that the usual blackness before my closed eyes seemed somehow different. If you close your eyes you might describe what you are seeing as a flat, two-dimensional, blackness, like a television screen tuned between active channels. Further, you might describe this two-dimensional blackness as not uniform. Some areas may appear lighter or darker than others. If you move your closed eyes from side to side, this two-dimensional blackness does not appear to move.

The 3-D Blackness I occasionally stumbled into was completely different from the two-dimensional variety. Typically I would be in the process of relaxing or just drifting along, and suddenly realize I was peering into a blackness that had depth. An instant after this realization, I'd be seeing the flat two-dimensional blackness again. I focused on becoming hypervigilant, in an attempt to recognize this 3-D Blackness and to stay focused within it. For a long time I got nothing more than brief glimpses, but eventually I discovered that focusing on relaxing after stumbling into the 3-D Blackness allowed me to stay in it longer. I had to resist my natural inclination to attempt to gain control of the situation.

Once I was able to remain in it for about three to five seconds by relaxing, I found that peering into its depth allowed me to remain in it for longer periods of time. Once I came to recognize the *feeling* of being in the 3-D Blackness it became easier to intentionally shift my focus of attention there. That feeling is very similar to one I've experienced in the physical world.

A number of books have been published that contain images that at first appear to be flat, two-dimensional collections of random dots or small patterns. One of the names these images go by is *Magic Eyes*. If you look at one of these images with your eyes crossed just right, you see a completely different three-dimensional image. While many people find it difficult to see the three-dimensional image, it is something you can learn with practice. If you can find one of these *Magic Eyes* books, learning to see the three-dimensional image can help you learn to focus your attention within the 3-D Blackness. When I am seeing the three-dimensional image within one of these *Magic Eyes* images, the feeling I experience is very similar to the feeling of being within the 3-D Blackness. And by the Hemi-Sync Model of Consciousness, if you remember the feeling of an area of consciousness to the point of reexperiencing that feeling, your attention will automatically be shifted to that area of consciousness. If you add to this placing your intent to experience the 3-D Blackness, you will begin having experiences of being there.

One feature of the 3-D Blackness that sets it apart from almost all other areas of consciousness is that it is easily recognized. It is normal for someone just learning to meditate, for example, to wonder whether or not they are doing it right. What sets the 3-D Blackness apart is that the cues indicating you are there are unmistakable. The visual cue is the difference between looking at a flat screen and looking into the depth of a scene. The 3-D Blackness has depth and images there have a three-dimensional, holographic quality. So, seeing a person there is not like looking at the image of a person on a movie screen. It is more like seeing a hologram of that person as a three-dimensional object. In my experience these holographic images are typically grainy, black-and-white images. The 3-D Blackness also has a uniformly black intensity, and a uniformly grainy texture similar to black velvet. In fact, Monroe called it the Velvety Blackness. Once you have learned to recognize the 3-D Blackness, and are able to maintain your focus of attention there for more than a few seconds, you can begin to explore its use as a tool of exploration.

From the experiences reported by many who routinely enter the 3-D Blackness, this appears to be an area of consciousness that can be thought of as a central hub in a transportation network. It is as if this place contains numerous interdimensional doorways, or portals, leading directly to other areas of consciousness. Those who enter the 3-D Blackness routinely do so to utilize this feature. For example, if such a person desires to explore a specific location such as the Education Center in Focus 27, a dimensional doorway or portal within the 3-D Blackness leads directly there. Or if an afterlife explorer desires to visit a specific person There, one of these portals leads directly from the 3-D Blackness to that person's location. The following edited excerpt from the chapter "Sylvia's Retrieval," in *Voyage Beyond Doubt*, describes using the 3-D Blackness as a shortcut to the location of a specific deceased person.

I closed my eyes, felt the shift in my perception, and realized I was peering into 3-D Blackness. Against its uniformly random quality, any shape within it stands out from the background and draws one's attention. Sometimes it's just a small patch that looks different from its uniform surroundings or has some movement or motion in it. When a small, solid, black swirl appeared, I focused my attention on it and felt movement toward it. The large, round, smiling face of Dopey, one of Walt Disney's seven dwarfs, popped into view. A perfect image for someone with a "moon face," a side effect of prednisone, who died under the influence of morphine!

The small, solid, black swirl is the dimensional doorway, or portal, that led me from the 3-D Blackness to Sylvia. In my early explorations I did not notice these portals until I inadvertently entered the 3-D Blackness after having placed an intent to reach a specific nonphysical destination. Idly peering into the depths of the 3-D Blackness, I'd noticed a small, darker area with a different texture, in the shape of swirl. These differences drew my attention and as I focused on the swirl, trying to see it more clearly, the next thing I knew I was at the intended destination.

Sometimes, very, very rarely in my experience, the portal presents itself as a small patch of color. The following edited excerpt from *Voyage Beyond Doubt* occurred before I knew much about the 3-D Blackness. This experience occurred while working with a group attempting to learn how to assist some of the 68,000 people who died in an earthquake in India. This portal led from the 3-D Blackness to an area in Focus 23 in which Helpers were providing assistance.

I peered intently into the 3-D blackness before my nonphysical eyes, and a small patch of bright, vivid green appeared and attracted my attention. I felt myself accelerating toward the patch. I emerged from its other side, flying perhaps eighty yards above the ground. In full 3-D color, I was cruising along at a pretty good clip, over low, gently rolling, lush, green hills. It was a clear, bright, blue-sky sunny day. On the horizon I could see two thin columns of white smoke rising, close together, into the clear blue sky. I turned and headed for the columns of smoke.

The next thing I remember is standing at the edge of what looked like a small tent city or relief camp. The tent flap entrances to all the tents were closed, giving the impression they were occupied. Areas resembling narrow streets between the rows of tents were conspicuously absent, except for one leading through the center of the camp from my left to my right.

People in small groups or by themselves were walking toward this tent city from the surrounding countryside, feeding a line that entered the camp. The victims of the quake entered the camp and were greeted. Camp workers handed out blankets, cups, water, and food. The distance between the tables was so narrow it forced everyone to walk single file. Each worker handing out supplies instructed the quake victims to follow closely behind the person in front of them.

I recognized cooking fires as the source of the thin columns of smoke that were rising straight up, high into the windless sky.

Hopefully you will recognize the 3-D Blackness when you experience it.

Since it is an easily recognized area of consciousness by virtue of its visual cues, and makes travel from one area of consciousness to another such a simple matter, it can be used as a primary tool of exploration. As you begin the retrieval and other exploration exercises in this *Afterlife Knowledge Guidebook* be aware that the 3-D Blackness exists, and when you enter it, explore it.

The Flying Fuzzy Zone

The Flying Fuzzy Zone comes under the heading of an interesting area of consciousness as yet unexplored (by me). I have entered it many times, only to exit immediately after realizing I was there. None of these visits has ever lasted more than a couple of seconds. Perhaps in your own explorations you may stumble into this Flying Fuzzy Zone and maybe you will be able to learn how to stay there long enough to more fully explore it.

My first encounter with the Flying Fuzzy Zone occurred during a program at The Monroe Institute. During the beginning of one of the tape exercises it suddenly felt like the top of my head was pushing against a thin, tightly stretched, sheet of rubber. As I pushed harder against it I felt something go pop and my head went through it. My visual field had a completely black background and was filled with zillions of fuzzy little points of light all flying in very fast, small, tight circles. These fuzzy little points of light, and the patterns of their flight, are reminiscent of the way moths look buzzing around in a bright light against the backdrop of the black night sky.

Since that first encounter I have entered the Flying Fuzzy Zone many times, though the sensation of my head pushing against something has not reoccurred. The result has always been the same; as soon as I recognize I am there I immediately exit the place. There is not much more I can tell you about the Flying Fuzzy Zone. Others have reported entering it, but none have been able to stay there long enough to explore it. Perhaps you will be the first. If you do, then—as Bob Monroe used to say—"come back and tell me, and then we'll both know."

PART IV

Retrieval-Based Exploration

19

The Art of Retrieval

If you have ever had a nightmare in which a horrible beast was chasing you, and you knew if it caught you something terrible would happen, you may remember how real your terror felt. The elements of the dream made you believe you had no option but to keep running. Your belief that it was real made escape through your own efforts extremely difficult, if not impossible. It's a vicious circle. Feeling the terror of being chased keeps your attention focused on the terror of being chased, limiting your awareness of other options to near zero. You have become *stuck* in a dream.

For you to escape your nightmare something must get your attention and serve to shift your awareness at least to a place where you can think more clearly. Anything that served to shift your awareness back to physical reality would *retrieve* you from your nightmare. A ringing alarm clock might retrieve you—that is, shift your awareness away from dream consciousness and back to physical reality consciousness. A splash of cold water might do the trick. To retrieve you from your nightmare something or someone existing *outside* your dream would have to assist you to shift your focus of attention out of your dream. There are many parallels between this example and being stuck after death in Focus 23.

A person's beliefs and expectations about what happens after death—or the circumstances of death itself—can create a dream reality that the person enters at death. In their self-created, dreamlike reality they will react to the elements of that reality as if they are real, just as you did in your nightmare.

The difference between you in a nightmare and someone in Focus 23 is the alarm clock. Someone stuck in Focus 23 after death needs something like an alarm clock.

Let's carry the analogy a little further. If a second person who is also asleep and dreaming could find a way to enter your dream, that person might realize you are stuck in a nightmare. That person might be able to see the horrible beast chasing you and see that you are running in terror. You can think of the Art of Retrieval as someone entering your nightmare and assisting you in shifting from ordinary dreaming to a lucid dreaming state. They might create a door with a huge sign over it that says, *The Perfect Hiding Place*, and yell, *"Hey! Buddy! Quick! In here!"* Once you are through the door with your awareness of the horrible beast blocked, the person who entered your dream and created the perfect hiding place might say, *"Oh, by the way, you're asleep and dreaming right now. There is no real beast chasing you. This is just a dream."* If you buy the person's story, it may trigger your shift from ordinary dreaming to lucid dreaming. Now perhaps you can think a little more clearly and realize you have other choices. The huge sign and door are just the sort of thing a nonphysical Helper might do in an attempt to retrieve a person stuck in Focus 23. Helpers are very often successful using such ploys. But sometimes, no matter what they try, they are not successful and the stuck person just keeps on running.

That's where we come in. Often the deceased person either cannot see or hear the Helper or refuses the Helper's assistance. Our advantage is that the deceased can see and hear us.

(By the way, because my books are filled with retrieval stories, some folks worry that most people get stuck after they die. That's not true. The reason there are so many retrieval stories in my books is that the Art of Retrieval is the way I first learned to explore our afterlife. The only deceased people I actively sought out were those who were stuck after death, so naturally those are the kinds of people I found. This does not mean that the majority or even a large percentage of people get stuck after death.)

Helpers are always there as people make the transition out of physical reality at death, and many of us have heard stories that demonstrate this. When Grandma is in Hospice in the process of dying and she begins talking to people in the room no one else can see or hear, she is talking to the Helpers who've come to assist her in making her transition. Often these Helpers are friends or relatives who predeceased her. Most often, they can assist her to make her transition and can escort her to her new life in the afterlife. But things can happen that interfere with the Helpers' attempts.

Some family members holding vigil with Grandma may believe she is delirious or hallucinating when she insists that a deceased relative is standing in the room, talking to her. If she starts talking about bright lights or angels in the room, some may become concerned that Grandma is losing touch with reality. It's probably fair to say Grandma *is* losing touch with physical reality as she makes her transition to the reality of the afterlife. And those people she sees, hears, and talks with are Helpers who have come to assist in making her transition to the afterlife a smooth ride. If they can get and hold her attention she'll never get stuck in Focus 23 or any of the Belief System Territories (BST).

But what if someone in the room convinces Grandma she's just hallucinating and those people she's seeing, hearing, and talking to don't really exist? If Grandma accepts that belief, her awareness of those Helpers may become blocked and close down. If she carries that belief into her afterlife existence, her awareness of nonphysical Helpers could remain closed down. Grandma could then get stuck in a self-created, Focus 23 reality in which Helpers do not exist. If Helpers attempt to enter Grandma's Focus 23 reality, her beliefs and expectations may block her awareness of them. Lacking awareness of the Helper's presence, Grandma may remain stuck for a very long time.

In medical treatment of the dying it used to be common practice to attempt to *reorient these apparently delusional patients back to physical reality.* Caregivers were trained to try to talk dying patients out of supposedly *delusional states* in which they claimed to be communicating with deceased relatives. In my view this does their patients a great disservice. Any nurse, doctor, or other caregiver who keeps forcing such a patient to refocus their attention back into physical reality and deny the presence of Helpers can cause great harm. In my view, such doctors, nurses, or caregivers should not be allowed to continue treating dying patients until they understand more about what death really is.

One common characteristic of those stuck in Focus 23 is that they don't realize they've died. From their perspective they are fully alert and able to see and hear those still living in physical reality. This may convince them that even though there are some pretty odd things going on, such as the physically living people in the room ignoring them, they are still physically alive. One could say that such people are continuing to focus their attention through their physical senses. Of course, they don't really have physical senses anymore, but focusing their attention *as if they do* keeps their physical-reality beliefs in force. Their physical-reality beliefs can block awareness of nonphysical Helpers.

Using the example of Grandma in Hospice, what do you suppose would happen if Grandma died in her sleep and awoke believing she was still physically alive? Her hospice room would probably look the same to her as it always did, except that all her physically living relatives have left the room. Of course they've left; Grandma died and they all went home, but she doesn't know that. Not realizing that she died, Grandma might decide to just wait until those people come back. Grandma has now created a Focus 23 reality in which she believes she is in a physical-reality hospital bed in a Hospice, waiting for her physically living relatives to come back into the room. This keeps her awareness focused within physical reality and can serve to keep her connected to the influences of her physical-reality beliefs. A Helper who enters Grandma's room to retrieve her now has a problem. Grandma's physical-reality-based beliefs may block her awareness of the Helper. If she is aware of the Helper, she may refuse to be retrieved since from within her *dream* she is still physically alive and waiting for her relatives to return to her room. In this case the Helper may not be able to retrieve Grandma for the simple reason that Grandma either can't see or hear the Helper or she refuses to leave the room.

The Density Factor

Another factor in a Helper's inability to make contact with someone stuck in Focus 23 after death is one I'd explain as similar to why we don't normally see or hear ghosts. A ghost to us is like a Helper to someone stuck in Focus 23. For most people ghosts do not exist within physical reality. Their bodies are made of far less dense material than our physical bodies. It's like the difference between rocks and air. Air is not dense enough for us physical beings to see it, and the stuff ghost's bodies are made of is far less dense than air. You can think of it like this: With our attention focused at the level of physical reality we don't see or hear ghosts because they're not dense enough.

Nonphysical Helpers exist in an area of consciousness, Focus 27, which is even further away from physical reality than Focus 23. In a sense, the Helper's body is made of stuff that is even less dense than the bodies of those who inhabit Focus 23. A person stuck in Focus 23 who believes himself or herself to still be physically alive is focusing his or her attention through the Focus 23 version of the physical senses. And just as we can't see or hear the less dense ghosts, ghosts can't see or hear the less dense Helpers as long as they hold their focus of attention within the more dense Focus 23 area of consciousness.

Although Helpers are sometimes unable to retrieve those stuck in Focus 23, in my opinion their attempts are most often successful. Helpers seem to be constantly cruising through the places people get stuck, looking for windows of opportunity. Just as some of our ordinary dreams may shift into lucid dreams when we suddenly realize that what we're doing is impossible, similar conflicts for those in Focus 23 may open a window of opportunity. When such an opportunity presents itself, all a Helper needs to do is step into the stuck person's now more lucid dream and assist that person to understand that other choices are possible. But when Helpers find a stuck person who is unaware of the Helper's presence, we can use our special advantage to assist Helpers in the Art of Retrieval. Our advantage is that we still live in physical reality, and our physical bodies are denser than Focus 23 stuff. That means that even though the stuck person cannot see or hear the Helper, this person can see and hear us.

Using Our Advantage to Retrieve Ghosts

If you somehow became aware of a ghost standing in your kitchen, you could face the ghost and say, *"Hi there! I can't see you too well, but I know you are standing next to the refrigerator."* The ghost would see and hear you. After the shock of someone acknowledging its presence and talking to it wore off, the ghost might be willing to listen to more of what you have to say. You could say, *"I'll bet some pretty odd things have been going on for you lately. I'll bet most people won't talk to you. They'll act like you don't exist. I'll bet you'd like to be able to talk to someone who could help you understand what's going on. I have a friend who would really like to talk to you. My friend is here in the room too, but you might need to look around a little to find her. She is standing right behind you. Look for my friend and she can help you get answers to your questions."* If you could see the ghost clearly, you might notice it turn and look behind itself, and then disappear.

In the Art of Retrieval your advantage over Helpers is in making first contact and communicating with those who are stuck. If in your communication you can get the ghost to shift its focus of attention away from physical reality, toward the area of consciousness where the Helper exists, there's a very good chance it will see the Helper in some form, often as a light. Once it is able to perceive the Helper, that Helper will take the ghost to a better place.

This works fine for ghosts stuck so close to physical reality they can see and hear us within physical reality. But what about people stuck within self-created realities that have no awareness of the physical world? How can we use our advantage over Helpers to retrieve them? When we shift our focus of attention to nonphysical realities, like Focus 23, our physical body keeps a portion of our awareness anchored within physical reality, and our Interpreter sees to it that we carry our physical reality habits and beliefs along with us. This keeps our awareness focused in an area of consciousness where we're made of stuff that's just a little denser than folks in Focus 23. When we shift our focus of attention to Focus 23 this density difference means the folks stuck there can still see and hear us, even though they can't see or hear the less dense Helpers. We can still use our advantage in Focus 23 and the Belief System Territories (BST) to make contact and communicate with folks stuck there who have no contact with physical reality. If through our communication we can assist them in shifting their focus of attention toward the Helper, their retrieval is a *fait accompli.*

Simply stated, our role in the Art of Retrieval is to make first contact and communicate with those who've become stuck after death and assist them in becoming aware of the Helper's presence. Once the stuck person is aware of the Helper, your role in the actual retrieval is completed. However, as you'll soon discover, a window of opportunity to explore much deeper into our afterlife existence and beyond has just opened.

20

The Retrieval Process

The retrieval process is:

• the Preparatory Process,
• contacting a Helper,
• the Helper guiding you to a person who is stuck,
• contacting and communicating with that person,
• gathering information from that person,
• introducing that person to the Helper,
• observing interaction between the Helper and the person,
• observing where the Helper takes that person,
• observing what happens there, and
• further exploration.

The system of afterlife exploration I teach is centered on the Art of Retrieval for many reasons. Even in my earliest explorations, one of the most compelling reasons to continue practicing the Art of Retrieval was compassion for my fellow human beings who had become stuck after death. Some are stuck in pain, anguish, loneliness, or terror. Knowing that many would remain imprisoned in their own self-created delusions drove me to continue practicing the Art of Retrieval to free as many as I could. With each retrieval, I learned more about our afterlife existence. With each verification, my perception opened further. My relationships with Helpers began to feel like genuine friendships. It was more than just my reliance on their assistance (in exploring) and theirs on me (in retrievals). Sometimes my explorations beyond physical reality were motivated by nothing more than a desire to visit those friends.

Somewhere along my retrieval path I lost my fear of death and my life changed. When you *know* you will continue to exist beyond death it completely changes your life. The fear of death, even subconsciously held, has insidious, far-reaching effects and limitations that are only realized and understood when the fear is gone. It brought me a newfound freedom to really live my life to fulfill the purposes I intended this life to have. Eliminating the fear of death for as many people as possible became another reason to continue exploring through practicing the Art of Retrieval.

Then I was invited by Duncan Roads to speak at the *Nexus* magazine conference in Sydney, Australia. For the first time I had to find a way to condense years of afterlife exploration and what I'd discovered into a one-and-a-half-hour talk. And I had to start thinking about how I could teach the Art of Retrieval. After the conference, as I climbed into a taxicab for the ride to the airport and my flight home, Duncan suggested strongly that I needed to develop a workshop to teach people how to explore the afterlife.

The retrieval process description you're about to read has evolved over several years of teaching workshops in countries around the world. Before you embark on your first retrieval exercise, I'd like to give you a step-by-step, detailed description of the retrieval process, along with some tips about how it's done.

As with other exercises in this *Afterlife Knowledge Guidebook*, the retrieval process begins by sitting or lying down in a comfortable position in your quiet place and closing your eyes. Then begin your Preparatory Process.

Throughout the retrieval exercise, if at any point you notice you are not relaxed, take in more Deep Relaxing Breaths (DRB) until you feel relaxed again. If it feels like you're just not getting anywhere, take in more DRB and then more Energy Gathering Breaths (EGB).

Reexperiencing the feeling of love is so much more important than most people realize. This helps to automatically open your perception beyond its normal limits. As Love Energy expands and fills your body and the space around you, it also serves as a cocoon of energy that has other very useful properties. Any point during the retrieval exercise in which you feel like you do not clearly perceive or understand what's going on should be your cue to again remember the feeling of love.

The Prime-the-Pump Exercises. The written scripts for all the retrieval exercises contain a guided meditation that serves as the Prime-the-Pump Exercise. This serves to stimulate the nonphysical senses to use imagination as a means of perception. It is important to remember that it is okay to pretend during *any* step of the retrieval process. It is especially important to allow yourself to pretend during the Prime-the-Pump Exercises. If you find yourself saying, I can't see, hear, or perceive a single thing he's describing in any way, PRETEND THAT YOU ARE! I know how hard it can be to allow yourself to pretend, but remember the *Gramps was a bank robber* story. Pretending can be a way of starting the process that leads from perceiving fantasy information to gray-area information to verifiably real information. *Pretending is a key to learning how to explore beyond physical reality.*

Place your intent and state the affirmation given in the exercise script. If you haven't yet identified the feeling of placing intent from the Silly Little Finger Bending Exercise, just remembering the act of doing that exercise is a way of placing intent.

Ask for a Helper to come, and become aware of the Helper's presence, or pretend you do. Your perception of the Helper may run from no feeling of a Helper's presence at all, to a 3-D, real-time interaction, or anywhere in between. No matter what your perception, Helpers *always* come when called. If you have no perception of a Helper, pretend you do and continue with the exercise. If something shows up after you ask for a Helper to come that you don't think is a Helper (a stained glass window, for example), pretend it's the Helper and continue with the exercise.

Ask the Helper to guide you to a person who needs retrieval. Follow the Helper, or pretend to, to that person. Again, your perception of this activity may vary along the full range of possibilities. If you have no perception of the Helper at this point in the exercise, pretend you do. If you have no perception of the Helper taking you to the person you are to retrieve, pretend you do.

At this point in the retrieval process, you will begin gathering impressions of, and making contact with, the person you are to retrieve. Be willing to accept any impressions of this contact as potentially real, withholding judgment at least long enough to fully gather the impressions and record them after the exercise. As I said earlier, my biggest mistake was to discard information due to my beliefs and expectations about its accuracy before recording it.

You will then be guided to introduce yourself to this person. This can be done in much the same way as you would introduce yourself to someone you just met. It can be as simple as just walking up to them and saying, *"Hi, my name is Bruce, what's yours?"* Sometimes the situation will point to some other way to introduce yourself. And again, it's okay to pretend to introduce yourself.

You will then be guided to join into this person's reality. Joining into their reality might best be described as playing along with wherever that person believes himself or herself to be, or the situation they believe themselves to be in. In the example of the woman who died and believed she was still at the bus stop waiting for a bus, the participant joined into the woman's reality by introducing herself and complaining out loud about how poorly buses kept to their schedules. As you gather impressions of the person and the scene, find a way to play along, and if you have any difficulty, remember you can ask the Helper to assist you in finding a way to join into the person's reality. Playing along can be a continuation of Priming the Pump in a way that shifts your awareness into the stuck person's self-created reality.

The next step in the retrieval process could be described as evidence gathering. You can ask specific questions. The answers that person gives may later lead to verification of the experience. However, very often it is the small details, rather than the answers to direct questions, that bring validating evidence. For example, it might be your impression that the person is dressed a certain way, wearing a piece of jewelry, or a symbol, a military insignia or uniform. After you return from this retrieval exercise it is important to write down every detail you remember. This may include drawing sketches of things you saw or pretended to see, to help you remember them long enough to keep the possibility of verification open. It may be that a week after the exercise you'll happen to be paging through a *National Geographic* magazine, scanning an article on an archeological dig, and see a photograph of a military medal that looks just like the one you made a sketch of. These tiny pieces of information may be the things that lead to verification of your experiences.

Introduce the person to the Helper, in any way that seems appropriate. You might just say something like, *there's someone here I'd like you to meet.* If you've had no perception of the Helper up to this point, you may be very surprised at what happens next. One workshop participant was in contact with a man who didn't know he had died in a mountain climbing accident. This participant had no perception of a Helper, but pretended to introduce the Helper by saying there was a doctor with him who might be able to help. The workshop participant then saw a Helper, dressed like a doctor, walk into the scene immediately and begin talking to the man and tending to his injuries. Remember, if you feel like absolutely nothing is happening in your retrieval experience, it is still okay to pretend.

After introducing the Helper to the person, you'll be guided to observe any interaction between them. This point in the process often begins to reveal just how skilled Helpers are, and may teach you techniques you can use later.

At some point it will become apparent that the Helper and the person are getting ready to leave the scene. When they start to move away you'll be guided to follow the Helper. Though you're probably getting sick of hearing me say it, *it's still okay to pretend* that you follow them.

At some point the Helper and the person will stop moving. When they do, stop with them and you'll be guided to gather your impressions of where they've stopped.

At some point the Helper's role in the retrieval will be completed and the Helper will be ready to move away from the person. When that happens you'll be guided to stay with the Helper.

Once you and the Helper are alone, you'll be guided to ask the Helper for information that might clarify any questions you have about the retrieval you've just participated in. Feel free to ask the Helper any other questions you might personally have about any aspects of the retrieval.

You are also free to ask the Helper to guide you to any other nonphysical place you'd like to visit or explore, or a source of information for other questions you might have that are not related to the retrieval you just participated in. That's what Helpers are for, to provide assistance for any request you make.

When you feel complete with your experience in the exercise, express your gratitude to the Helper and open your eyes. Immediately begin recording your experience in your notebook. Write down every single detail you can remember, especially any event that was unexpected—the Gray Area events. You may think you made up some detail. This is not a good reason to not document your experience.

After you've written down everything you can remember, in great detail, including sketches, close your eyes again, relax, and remember any feelings you experienced during the exercise, particularly any feeling you experienced while in contact with the Helper or person you retrieved. This uses the Hemi-Sync Model of Consciousness and State-Specific Memory to help you remember more details of your experience. Remember, write down every detail you remember no matter how insignificant, unrelated, or fantasized it seems. You don't have to try to explain these details or try to interpret or understand what they mean; just write them down. Their relevance, meaning, or interpretation may pop up later.

Throughout the retrieval exercise, use the tools you learned earlier in this *Afterlife Knowledge Guidebook*. If the images or impressions you are getting seem too outlandish to be real, remember about Interpreter Overlay. Let go of the image and place your intent to connect again with greater clarity. If things seem to be moving along and you suddenly realize you are being blocked from doing something you desire to do, remember the process of dialoguing with an Aspect of Self to change or eliminate the blocking belief. If you notice the feeling of tension creeping in, remember you can take 3DRB and 3EGB at any time. Remember to *feel* love as a way of opening or clarifying your perception, and remember to project love to open and clarify the perception of the person you are retrieving. Above all, remember that it is okay to pretend at any point in the exercise. Some information may later prove to be fantasy, and some may later prove to be verifiable. During the experience of gathering the information it is almost impossible to discern what's real and what's fantasy. Pretending can be the beginning of the process that moves your perception from fantasy to unexpected events to validated or verifiable information. One important goal of learning the Art of Retrieval is to use the Basic Premise to prove to yourself our afterlife is real. Pretending is a key factor in accomplishment of that goal.

Know that workshop participants may report that it felt like they were pretending and fabricating the entire experience as it happened, even if almost all of the information they gathered is verified. It can feel like you are making it all up even when you're not. That's just part of the nature of learning how to explore the afterlife.

After the exercise, as time and opportunity permit, look for ways to verify and validate any of the information you gathered during the exercise.

With that, you're ready to do your first retrieval exercise.

21

First Retrieval Exercise

You are now ready to begin actively exploring our afterlife. In this first retrieval exercise, the Helper will select the person you are to retrieve. As I mentioned before, Helpers are constantly cruising the areas of afterlife consciousness where people are stuck. They are always looking for opportunities to utilize your services and your first-contact and communication advantage.

This exercise is a verbatim transcript of the Focused Attention exercise from a workshop. If you did not purchase the exercise tapes or compact disk (CD) along with this *Afterlife Knowledge Guidebook,* I recommend that you use the script below to record your own audiotape for this exercise. Without an audiotape your attention will be divided between remembering the instructions for the exercise and doing the exercise. With the audiotape it will be far easier to focus your attention on doing the exercise, with far more productive results.

If you record your own exercise tape, use a soft, calm, relaxing, soothing voice. As you do this exercise, if your retrieval experience begins to go in a direction that conflicts with the recording's verbal guidance, ignore the recording and follow your experience. You might consider doing this exercise several times before moving on. Each time you do this exercise it's an opportunity to remember and use more of the tools you've learned in this guidebook.

First Retrieval Exercise: Script

This is a Retrieval Exercise. (Wait 5 sec)

As you get ready to begin the exercise, adjust the volume of this recording so that you can comfortably and easily hear and understand my voice. You may do this exercise either sitting or lying down. (Wait 10 sec)

When you're ready to begin, please close your eyes. (Wait 10 sec)

To begin this exercise move your body into a comfortable, relaxed position in your quiet place. (Wait 30 sec)

Complete your Preparatory Process, remembering and imagining each of the individual feelings, images, impressions, and details as you do each step in the process. (Wait 10 sec)

Take in Three Deep Relaxing Breaths. (Wait 45 sec)

Take in Three Energy Gathering Breaths to establish the flow from below. (Wait 45 sec)

Take in Three Energy Gathering Breaths from Below. (Wait 45 sec)

Take in Three Energy Gathering Breaths to establish the flow from above. (Wait 45 sec)

Take in Three Energy Gathering Breaths from Above. (Wait 45 sec)

Remember a time when you were feeling loved or loving. (Wait 30 sec)

Let this memory help you to remember and reexperience the feeling of love. (Wait 20 sec)

If the feeling fades that's okay; just remember another time when you felt love and let that feeling build. (Wait 20 sec)

Remember, it is okay to pretend during this exercise. (Wait 5 sec)

Take in at least three more Deep Relaxing Breaths. (Wait 30 sec)

Remember when you first began to wake up this morning, your eyes still closed, still under those nice, warm, cozy blankets. (Wait 15 sec)

Remember the feel of the warm bedsheets and blankets against your body. (Wait 10 sec)

Remember as you woke up and first opened your eyes. (Wait 10 sec)

Remember where you were and what you saw. (Wait 10 sec)

Remember that it's okay to pretend. (Wait 10 sec)

Remember the furniture in the room, the doorway, and windows. (Wait 15 sec)

Remember anything you heard as you slid out of bed, the feel of the air against your skin, and what you did next. (Wait 15 sec)

Remember as you were choosing the clothes you would wear today. (Wait 15 sec)

Remember the colors, shapes, and textures of the fabrics. (Wait 10 sec)

It's okay to pretend. (Wait 5 sec)

Remember the texture and feel of the fabrics sliding against your body as you dressed. (Wait 10 sec)

Remember walking into the room you are now in, and preparing to begin this exercise. (Wait 15 sec)

At your own pace, take in at least three more Deep Relaxing Breaths, and as you let each breath out, feel yourself relax a little deeper. (Wait 20 sec)

Remember the feeling of placing intent, or just imagine doing the Silly Little Finger Bending Exercise. (Wait 20 sec)

Reexperience the feeling of placing intent as you say in your mind, **I deeply desire to contact** (wait 5 sec), **to communicate with** (wait 3 sec), **to gather information from** (wait 5 sec), **and be of service to a person needing retrieval** (wait 5 sec) **whose existence can be verified.** (Wait 5 sec)

Ask for a Helper to come. (Wait 10 sec)

Feel for the presence of a Helper, remembering it's still okay to pretend. (Wait 10 sec)

Is this Helper dark or light? (Wait 10 sec)

Is this Helper large or small? (Wait10 sec)

Is this Helper near or far? (Wait 10 sec)

Male, female . . . or something else? (Wait 10 sec)

Young, old? (Wait 10 sec)

Is this Helper beside you, behind you, or perhaps in front of you? (Wait 10 sec)

At your own pace, take in two more Deep Relaxing Breaths and then two more Energy Gathering Breaths from Below. (Wait 20 sec)

Introduce yourself to the Helper, or pretend to. (Wait 15 sec)

Ask the Helper to guide you to the person who needs the service of retrieval whose existence can be verified, and follow the Helper there (wait 3 sec) or pretend to. (Wait 15 sec)

Feel for the presence of this person. (Wait 10 sec)

Is this person behind you, beside you, or perhaps in front of you? (Wait 10 sec)

Is it your impression you are indoors or outdoors? (Wait 10 sec)

Let your Perceiver and Interpreter perform their functions as you first begin to become aware of this person's presence; gather in your impressions of this person and the scene they are in, or pretend to. (Wait 15 sec)

Is this person young or old? (Wait 10 sec)

Large or small? (Wait 10 sec)

Male or female? Gather in your impressions, or pretend to. (Wait 10 sec)

Take note of any feelings or sensations you are experiencing. (Wait 10 sec)

As you become more aware of this person's presence, gather in more impressions of this person's appearance, how they are dressed, and the scene they are in, or pretend to. (Wait 15 sec)

How is this person dressed? (Wait 10 sec)

Do you notice anything unusual about this person's dress, situation, location, posture, or mannerisms? Gather in your impressions. (Wait 15 sec)

Are you aware of any objects in the scene? Gather in your impressions. (Wait 15 sec)

As you are more and more aware of this person, introduce yourself to this person—or pretend to. (Wait 15 sec)

Join into this person's reality, play along with where they think they are, and continue to gather in your impressions. (Wait 15 sec)

Ask this person, "What happened to you?" (Wait 15 sec)

Ask this person, "Why are you here?" (Wait 15 sec)

Ask this person, "What is this place where we are?" Gather your impressions. (Wait 15 sec)

Ask this person, "What is one of your favorite things to do? Do you have a hobby or special interest?" (Wait 15 sec)

Ask this person, "What is your name and where do you live?" (Wait 15 sec)

Ask this person, "How old are you? (Wait 2 sec) Where were you born? (Wait 2 sec) And what year is this?" (Wait 20 sec)

Ask this person, "What do you most wish for?" (Wait 20 sec)

Ask this person, "Can I help you with something?" (Wait 20 sec)

Ask this person to show you, tell you, or give you something that would prove to someone they know that you have visited with them. (Wait 30 sec)

Introduce the Helper to this person in whatever way seems appropriate to you, or pretend to. (Wait 15 sec)

Gather in your impressions of any interaction between the Helper and this person. (Wait 20 sec)

As you observe any interaction between the Helper and this person, this might be a good time to take in more Deep Relaxing Breaths, or Energy Gathering Breaths if you feel the need. (Wait 30 sec)

You will know when the Helper and this person are getting ready to leave—when they do, follow them—or pretend to. (Wait 15 sec)

You will know when the Helper and this person stop moving; when they do, stop with them. (Wait 15 sec)

As you become aware of where you've stopped, gather in impressions of your surroundings. (Wait 15 sec)

What is this place where you've arrived? (Wait 10 sec)

Are there other people there? (Wait 10 sec)

If there are, what's your impression of what they are doing, who they are, and why they are here? (Wait 15 sec)

As you continue to observe these people and your surroundings, you will know when the Helper is getting ready to leave this person with the others. When the Helper moves away from this person, stay with the Helper. (Wait 15 sec)

When you are alone with the Helper, ask the Helper how this person died. (Wait 15 sec)

Ask the Helper, "Who was this person and why did this person need retrieval?" (Wait 15 sec)

Ask the Helper, "Why was this person chosen for me to retrieve and who made this choice?" (Wait 15 sec)

Ask the Helper, "Who were those other people I saw and why were they there?" (Wait 15 sec)

Ask the Helper, "What is this place where we've arrived, and why was this person brought here?" (Wait 15 sec)

Ask the Helper, "Where will this person go next and what will they do there?" (Wait 20 sec)

Ask the Helper to show, tell, or give you something that will prove to you that this retrieval experience was real. (Wait 20 sec)

Ask the Helper for any other information or guidance you desire. (Wait 30 sec)

If there is some nonphysical place you'd like to explore, or information you'd like to access, ask the Helper to assist you. Take as much time as you need and only when you feel complete with this experience, express your gratitude to the Helper and open your eyes. Then immediately begin to write about your experience and use the debriefing section in the *Afterlife Knowledge Guidebook* to assist you in recording your experience.

(Do not record this note: you may either keep your tape player running to leave a very long blank space on the tape, or you may choose to leave a short blank space and plan to turn off the recorder for the remainder of your exercise experience.)

Debrief of the First Retrieval Exercise

Remember to write down every detail of your experience in your notebook, and use State-Specific Memory to remember more of your experience. It may be helpful to reread portions of the exercise script above to trigger more memory. Pay particular attention to recording whatever the person or Helper gave you that could prove your contact was real. Make sketches of any objects or scenes that were a part of this experience. Look for ways you might be able to verify the experience as real.

Consider sharing your retrieval experience by posting it on the Conversation Board at my web site, www.afterlife-knowledge.com. You may get some feedback from more experienced Conversation Board visitors. I check this board often and when time permits I'm happy to comment on your experiences.

Tips for the First Retrieval Exercise

Many participants report that the story of their retrieval experience unfolded in such an unexpected way that they realized they couldn't have made it up. The pace at which events unfolded and the internal consistency of those events were so unexpected in and of themselves that they felt the experience had to be real.

As you review your retrieval experience, think about the tools and techniques you forgot to use:

Did you follow an Interpreter Overlay when it might have been more productive to let go of the image and reconnect?

Was there a point when you didn't know what to do next and you forgot to ask the Helper for assistance?

Did you forget to take in Deep Relaxing Breaths when you began to feel tense or fidgety?

Did you lose your Balance on the side of the Interpreter and get sidetracked with talking to yourself?

Sometimes a little post-retrieval analysis on your part can help you remember to use more of the tools and techniques next time.

A retrieval exercise can be an ideal time to eliminate blocking beliefs. It is entirely okay if you realize that your perception is being blocked and you abandon the remainder of the recorded exercise in favor of exploring the belief and its effects, and using the exercise to change or eliminate that belief. Recall the experience of a man named Al during a workshop in which he decided to visit a deceased friend during one of the retrieval exercises. After he placed his intent for the visit, an image of his friend began to form in the blackness in front of Al. The image got clearer and clearer and then began to fade back into blackness. Al realized he was being blocked from doing something he desired to do, and that blocking beliefs were probably responsible.

He used a modified form of the Dialoguing with an Aspect of Self Method of eliminating beliefs. In his mind Al said, *"I want to know every belief that is preventing me from visiting with my friend."* During his debriefing after the exercise, Al said it was like watching firecrackers go off in front of him as beliefs about the dangers of communication in the spirit world from the religion he was raised in came into his awareness. Five or six such beliefs came into his awareness in a matter of seconds. Al explained that he looked at all those beliefs, saw where they came from, how and why each one was enforced, and then said to all of them, *"You're all a bunch of crap, be gone!"* He reported that moments later his friend's image came back into view and they had a very nice visit during the remainder of the exercise.

A few participants report experiencing strong emotions while in contact with the person they are retrieving. In rare cases these emotions can feel overwhelming. Often this occurs due to the perspective from which you are observing, and a shift of perspective is an effective way to reduce the emotional impact of the experience. One effective technique is to pretend that you step behind a window that is between you and the person you are retrieving. You can still observe and communicate with the person, but you are not *in the scene with the person.* Being *in the scene* with the person carries the assumption that you are experiencing the action of the person within the scene, including the emotional content. Stepping behind the window removes you from the scene and shifts your perspective to that of an Observer of the action rather than a participant. This might sound silly, but if you find yourself in an emotionally overpowering experience, pretend to step behind an imaginary window and see what happens.

Many participants report that they felt like they were making up the entire experience. This is a very common perception even when nearly all of the information gathered during the exercise is verified immediately after the experience. Even if you feel you made it all up, write it all down in your notebook. You just never know which seemingly insignificant little detail that you're sure you fantasized will turn out, in the future, to verify your experience.

Verification of your experience can sometimes come through the clothing style of the person you retrieved. For example, if your retrieval experience took place in fifteenth-century Italy, and you didn't know the clothing styles of that culture and time, a trip to the library to do a little research on clothing styles in Italy may be fruitful. Similarly, ancient weapons or hand tools, military insignia or uniforms, means of transportation, images on money, the kind of sink in a kitchen, vehicles, and other such details from your retrieval experience may lead to verification.

Verification can come in some very strange ways. Several weeks after attending the workshop one participant happened to be flipping through cable TV channels one night and stopped when she realized she was looking at a picture of a man she'd seen during a workshop retrieval exercise. During the exercise she'd encountered an over-the-road truck driver who acted strangely. She had seen his truck and trailer during her experience. The television program showing this truck driver's picture was called *Unsolved Mysteries*. It told how the truck driver had disappeared, and showed home movies of his truck and trailer, the same model and color she had seen during the exercise. This man disappeared less than 50 miles from the site of the workshop.

There is a pattern in the progression of the *degree of complexity* for retrievals that I've seen in my own experience and that of some workshop participants. The early retrievals are usually a simple matter of making contact. As the retriever gains more experience and understanding of various retrieval situations, Helpers apparently take notice of the increase in the retriever's capabilities. After some number of *easy* retrievals the Helper may guide you to someone who is stuck in a more complex way. I don't see this as *testing*. Some retrieval situations just require a more experienced retriever. This pattern of the progression in the degree of complexity of retrievals feels to me like *on-the-job training*. (It reminds me of working as an apprentice carpenter.)

Many folks ask if they'll always get the same Helper in each retrieval. Experience shows that this varies. Sometimes the same Helper will work with you for a few or several retrievals. Sometimes you'll go for a stretch where it's a different Helper each time. There do appear to be some Helpers who return to work with a retriever on a regular basis. Over the years I've been doing retrievals and exploring I've formed relationships and friendships with some Helpers. It's a lot like having a friend in the physical world, except they don't live in the physical world.

Do Helpers have names? In my experience some do and some don't. Names don't seem all that important to some Helpers, but they are almost always willing to let you use a name to refer to them. Some of them have names that sound like music.

Is there such a thing as a *bad* or *evil* Helper? It is surprising to me how often this question comes up. I have never encountered a *bad* Helper. Recall that I have rules for relationships with nonphysical people. If that person ever tries to force their will or their beliefs on me, that person is not a Helper and I refuse to have anything else to do with them, no exceptions. Helpers will sometimes guide me to experiences that cause me to question my morals or beliefs, but they will *never* suggest or demand that I accept theirs over mine. Again, no exceptions.

Remember, at any point in any retrieval you can ask the Helper for assistance and the Helper will do their absolute best to provide it.

Tips for Dealing with Fleeting Images

The following is excerpted from my web site's Conversation Board. It's a visitor's question about dealing with indistinct and fleeting images and my response. This person's experience is fairly common when first learning to explore the afterlife and you might find this highway sign analogy useful.

VISITOR: I'm doing the exercises as you taught in the tapes. It's a bit confusing . . . a lot of "nothing happening" . . . images coming, fleeting, clear for a second and then vanishing . . . saw twice the face of a man with long white hair and beard. No words . . . barely visible scenes sometimes . . . I think that maybe I'm trying too hard to "see" or to be aware . . . sort of pushing. Should maybe relax more.

MY RESPONSE: If you are like me, the problem is in the definition of *seeing*. I expected that seeing within a nonphysical reality would be exactly like seeing within physical reality. I, too, would have said things like all I was getting was *a lot of nothing happening . . . images coming, fleeting, clear for a second and then vanishing . . .* before I understood what *seeing* means.

At the time I didn't realize that what you are describing is the most common form of nonphysical seeing, and I didn't know how to use that form. From my present understanding of *seeing* I'd say you're getting exactly what I get most of the time. What I learned to do (with a fleeting image that might be clear for a second or two and disappear, for example) was to focus my attention on what I had just seen instead of trying to force myself to see it, or more, again. In this case *focusing my attention* just means remembering what I had seen. I discovered that even though I didn't see that image again I began to have thoughts which I interpreted as information that came from or through that image. I then just continued to follow the *natural course* of those thoughts. That fleeting image can be thought of as one of the unexpected events I talk about in the workshop. One then just plays along with that unexpected event to follow where it goes.

Think of these fleeting images this way. You're driving down the freeway in the dark of night at 70 mph and your headlights illuminate a road sign ahead. At first it's too far away to read; it's fuzzy and unclear. You zoom past the sign so fast you might only get a brief glimpse of it, maybe just enough of a glimpse to know it says, Rollinsville 5 Miles. You only saw it for a few short seconds as you sped past, but it gave you information about what's ahead of you. You're on a road that leads to Rollinsville. What sense would it make to get off the freeway and try to find a way to drive back to where that sign is to read it again? It's already given you all the information it can and probably all the information you need. Worse, you've diverted yourself off the road that was leading you to where you wanted to go. The sign told you that you were on the right road and if you keep driving on that road you will arrive at Rollinsville.

Consider treating the fleeting images you describe in the same way you'd treat that road sign. You placed your intent to retrieve someone and then saw a brief fleeting image of a man with long white hair and a beard. It may be that this is just a road sign indicating you are on the right road and headed in the right direction.

To continue my metaphor . . .

Once you saw the Rollinsville 5 Miles sign, you might start focusing your attention on that sign, just remembering what it said without trying to see it again. This is like continuing to drive on the road. As you do this you might *see* another fleeting image, another road sign that might say, Joe's Cafe 4 Miles. By focusing your attention, just remembering that road sign might bring another fleeting image to mind. If you try to turn around and drive back to any of these signs, you're diverting yourself off the road that leads to the person you were going to meet and retrieve who is probably sitting in Joe's Cafe in Rollinsville.

As you continue this process you'll discover that thoughts, ideas, feelings, emotions, images, etc. come with each road sign. By focusing attention on them you are making a stronger and stronger connection with the person you are going to meet. At some point of the story, these images, feelings, etc. will take on a life of their own. At this point, like when Grandpa said he was a bank robber, it's time to just play along and see where the story takes you.

Know that it will probably feel like you are making this all up, but keep following the story and ask questions of anyone or anything you perceive. Ask to be shown, given, or told something that will prove this experience is real; that's a key to getting proof. If you use this process, at some point (as for many, many other explorers) you'll begin getting evidence. And at some point you'll start getting evidence that proves that at least part of what you are experiencing is real. When that happens, the process of removing blocking beliefs is well on its way and this leads to clearer perception, more evidence, etc.

VISITOR: Do you still have to pretend as a starting point to phase in the inner realities? You teach that it's okay to pretend, and I understand that as being a crutch, or better still, a tool for beginners, that once you are beyond doubt, you directly phase in. Am I right?

MY RESPONSE: What I do now, at most, is a short Prime-the-Pump Exercise. For example, I might say to myself that I want to see an image of the number 12, or of a banana, anything. Once I see that image, whether it's 3-D, holographic, full color, or the briefest fleeting, fuzzy, barely discernable, black and white, I assume my nonphysical sense of sight is stimulated enough to use and go ahead down the freeway from there.

I've been exploring for so long that I am completely confident that if I place intent to contact someone, the contact is going to happen. Contact often begins with a fleeting image, a feeling, a thought, etc. I've come to accept that since I placed intent to make contact, my next thoughts or feelings which are the least bit unexpected are the road signs directing me to the person. I just follow those road signs knowing the person is up ahead, not the least bit worried about the image quality of those road signs or of the person I find when I arrive at their location.

Also, I've been exploring for so long and have had so many experiences verified as real that I've come to recognize a feeling during these experiences that indicates the experience is real. It's become easier to recognize real experiences as they are happening.

Using Fleeting Images

The power of sharing experiences on the Conversation Board at the web site is illustrated in a later post by another web site visitor. This visitor had read the previous exchange and decided to try to use the highway metaphor to explore for verifiable afterlife contact.

VISITOR: I would like to share with you some very interesting results achieved by means of Bruce's recently posted "highway metaphor" for analyzing fleeting nonphysical signs or indications and "driving" along in search of evidence. This experience took place in five separate sessions. A friend of mine, who knows about my afterlife interests, asked whether I would mind trying to make contact with a person who had recently died here in Italy. I said I would try and she gave me the name of a man, Ivo, and the name of the town he lived in. That's all.

During my first session, I sort of deliberately visualized the welcoming sign you find on the road when you enter a new town, with the name of the town my friend had given me on it. I had never been in this town, nor did I know where it was exactly, but I sort of expected it to be in a flat country, whereas in this first session I visualized it in a hilly area. At the same time I got the inner feeling that this man was alive, and I started fearing that my friend had been trying to tease me. Upon reporting back my experience, I found out that the town is actually in a hilly area, and that evidence of survival was the very first thing Ivo's family was looking for. She had not been teasing me. I was told he was alive, because that was the basic fact I was to report back to start with. Furthermore, there had been circumstances related to Ivo's death (which my friend did not clarify at the time, in order not to provide information) which related to his identification, and which had made it harder for his wife to accept that the person concerned was actually her husband.

In the following session, which took me a couple of minutes, as I was sitting in my chair waiting for my PC to switch on and for the Windows operating system to load. I saw myself driving along this road, stopping at a coffee bar where a number of light motorcycles were parked, entering the bar, and asking for a cup of coffee. In the meantime I looked around for Ivo. I saw a number of people playing billiards and among them was my man; he looked a young man, very slim, with straight dark hair combed backwards, and he was in the middle of the game when two or three policemen broke in and "arrested" him for gambling. Ivo was handcuffed and taken to prison. Note: in Italian gambling is "gioco d'azzardo" and (I was not told at the time) in Ivo's death the possibility of "hazard" had to be investigated. I did not have a clue as to all this, but my friend said it all made sense, and had to give me some minor extra information: after his death, Ivo's body had been "confiscated" and locked away by the police for 48 hours. For two days his family had been unable to see him. During my third session with Ivo, I saw him in prison, and then suddenly the picture opened up like a pair of scissors, and I saw a beautiful countryside, and Ivo meeting up with a dog and hugging it as if they had not seen each other for quite a long time. He pronounced a name which I could not grasp, but it started with B (Buddy, Bobby . . . I could not catch it) and he then realized: You are dead. If I am here with you . . . then I am dead too. . . . My friend checked on this last detail with Ivo's wife and was able to confirm to me that, before getting married, Ivo had a dog called Briciola, who had died many years earlier. Fourth session: this time I only saw a symbol, which reminded me of the "M" of Motorola. My friend called me again yesterday, after a few days' stalemate, and told me that she had checked. The Motorola symbol did not seem to apply to the story from a cell phone point of view, and could I please try and relook at that symbol, maybe from a different perspective. As we were on the phone, she had to answer another call (on her cell phone, ha ha!) and so I was given a couple of minutes to think. I realized the symbol wasn't the "M" of Motorola, but the "H" of Honda, and then I immediately saw a high-powered motorbike driving along an extra-urban road, some living being crossing the road as the motorbike was approaching, and then the vehicle careening off the road, with blood staining the driver's crash helmet. I actually "felt" a gush of blood coming from my face and hitting/staining the helmet. My friend got back and when she heard this, she thought it was about time to provide me with full feedback.

Ivo was 42. He was on his way to meeting his friends at a coffee bar a few kilometers out of town with his high-powered motorbike, when for no explainable reason, he had careened off the road and had been killed. He had definitely not fallen asleep, he was absolutely lucid, no tire marks were found on the road, and he had been seen driving at a very reasonable speed only just before the accident, when the motorbike (seen from behind) had suddenly started losing control.

He used to meet with friends at the bar, and one of his recent passions had been billiards. When the accident took place, a car with two or three policemen (his wife was not sure about the number) had reached the scene and confiscated Ivo's body and motorbike, as mentioned above. His looks had been exactly as I had described them. To date, the cause of the accident has not yet been ascertained, but due to the nasty cut on his forehead, which followed the crash of his helmet, his wife had not been allowed by her relatives to see her husband's face, so that she would not have been traumatized. This was the identification detail I had not been given so far. That's all.

As a first attempt on this I feel very pleased with the results, and as a motorcyclist myself, I can confirm that if a cat or any other living creature suddenly crosses your way when you are driving, even at a low speed, you can find it very difficult to control a motorbike. As you might have realized, I have asked a friend to help me with the translation into English, so as to have this published on the Board as soon as possible.

Love to you all for listening, and thanks to Bruce for providing such a powerful range of hints.

A Note about the Role of Pretending

Throughout these exercises I've stressed that fantasizing and pretending have a vital role in the process of exploration beyond physical reality and the afterlife. Pretending is a way of engaging and activating our nonphysical senses, using imagination as the means of perception. In early workshops I led some folks astray because I didn't stress that following the trail pretending leads you to is important, and that playing along with any unexpected event is the continuation of the process. I'll use the workshop exercise experience of a participant I'll call Robert to illustrate what I mean.

Robert began by actively pretending that he was meeting a Helper and being guided to the deceased person he was to contact. Something unexpected happened. He began to get impressions of something *cloaked in a surrounding darkness,* as he put it. I would say that this unexpected event was the beginning of the trail of impressions Robert's Perceiver was following that would have led to solid contact and communication with that deceased person. But Robert decided that if the person was surrounded by darkness he probably wouldn't be able to see him or her, so he actively pretended the person was instead surrounded by light. From that point on in the exercise Robert described his experience as a series of completely pretended information that was useless. It was obvious to me that I hadn't explained the role of pretending clearly enough.

When something unexpected happens, it's a sign you are moving along the continuum of information perceived by using imagination toward the real, verifiable information end of that continuum. If when Robert had the impression of something cloaked in surrounding darkness he had said to himself, *I just had the impression of something cloaked in surrounding darkness; okay, I'll pretend I'm making contact with something cloaked in surrounding darkness,* he would have stayed on the trail. Instead, he decided to actively pretend something else, which moved him back toward the fantasy end of the continuum. Thereafter, throughout the exercise, each time something unexpected happened, Robert went back to the fantasy end of the continuum, forcing his Perceiver to search for another trail. It's important to use pretending *correctly* and by that I mean *use pretending to follow the trail of the experience* as it unfolds even in the face of feeling like you're making it up. I made the same mistake as Robert many times when I was first learning to explore our afterlife. I'd sum up by saying, use active pretending to find and follow the trail of impressions you are perceiving, instead of looking for a new trail. The more you practice the above retrieval exercise, the more opportunities you'll have to bring more concepts and techniques into the experience. At any time during an exercise you may, for example, realize you're being blocked from doing something you desire to do. That's an excellent time to use the technique of dialoguing with the Aspect of Self that is holding and enforcing the blocking belief, to change or eliminate it. Some things, like learning the Balance between the Perceiver and Interpreter, need practice sessions.

Sometimes you may feel that the contact with the person you were to retrieve was lost before you completed your role in the retrieval. You can return to the retrieval experience by remembering a scene from the experience and the accompanying feelings. Those of you who have read *Voyages into the Unknown* might remember the story of Benjie's retrieval. On my first attempt I couldn't convince him to leave with me because his parents had taught him to never go anywhere with a stranger. More than a week later I attempted to retrieve him again, and found him by remembering the scene I last saw him in and the heartbreaking feelings I was going through as I'd left him there on my first attempt. That second retrieval attempt was successful.

Deeper Exploration

Just as you can rejoin and continue a retrieval experience that you feel was unfinished, you can rejoin a retrieval as a way of deeper exploration of our afterlife. For example, remembering the scene the Helper took a person to and the feelings you experienced there can bring you back to that point in the experience. You could then ask the Helper to guide you to where this person went next and explain to you what happened There. In this way you may discover areas of our afterlife previously unknown to you (or to me for that matter).

Your Growing Body of Afterlife Knowledge

Each time you perform the Art of Retrieval there is the opportunity to learn more about our afterlife through your interactions with stuck people, Helpers, and other inhabitants. Through your own direct experience you'll discover more of the ways people get themselves stuck after death, and more of the *tricks of the trade* Helpers use to retrieve them. Helpers seem to fulfill their role not only in the retrieval, but also in taking every opportunity to assist you in learning more about our afterlife and its inner workings. And each time you are able to accept any part of your retrieval experience as real, you are removing beliefs that block perception. Each time this happens, perception opens further, making it possible that your next experience will be easier and will contain more verifiable information.

22

Focus 23 Retrieval Examples

The Focus 23 retrieval examples in this chapter are taken from workshop participant and web site visitor experiences. I've included them to encourage you to continue practicing. As you continue to practice the Art of Retrieval you will no doubt find more tricks of the trade. The following experiences are firsthand accounts.

Linda's First Retrieval

The following account was posted by a web site visitor I'll call Linda, who learned the Art of Retrieval using a set of audiotapes that was a live recording of the workshop in Friday Harbor, Washington. From previous posts on the web site's Conversation Board it was apparent that Linda had to overcome strong belief-based fears about exploring our afterlife. Working up the courage to make her first attempt was a huge step.

After mentally reviewing what transpired with my first retrieval, I have realized that I actually conducted my first RETRIEVAL!!!! For four days I've been feeling like it was all made up by my vivid imagination. However, another visitor's post gave me hope when she said that sometimes retrievals seem to be all made up, which was exactly what I felt about my first!

I was listening to Bruce's Friday Harbor tapes (#7), and he was doing the retrieval exercise with the group. I remember flying over a lake. There was a big house or mansion situated close to the lake. Next thing I knew my Helper and I were standing near the doorway of a study room looking at a man in his forties staring at his bookshelf. I couldn't see his face, but I had the impression that he was wearing a robe. With Bruce's cue (still listening to the tape) I began talking to the man and asking him questions. I found out his name was Bill Morton and he was a lawyer in Minnesota. I pretended to be interested in his book collections and told him how much I love reading, and asked if I could borrow one of his books. I then asked him if my friend could look at his books.

That was when I felt my Helper walk toward him. For the first time, I saw my Helper. My Helper was a female with blonde hair and blue eyes. She was wearing a long, flowing dress. She shook Bill's hand and said her name was Dorothy. She pretended to be interested in his books too. While he was showing her his books I said to him, "Hey, I know where we can go with many books, the library! Do you want to go?" He said "yes." Dorothy took his hands and walked off into the blackness. I was following from behind. The study room faded—it was replaced by blackness for a split second.

Next thing I saw was green grass, a sidewalk, people walking to their destination, and a big, magnificent, white building. We walked up the stairs to the library's entrance. Inside, the place seemed spotless and very white. Bill and I were in awe with the place. While we were admiring the library, a lady walked towards us. Bill recognized the person. He ran and hugged her. He looked really happy. They walked off together. I stayed behind with Dorothy. I thanked her and came back to C1. In hindsight I am slowly getting excited about my retrieval because I am realizing that I truly did not make this up. This is an actual retrieval! Yippee!!!

Alice's First Retrieval

This next retrieval was posted on the Conversation Board at the web site by a woman I'll call Alice. She'd been experimenting with the retrieval process while physically awake and her first retrieval occurred during a lucid dream.

My first real-seeming retrieval took place in a lucid dream where a boy popped up twice and I called for a Helper. I had been using my imagination earlier in the day but it didn't seem real enough so I thought, well, I'll wait and see what develops, maybe I'm not the retriever type after all. I went to bed under an electric blanket, and thought maybe electric blankets have a counter effect on afterlife exploration, then again maybe eating a bowl of chili does too. I'm here to tell you that neither of those things has an effect!

I started drifting off around 3 A.M. and got those pleasant vibrations, which usually cause me to come back to C1 consciousness, but this time I just watched the show and let it happen. I managed to think a thought and state an intention to do a retrieval with a question mark at the end of my affirmation sentence. I threw in for good measure that I wanted it to seem more real this time and that I wanted to bring back evidence.

I clicked out and when I regained consciousness I found myself on the second floor of a rooming house for students, in a room where the kids hang out. I saw a very pretty, forlorn-looking girl sitting on the floor with her back against a couch. I went close to her and the feeling was that I was in my physical body as I sat down next to her. I touched her and she seemed solid. This was a totally new and different kind of experience for me.

I looked in her eyes and we both smiled. I started gathering PUL (Pure Unconditional Love) just like I've been practicing daily. I asked her name and as close as I can get was that she said something like Cami. I asked her how old she was and she said sixteen. Somehow the subject got around to her aunt and whenever we spoke about her aunt Cami's face took on a clouded and confused look, as if something was blocked from her conscious awareness. I sensed it was too traumatic for her to think about.

Then there was a lot of commotion and a group of young people (Helpers) took her off somewhere. I felt she was in good hands so I didn't follow them to see where the Helpers took her, instead I started exploring my surroundings. I was standing near the front of the structure where I'd found Cami and I gazed across the street where a very old bungalow stood with a fresh coat of white paint. I felt the town was very old in places when I saw other houses like this. I felt the pride that people had in their neighborhood and I was about ready to leave when three people came up to me in the guise of hotel clerks. They thanked me for coming and were very hospitable, then they handed me checks. I'm not going to touch that gesture here; it was comical and unexpected though. I asked them what state I was in, feeling foolish for asking. They said this was South Dakota and that the nearest town was Langford.

Next I went outside and saw that there was a room for rent in the same building I had been in and immediately wondered if the room was where Cami had stayed. I saw a note on the door from another student who was interested in renting it. I felt the suddenness of Cami's departure from the physical plane.

Then my daughter drove up and asked me if I was ready to leave yet! I was thrilled to see her. She is starting to be aware that she goes traveling at night and hangs with a group of people who are familiar to her but she can't quite place who they might be in C1. My daughter frequently pops into dreams of mine, and just hangs back watching. I don't know if she's learning something or just seeing that I don't get in trouble! She says she was my mother in another reality and that may be the case.

Immediately after my daughter arrived in my dream I woke up, finding myself in bed and with a clear memory of every detail of the experience. I jumped out of bed and ran over to get a map and looked for Langford, South Dakota. I was a little surprised to find there actually is a town called that up in the east corner of the state, near Aberdeen. I have absolutely no doubts now about retrievals, not so much because of getting names of towns or numbers, but I got a sense of knowing that I cannot impart to others in words. All I can do is write it down for you, share it with my mouth hanging open. I've been studying retrievals for a year and I now understand that using the imagination as a gateway into this exploration is what prepares us for further forays out there, or in here as the case may be, but without the PUL, it wouldn't have happened at all.

Jim's First Retrieval

This retrieval was posted on the Conversation Board at the web site. The doll described in this experience, and how Jim reacted to it, is a fine example of what I mean by playing along with unexpected events.

I've been doing Bruce's home-study course slowly. At first it was slow but purposeful, and then, when he talked about the identity crisis, I realized he was describing symptoms I'd experienced that I thought indicated I was a walk-in. Bruce's description of a belief system breaking down a supporting structure of our ego made sense to me.

After I completely woke up this morning I immediately thought I'd try to do a retrieval. I did the Three Deep Relaxing Breaths, Three Energy Gathering Breaths, and the Feeling Love Exercise. Then I mentally dressed myself in something casual, my version of the Priming-the-Pump Exercises. Then I called for a Helper who I felt had just been waiting for me to ask, saying, "I would like a Helper to do a retrieval."

"Come with me," I heard the Helper say. I reached out and held my Helper's imaginary hand, then we took off and we went in kind of a rush through darkness. We stopped in the darkness and a little baby came into view. I thought, *"Cute, baby steps for my first retrieval."* As I watched this little baby it was walking very stiffly, and then it turned into a doll. The Helper said, "Get the doll, you're going to need it."

As soon as I grabbed the doll we went rushing off through the darkness again. Then we stopped and a little girl came into view. As she started to focus on my presence it was the doll that really got her attention. "My doll!" she exclaimed. I handed her the doll and picked her up, talking to her as if she was my own child. As we were talking I could see she was looking over my left shoulder, behind me. Suddenly she excitedly said, "Daddy." I turned around and handed her off to the man standing there with the feeling of love surrounding the whole scene. I watched them disappear as they left the scene and then I was left alone in Focus 23. I was so amazed I decided to look around. I asked the Helper for another retrieval and I thought about feeling the rushing blackness again. The next thing I knew I was lying in my bed staring up at the ceiling wondering, *"When did I open my eyes?"* It was so simple that my Interpreter wanted to deny the whole thing.

Preston's First Retrieval

This next retrieval account was posted on the Conversation Board at the web site by from someone I'll call Preston. He is very thorough in detailing and analyzing his experience.

I've been working through one of Bruce's tape sets for the last three months. Don't ask me why it's taking me months to work through a two-day seminar, I don't know. I finally got to the first retrieval exercise on tape #7 tonight, and thought it might be interesting to post my notes!

Just as a quick introduction: Though I first read Bruce's books back in 2000 I've never really tried retrieving anybody, except immediately after 9/11 when I gave it a flailing shot anyway. I figured they could use all the help they could get, bumbling or otherwise. I posted the results of that effort here at the time. I've also never had an OBE, though I've gotten fair-to-middling at meditating from using assorted TMI (The Monroe Institute) tapes. The most "out there" experience I've ever had was hearing a distinct "not quite my" voice giving me advice a couple of times in autumn 2001. (I'm still working on repeating that one! :))

I started by listening to side 7b of the Virginia Jan '01 cassette set. I had to switch tapes part way through. I began at 18:00 or so, sitting in my relatively comfy chair, with the neighborhood dog occasionally barking outside. Dim lighting.

Before starting the tape, I was sitting at the computer idly moving energy from my feet, up and out the top of my head and back down around in a sphere-ish kind of way, focusing mostly on a general feeling of flow rather than obsessing about making sure the energy identifiably moves every step of the way. This was sort of a combination of Bruce's Energy Gathering Breaths, New Energy Ways, and a pseudo-REBAL. (You know, unless you know Bruce's techniques, and Robert Bruce's NEW stuff, and The Monroe Institute terminology, that sentence makes absolutely no sense, does it? Sheesh. . . .) At one point I just suddenly felt like this was a good time to close the computer and start the exercise. Fair enough—I try to avoid being oblivious. . . .

Following Bruce's instructions on the tape, I did the preliminary Deep Relaxing Breaths etc., etc., including the new addition of remembering assorted activities of the day. As always, my breaths are apparently deeper than average, as I found myself once again hurrying along to get three in before Bruce started telling us to do something else!

The moment I asked for a Helper, or even a bit before, while Bruce was still in the process of telling us to ask, a dark triangle shape quickly scooted into my left field of vision from off stage left. Dang, those Helpers are fast! It was darker than the rest of my closed-eye field of *vision*, which was interesting—haven't seen this sort of thing before. But anyway, a Good Sign. Focused on this a bit, but didn't manage to get more detail.

Note: Somewhere in the middle of the retrieval I noticed that my attention was occasionally wandering. I paused and asked for greater focus/clarity, and while there was no immediate effect, a bit later I suddenly sank into a more silent, focused mode without any effort on my part. Another first.

When I asked to be led to somebody who needed a retrieval, I got a few disjointed images: the base of a stone structure, a rough-rock/gravel-strewn ground, a man face-down against the slope of a long depression in the ground. (Not as fast as that makes it sound—the impressions lazily filtered in one by one.) I put that together to get the sense of a man lying in a rough ditch, perhaps at the base of the kind of wall you might have around an ancient city.

Asked the man what he was doing, and got a feeling of a reply that he just couldn't get up. I asked his name, and got a double image of first a triangle, and then above it what appeared to be a word with all the letters except the first letter covered up with a rectangle or something. The letter kind of looked like an unusual variation on a capital A, and this together with the triangle suggested to me a primitive version of the letter A (like from thousands of years ago when the letters of our alphabet were still forming from their original pictographs). Thought of him as "A———" from here out.

Asking the man what had happened to him, I got sort of a *Duh, I fell*, implying, "I'm lying in a ditch at the base of the wall, whadda ya think happened?"

Asking the man for something that would identify him, at least to his friends, I got an image of a puzzle/game with polished wood (?) pieces that you stack to form a structure or tower. The pieces were of assorted interesting shapes, and when put together make a pointy tower (in contrast to the square, flat-topped tower that you get with a similar game I've seen in the stores).

When the Helper took him away, I got an immediate sense of a moving vehicle, specifically of some form of tank treads (which certainly didn't match my working-interpretation so far, of a fairly early walled-city civilization). It was a solid sense of movement toward the left (say, in the direction of 10 o'clock). I tagged along with it, without much difficulty. When they stopped, my impressions were noticeably more vague of the inside of some structure, perhaps a hangar or similar "functional" building.

When I left with the Helper, I got another feeling of movement from our retrievee, in a vehicle moving somehow similar to the way a submarine would glide through the water while surfaced, but with the impression of a largish open area in the top of the vehicle where A——— apparently was (along with others?) (This suggested the previous structure might have been something like a sub hangar/base? Dunno.) I then asked for any other information from the Helper that might help me understand:

Image 1: A———, among a dozen or so men in a cramped room, dressed all in black (uniforms? Either pants and long-sleeved shirts, or black coveralls), apparently standing at attention along the three sides of the room that I could see. Got the impression that someone was talking intently at them, perhaps they were receiving orders, or being chewed out by him. . . .

Image 2: A lone image of an indoor gallows (with guillotine), followed by a silhouette of an unidentified man hanging from a noose. At first this suggested suicide to me, but the guillotine seemed to imply more of a deliberate killing. Could he have been pushed off the wall?

I asked the Helper if there was anything else, and got an image of a stylized eye, which I interpreted to mean *If you're interested, go look for yourself.* Since that seemed to be it, I thanked the Helper, and got up to get my PowerBook to write this down.

Self-Debrief: Confidence

It's probably a good sign that it never occurred to me to question what I was "seeing," or agonize during the times when nothing was coming in. It's only after writing this that I can look at it and say that I appear to have been rather successful, at least in terms of getting at least some sort of results. I wouldn't say I felt "confident" doing it, but rather I just *forgot to feel not-confident* (if that makes sense . . .) despite my lack of experience. Not that I'm complaining.

Writing

I definitely want to keep writing detailed reports like this. The contrast between my overall image of the retrieval at the moment I finished it, and now that I've written it out, is like night and day. When I first opened my eyes, I was thinking, *I perceived some stuff, but not that much. Well let's write it down anyway.* But sitting down to make notes allowed me to focus on it more, and it looks like I remembered a lot more than I thought I had.

I started by just jotting down disjointed bits here and there, and then going back and filling in the details, which allowed me to get a quick overview of the whole experience and helped cement it in my mind. Then when the basics were covered, it's like my mind was now free to go back and pull out memories of more details here and there, so I put those in too. Looking back on what I wrote, it looks almost coherent! What a concept!

The Tape

Though having the tape end part way through this exercise, thus requiring me to put in the next tape, wasn't what I'd anticipated, interestingly enough it didn't bother me. That's probably because Bruce's method doesn't require you to enter a massively deep meditative state like, say, OBE training wants you to do. If an OBE tape had stopped part way in I'd probably have been bumped out of the relaxed state, but when this tape ended in the middle of things, I just smiled and put the new tape in, and off we went. It helps that this isn't the kind of tape you're supposed to listen to every time you use the technique. That's somehow freeing.

It's nice having somebody (i.e., Bruce) walk me through the process, rather than just reading about it. Reading is nice, and useful for assembling a list of things to keep in mind, but whenever possible I prefer to metaphorically look over somebody's shoulder to get a "feel" for an activity. That's the way I learn the best. Just to get the feel for the timing, the level of intensity or laid-backness, that sort of thing. In that, and looking at the results, I'd say the tapes just paid for themselves.

Preston's Second Retrieval

Preston's second posting is a fine example of how being willing to pretend continues to prime the pump of imagination as the means of perception, and his style of documenting his experience brings out details beginners might find useful.

I wrote this up two weeks ago but didn't post it here for some reason. Jeff's asking about the process of retrieval last week reminded me that I should probably post my experiences for the benefit of other beginners, non-earth-shattering as they may be. So, this is my second retrieval exercise.

I did this second retrieval exercise using Bruce's workshop tape set, tapes 8b–9a. This time I didn't do any NEW energy work beforehand—I just started the tape and jumped in. First the standard Energy Gathering stuff (3x3x3), then an interesting guided imagery of walking through a park—getting things rolling with deliberate imaginings like this is a good idea, I think. Feels right.

At the beginning when I asked for a Helper I got no clear impressions, unlike last time. I didn't know whether to wait around till I perceived something or not, but eventually I just went with imagination. I optimistically assumed a Helper was there, said "Hi" to nothing in particular, and left with him.

No immediate visuals of the retrievee either. A couple of unclear abstract feeling/images came at first, but I couldn't put them into clear thoughts much less words. Then I got a vague image of somebody inserted into something, the impression of someone's feet sticking out of a pipe. Slowly I got an image of somebody who'd crawled into a drainage pipe, like you might find crossing under a rural road. I had the impression of following an animal or pet into it and then getting stuck. Then an impression of an isolated area that I figured meant there would have been no one around to hear if he'd called out.

I asked the person stuck in the pipe for the year and at first got 1957, and when I asked for confirmation it changed to 1927. I asked for hobbies, or something that could be used for verification, and got an image of a frog jumping—possibly a reference to playing leapfrog, but more likely that he liked chasing frogs. I was starting to get a feel that this was a child. Up to this point I'd assumed that he was an adult. I never got a particular feel for one sex or the other, but based on the hobby I arbitrarily assumed a guy.

I asked the (still not visible) Helper how this person got stuck, and got a different impression: that he'd been assaulted in some manner, and perhaps put here in the pipe (after being killed?). Don't know the reason for the difference in the image compared to what the child had said.

Then the Helper showed up, taking the form of a burly workman in blue overalls with a bushy mustache (not a 1950s look, more an early turn of the century immigrant-worker image), and I pointed out to the child that help was finally here. At this point I tried sending him some PUL, though I'm not particularly good at even feeling it myself, yet. Together (?) we opened up the pipe by just peeling the metal open like it had a seam in the top. The child stood up, and immediately grabbed onto the Helper, who picked him up and held him tightly.

I followed as the Helper started walking away. He walked very slowly and very deliberately up a sloping path. The way he was walking was convenient for giving me something to practice focusing upon, if nothing else. Upon cresting the hill we continued walking down to an area where I got the impression of *something* being there, some complexity that I wasn't perceiving clearly. After a bit I noticed that the child was met by a woman, with a second person standing nearby, who might have been male. I thought the woman could have been his mother at first, but then the idea of older sister came to mind. After that I noticed a second woman standing slightly apart from them. I now thought that this might have been the mother though I didn't get a clear impression.

Though I was automatically just continuing to look at the people in front of me, when Bruce said to go with the Helper when he backed off, that also seemed appropriate—after all *it wasn't my reunion.*

As we left I asked the Helper: "How can I improve my perception?" Non-verbal reply: "Do more energy-raising work like NEW, and some physical exercise might not hurt. . . ." Also got an echo of the message on Bruce's forum that I left just today concerning confidence: Just keep doing it, and let the accumulating experience erode away my doubt. I'd intended the advice for the person who posted the message about doubt, but my own answer was applicable to me just a few hours later.

Self-Debrief: Perception

The lack of immediate perception of a Helper this time was unnerving, compared to how easy it'd been during my first exercise last week. The fact that I hadn't been doing any Energy Gathering/NEW beforehand may have been a contributing factor—my energy level today was pretty generic, rather than the slightly ramped-up level I'd been at last time. It'll be interesting to see what factors contribute to clearer perception.

From around the time that the Helper showed himself in the guise of the worker, my perception had improved (or perhaps my improving perception allowed me to see the Helper who'd been there all along!) to the point that I wasn't worrying about it anymore, and just going with the flow. I wasn't doing this at first since it's tough to go with the flow when there's initially no flow to go with.

For the record I'd describe my perception as "not quite visual," though that's admittedly not much of an explanation. Every so often in my life I've had stunningly clear visual images appear unbidden in my mind's eye (though without any particularly deep content . . . A cute "eyeball critter" once, and assorted generic architecture. . . .), but this was *not that*. Nor was it my everyday vague-to-middling visualization. It was somewhere in between, or maybe slightly "off to the side" away from visual perception. I'll have to get more experience before I can really describe it well (if then). I'd say the idea of what it'd feel like to be using a rarely used but not-quite-unfamiliar sense seems to fit. As I said, "not quite visual." Hmm.

Emotional

The clear reaction of the child to the Helper helped me to feel that I was actually doing something to, well, ah, help. Up until that point there hadn't been any particular emotion to the scene (or in my previous retrieval) at all, or at least I'd been unable to perceive any. This time I was at first preoccupied with the fact that I wasn't perceiving anything, then I drifted towards just focusing on what I did begin to perceive.

Data

Two things changed during the process. First, the date dropped thirty years, then the manner of death switched drastically. The appearance of the Helper-as-workman was a closer match to the earlier date, for what that's worth. As for the manner of death, it's easy to speculate about the kid not comprehending what had happened, or perhaps building a more comfortable memory in the intervening time, but I honestly got nothing but those two data points—anything I say connecting the two would be just my creation. For what it's worth, there you have my second retrieval!

Maria's Retrieval

This retrieval is not a first, but it's early in the retriever's experience. It demonstrates that sometimes the unexpected event is more within the structure of the retrieval than the activities taking place.

This morning I did the following retrieval, which seemed very strange to me. I was in a jungle setting, with a river full of crocodiles. I found a little boy wandering around. I tried talking to him but he couldn't understand me. He was smiling and seemed happy. I KNEW he had died and had been eaten by a crocodile. I asked in my mind where we were, the date, etc. but got absolutely nothing except that *Amazon* sort of popped into my head.

I picked up the boy and off we went, but we didn't go where I expected to. We landed in another jungle setting and I thought this was very strange. Then people came running to us and greeted the boy, and then they led him off into the jungle. He was very happy to see them. Then I realized we were in Focus 27 but it was an area of Focus 27 created to look like a place he would recognize, not the place I normally take someone to like the Park or the Reception Center. I'm accustomed to bringing those I retrieve always into the same basic scene so this threw me until I had time to reflect on it. Maybe my Guides are trying to prepare me for Lifeline.

Rick's First Retrieval

Beverly, I'll call her, attended the workshop in Lillian, Alabama. Her husband, "Rick," had driven them from North Carolina but had no intention of attending the workshop. He'd planned to just hike the beaches and spend a few days on his own. That changed when Rick attended a lecture I gave the night before the workshop and he became intrigued by the possibility of actually learning how to explore the afterlife on his own. A week or two after the workshop Beverly posted the following to the web site, describing Rick's experience in the first retrieval exercise of the workshop.

A while back I posted a note saying that my husband, Rick, and I were at the Lillian, Alabama workshop last December, and that I would eventually post one of each of our exciting retrieval experiences. Well, to start, here is an account of my husband's first retrieval experience: Rick found himself standing outside a house that he immediately recognized as being the house of a woman (Mary), who used to be our neighbor when we lived next to her many years ago in West Hartford, Connecticut. Now, just to give you a little background info on Mary before I continue. For 10 years, after her husband's death, Mary remained in her home 24 hours a day, refusing to leave it, and spending most of her time just staring out the living room window, looking at the surrounding neighborhood. And also, I'd like to mention that Mary was absolutely terrified of men, but she did inform me when we were neighbors that she liked my husband, just by viewing him at a distance. (Now back to the retrieval.)

Rick approached Mary's front door, and since she was looking out the living room window as he approached, and she recognized him, she opened the door for him. Rick, after greeting her, then asked her, "Mary, why haven't you left this house?" She said it was, "Because I'm afraid I might see or bump into my husband somewhere." (As another aside here, while Mary and her husband were both alive, they used to fight viciously and constantly, like cats and dogs! So apparently Mary had stayed in her house all these years in her afterlife state, in order to avoid seeing her husband!)

Then Rick said, "Mary, how have you been spending your time in the house lately?" and she said, "Well, I've been looking out the living room window at the vacant house across the street, because someday I'd love to have my son buy that house, so that he could live next door to me, and we would then be close together." (As another aside, Mary's son is also deceased, but Mary was totally devoted to and very close to her son while he was alive.)

Then, all of a sudden, a FEMALE person, the Helper, just pops up, standing next to Rick, and Rick says to Mary, "I have a friend here who is a real estate agent, who would just love to take you to look at that house across the street, to see if that might be something your son would be interested in to purchase." Well, Mary's eyes lit up . . . and the next thing that happens is that the real estate lady is walking across the street, with both Mary and Rick following behind! (As another aside, Bruce suggested during the debriefing after this retrieval, this "crossing the street" could very well have represented Mary's crossing over into another "realm" or "dimension.")

After Mary had viewed the vacant house, she said, "I know that my son would just love to buy this house because it would be just perfect for him." The real estate lady then said to Mary, "I know exactly where your son is right now, and I could take you to him if you'd like." At that thought, Mary absolutely beamed and said she'd like to be taken to her son . . . so the real estate lady took Mary's hand and they both walked off . . . (into a very happy ending for Mary, having finally left the imprisonment of her house after so many years!).

Wow, this is just such amazing and incredible stuff, huh? And to think that Rick went into all of this *retrieval stuff* absolutely cold, not even knowing who Bruce Moen was before this workshop! And Rick was just thinking that he was going to give me a ride to some workshop in Alabama and hang out at the nearby beaches waiting for me . . . HA!!!!

A Later Retrieval by Alice

Alice's next retrieval account shows marks of progress in her technique.

I thought I'd try a retrieval while wide awake instead of at night where I never follow thru with the intention because I fall asleep too easily. After asking for the Helper to guide me to a person needing retrieval I saw an old man walking and looking at the ground. He was real gruff-talking, but a real cutey though.

I said, "Hey, you been here a long time, huh? How 'bout we go someplace else as you're not in a physical body anymore you know." The part about the physical body went unnoticed and he said, gruffly and impatiently, "I gotta git that thar gold!" Again, I repeated the part about him being a spirit now. He took my hand and said, "But I'm solid as ever," and it did appear so. I called Guides: ooh, GUIDES! Two Guides came but they wanted me to keep talking to Mr. Gruff, as he still wasn't willing to take this dumb girl's word for his situation. So, I said, "Yeah, you look pretty solid, but watch this!" I stuck my hand into his side and it came out his back. He was a little astounded. So much for using the gentle touch. He told me I was a ghost and we debated briefly about which of us was a ghost and which of us was solid. The Guides started to move in closer and the name Zed came to me. I hugged Mr. Gruff and told him I loved him, and for a minute, I did love him. I told him to come away from this place for a while, and if he wanted, he could return here later.

Then a guide put his arm around Zed and took him aside, in a conspiratorial tone said "Say Zed, I know where there's a good spot for panning gold. . . ." The last thing I saw before they left was the interested look on Zed's face.

I got the impression that the other guide was just there for training purposes, as he or she just observed. The thing that's different about retrievals I do now as opposed to those done two months ago, is there's more compassion and PUL energy at work than before. It's a real subtle change, but noticeable.

Peter's Experience

At a Mind, Body, Spirit Festival in Sydney, Australia, I did a two-and-a-half-hour version of my two-day workshop. No one in the audience knew before that day who I was or what I taught. They'd just picked my lecture/workshop out of curiosity from a long list of activities at the festival. I've included these first retrieval accounts because they demonstrate that no prior experience or understanding is necessary to experience and learn the Art of Retrieval. After lecturing for about an hour and a half, giving an extremely abbreviated version of the skimpiest of the basics, there was time for one retrieval exercise and for a few in the audience to describe their experiences.

Peter described himself as a computer programmer who was a logical, rational fellow with no previous experience of things metaphysical. When he asked for a nonphysical Helper to assist him at the beginning of the afterlife contact exercise, he didn't perceive her arrival so he decided to just pretend one had arrived. When he asked his imagined Helper to guide him to someone in the afterlife needing retrieval, he pretended to be moving through empty blackness. He suddenly found himself standing in a dark alley looking at a young woman who was sitting on the ground with her back against the wall of a building. In their conversation she told him her name was Valerie, she was 16 years old, and that she'd lived in Green Valley, a suburb of Sydney. When Peter asked Valerie how she died, he saw a scene in which she injected herself with a fatal overdose of heroin. As Peter described this scene in the debriefing session after the exercise, remembering that scene visibly shook him.

After gathering information from Valerie, Peter told Valerie there was someone he wanted to introduce her to, and the Helper came into view for the first time. He described the Helper as a woman who appeared to be a bright white light and gave off the feeling of a loving mother. When Valerie saw the Helper she stood up and followed her, leaving her backpack and drug kit on the ground.

Peter followed Valerie and the Helper through empty blackness until a sunlit field came into view. Valerie seemed to recognize three young women who were picnicking in the open field. They jumped up and began waving their arms and calling to her. Peter said he had the feeling these were friends of Valerie's who had previously died and were there to welcome her into her new life in the afterlife.

Mary's Experience

A woman in the same introductory workshop—I'll call her Mary—began by saying she had expected to have only vague impressions of anything. When she asked for a Helper to come at the beginning of the exercise, she was shocked when a clown, in full costume, walked toward her out of the surrounding darkness and stood next to her. (I gave a short version of this retrieval account earlier.) When she asked the clown to take her to someone who died and might need assistance, she experienced a sense of movement and then found herself in a hospital room. She thought it might have been in the Children's Hospital in Sydney. She could plainly see a small boy on a hospital bed that had a curtain drawn around it; a thin, frail, dark-haired boy named Jamie who didn't realize he'd died and didn't leave because during his mother's visits she had kept telling him not to leave. He was doing his best to obey his mother's demand that he not leave, but he was confused about why she hadn't come back to his room to visit him anymore.

Something gave Mary the idea to invite Jamie to a party, and after a little cajoling he agreed to go. When she told him it was okay for him to slide down from the bed he did so, and she decided it was time to introduce Jamie to the Helper, the clown. She expected Jamie would be excited to see the clown and was surprised when he held back and seemed afraid as the clown approached the boy. The clown then stopped, bowed deeply and removed his hat, revealing a baby chick that was standing on his head, hopping and peeping. Mary said the baby chick was so bizarre and extraordinary that Jamie smiled and was no longer afraid of the clown. The clown stepped forward, took Jamie's hand, and the two of them started walking toward the door to leave the hospital room.

Mary followed them down the hospital hall toward the elevator and waited with them for it to arrive. When the elevator doors opened she followed them in and stood behind Jamie and the clown, expecting that after the doors closed the elevator would go up toward Heaven. It didn't; it went down. She became concerned about the implications, I suspect because of her beliefs about the locations of Heaven and Hell.

When the elevator stopped, the doors opened onto a bright, sunny, green expanse of lawn filled with dogs and goats, ducks and bunnies, with many other children playing and having fun at a big party. A little dog walked up to the elevator's open door and Mary said Jamie seemed to know the dog, and the dog seemed to know Jamie. When the little dog barked and turned back toward the party, Jamie followed him out of the elevator.

Mary then took the opportunity to learn more about our afterlife by asking the Helper/clown if it was common for children to get stuck after they died. The clown explained that since children are so familiar and comfortable with fantasy they very seldom get stuck.

If Mary follows up on what she learned in her contact with Jamie, she might discover a little boy by that name had been a patient in the Sydney Children's Hospital. She may discover he looked as she saw him during her experience. Other details such as the room and equipment surrounding Jamie's hospital bed may give some level of verification. If she managed to find Jamie's parents, her description of Jamie might be further evidence. In my experience, it's often the little, seemingly insignificant details that end up providing the strongest evidence. For example, if Jamie had a little dog that died and fits the description of the one who met Jamie at the elevator, it could be more evidence that this afterlife contact was real.

Diane's Animal Contact

When Diane asked for a nonphysical Helper to assist her at the beginning of the exercise in the same Sydney workshop, she didn't perceive one at all. After asking this seemingly nonexistent Helper to bring her to a person she could communicate with in the afterlife, Diane moved through blackness. She then realized there was a little dog standing in front of her. Believing she was supposed to contact a *person* she kept looking around for someone to talk to. Not finding any person around her she looked down at the little dog wondering why he was there. A story unfolded in Diane's mind's eye.

She saw the little dog following its master around; wondering why he never called him or petted him anymore. She could sense he was starved for affection. She saw the little guy following the kids in his family around, wondering why they never played "chase" anymore. They used to run around the yard playing together. First the kids would chase him and then he'd turn and chase them. But the kids never played with him anymore. The poor little dog was worried that maybe he'd done something wrong and that his master and the kids were so upset with him they were ignoring him. Then Diane heard the little dog ask her if she knew what he had done to make his family so upset.

Diane told the little guy she knew what the problem was and that he hadn't done anything wrong that upset his master or the kids. It was just that he didn't have a physical body they could see anymore, so they didn't know he was there. She said the tremendous sense of relief the little dog felt washed over her and brought tears to her eyes. When Diane told the little dog that there was someone she'd like to introduce him to she expected the Helper would be a person. All the language I'd used as guidance in the exercise was based on both the retrievee and the Helper being people. But instead of a human Helper entering the scene, a large white dog walked from behind Diane toward the little dog. The two dogs introduced themselves to each other in the usual way that dogs do. Just before the two dogs left, the little

233

dog looked up at Diane and asked if she would mind holding him for a little while. It had been so long since he'd been held by anyone. With tears in her eyes Diane bent down, picked him up, and held him close. After a while the little dog thanked her and she put him back down. The white dog indicated it was time for the two of them to leave. Diane followed to see where they'd go and after walking a short distance through darkness they came upon a huge expanse of open pasture filled with other dogs and puppies playing. As soon as the little dog saw them he rushed off to join his new afterlife family.

Sometimes there isn't much information gained from an experience that can be easily verified. Diane felt that encountering dogs instead of human beings was an indication she wasn't making up her experience to match her expectations. She also felt that sometimes just being of service to someone in need means more than getting verification.

WWII Fighter Pilot

When Irene, in the same Sydney workshop, asked for a nonphysical Helper to assist her, a ball of blue light appeared and enveloped her. After asking the Helper to guide her to a deceased person, Irene described seeing a large, solid block of energy, like a refrigerator. Entering this she found a man standing in front of her, dressed in the leather jacket and headgear of a British World War II fighter pilot. When Irene asked his name and where he was from he said his name was Wallace Hepburn, from Blackpool, England. He had somehow lost his aircraft and was looking for it. She asked him to show her something that would prove to someone he knew that she'd talked him, and he showed her a photograph of a woman with dark, curly hair that he said was his wife. He expressed his concern for his wife having to live alone through such troubled times in the war. Wallace didn't realize he had died in a dogfight over England more than 50 years ago.

When she told him there was someone she'd like to introduce him to, the blue light surrounding her flowed out toward Wallace and enveloped him also. Then a huge open room materialized around them and Irene could see what she described as "energies" standing nearby. One of these transformed into a woman Irene recognized from the photo Wallace had shown her earlier. It was his wife, who had died since the war and was there to greet her husband just as he now became aware that he'd died.

If Irene, who lives in Australia, can find a way to research records dating back to WWII England and finds that a man named Wallace Hepburn, who came from Blackpool, was an RAF pilot who died in action, she'll have some level of verification her afterlife encounter with him was real. If by some chance she finds a picture of Wallace and his wife, it could be stronger evidence they both continue to exist over 50 years after his death.

Sam's Cat

One of my two-day workshops took place in a wonderful health resort called The Hideaway Retreat, not far from Brisbane, Australia. As the final participant-experience account in this chapter I'd like to share one that wasn't a retrieval at all. But the experience of a guy I'll call Sam still brings me a chuckle as it's so much like my own early experiences. It demonstrates just how resistant we can be to allowing our own direct experience to change our beliefs.

As one of the afterlife communication exercises began, I noticed the resort's huge Siamese cat, Sebastian, sitting in the lap of one of the participants. After making sure she had no objection to the cat being there, we continued on with the exercise.

After the exercise, Sam explained that at the beginning of the exercise he expressed to his Guides that he wanted to have an experience that would absolutely prove to him beyond all possible doubt that he had the ability to perceive beyond the physical world. In his debriefing after the exercise, Sam explained that after closing his eyes at the very beginning of the exercise he felt the cat, Sebastian, brush his leg as it walked by and stopped a short distance away. He then heard the cat jump up onto an empty chair next to him and felt it reach out and lay its paw on his arm. He said he could hear the cat's breathing, he smelled the cat, and felt its paw and fur on his arm.

At that point in his debriefing Sam explained that he doesn't like cats and that it took a bit of internal struggling not to interrupt the exercise by opening his eyes and shooing the cat away. He managed to keep his eyes closed and after a little while he was able to relax enough to continue with the exercise even though the cat still had its paw resting on his arm. As soon as he felt it was okay for the cat to be there, he said the cat pulled back its paw, jumped down off the chair next to him, and he'd heard the sound of the cat's paws landing on the floor next to him. The cat brushed up against Sam's leg again as it walked back toward the woman where he'd started, and he'd heard it jump back up into her lap.

Sam was in for a big surprise. During the workshop exercises I usually keep my eyes open to get a better feel for how participants are doing. I'd kept an eye on the cat during the exercise and I knew it had never left the woman's lap during the entire exercise. When I asked the woman to tell Sam at what point during the exercise Sebastian had left her lap, she explained that the cat had never left her lap at any point during the exercise. Sam jumped up and shouted that this was impossible because he had felt it brush his leg, heard it when it jumped up and landed on the chair next to him, smelled the cat, and felt its paw on his arm. Sam kept insisting that the woman had to be mistaken about the cat's whereabouts during the exercise. She and I both knew the truth. Sam had placed intent to have a completely convincing experience of his ability to perceive nonphysically. Sebastian, bless him, evidently played a role in fulfilling Sam's intent, probably by going out of body (OB) and playing with Sam.

The path to having contact and communicating with those living in the nonphysical world of the afterlife leads to learning to use our nonphysical senses. Sam's experience demonstrates both the power of placing intent for such an experience and the difficulty we can sometimes have accepting results that conflict with our beliefs.

23

Belief System Territory
Retrieval Exercise

Once I would have said that retrievals from the Belief System Territories (BSTs) were too difficult for physically living humans to perform. I took something Robert Monroe said to mean that an intimate knowledge and understanding of the specific belief system were required to have any chance of retrieving any of the inhabitants. As a result, I took on the belief that retrievals from this area of our afterlife were best left to Helpers who have a better understanding of how to use the intricacies of beliefs within a specific system to retrieve the inhabitants.

Something unexpected happened. Workshop participants started posting their experiences of doing retrievals within the BSTs on my web site's Conversation Board. As I read these accounts it was clear to me that the retrievals described were indeed Belief System Territory (BST) retrievals. Each retrieval took place in an afterlife area inhabited by deceased people who shared a set of beliefs. A Helper guided the Retriever to a single individual within one of these BSTs who had begun seeing conflicts between their experiences and the set of beliefs they shared with other inhabitants. It appears from these explorations that Helpers routinely monitor the experiences of individuals within the BST, a sort of watchful waiting for an opportunity to retrieve an individual. When such an opportunity occurs, Helpers sometimes perform the retrieval themselves, and sometimes circumstances seem to require, or at least benefit from, the services of a physically living Retriever.

At least three aspects of BST retrievals are different from Focus 23 retrievals. The first is in the level and character of interaction between the Retriever, the Helper, and the person being retrieved. The second is in projecting Pure Unconditional Love (PUL) for retrievals within the BSTs. The third is the area where these individuals are taken following the retrieval.

1. The differences in level and quality of interaction between the Helper, the Retriever, and the person being retrieved from the BST are often first noticed in the specific suggestions or instructions Helpers give about how to interact with that person. These take the concept of *joining* into the person's reality—*playing along* with where they think they are—a step further than Focus 23 retrievals, to *interacting within*, or *playing a role within* the person's reality. In a way, your experiences of *joining* into that person's reality in Focus 23 retrievals can be thought of as training for *playing a role* within the person's reality in BST retrievals. Perhaps it's a matter of degree.

2. BST retrievals also carry the projection of PUL (learned during Focus 23 retrievals) a step further. Often during early Focus 23 retrieval experiences, the retrieval can be accomplished without actively or consciously projecting Love Energy to the person you are retrieving. In many BST retrieval accounts, the Retriever reports that at a specific point in the retrieval process, the Helper suggests that they feel and project PUL energy to the person being retrieved. Sometimes this suggestion is reported as if the Helper directly asked the Retriever to do so. More often Retrievers report a sudden, strong urge to feel and project PUL to the person. In BST retrievals, projecting PUL is often described as the turning point. Retrievers report sudden and specific changes in how the person acts or reacts to their presence and the presence of the Helper, and an often-dramatic change in the course of the retrieval. When doing BST retrievals it's important to keep in mind that at some point you'll probably need to blast the person with PUL. When you do, pay particular attention to the response on the part of the person you are retrieving. As with your learning to *play a role* during Focus 23 retrievals, Helpers take note of your progress in learning to project PUL and look for opportunities to begin utilizing your ability in BST retrievals.

3. Focus 23 retrievals almost always result in taking the person to an area within Focus 27, but often BST retrievals have a completely different outcome. Very often the person is taken to a different, one might say less

intense, area of that BST. This could be thought of as taking the person from, say Focus 24 to Focus 25 or Focus 26. For example, a person stuck in the Heaven of their specific religion may have begun to doubt some of the aspects of living there. Often such a person will be retrieved to an area of that same Heaven where others with such doubts have gathered. In this area the person is freer to explore and come to understand the meaning and implications of their doubts, ultimately leading to later retrieval or some form of natural migration to Focus 27.

As you begin to learn the Art of Retrieval from the BSTs, I suggest you keep in mind the differences described above. Remember to ask the Helper for assistance, project PUL, and take note of and explore where the person is retrieved to. The BST retrieval exercise below is again written as a verbatim transcript of the Focused Attention exercise from a workshop. If you did not purchase the compact disks along with this *Afterlife Knowledge Guidebook,* use the script below to record your own tape for this exercise.

If you are recording your own exercise tape, use a soft, calm, relaxing, soothing voice. As you do this exercise using the audio recording, if your retrieval experience begins to go in a direction that conflicts with the recording's verbal guidance, ignore the recording and follow your experience. This exercise is one that you might consider doing several times before moving on to the next exercise. Each time you do this exercise it's an opportunity to remember and use more of the tools you've learned in this *Afterlife Knowledge Guidebook.*

Belief System Territory Retrieval Exercise: Script

This is a Belief System Territory Retrieval Exercise. (Wait 5 sec)

As you get ready to begin the exercise, adjust the volume of this recording so that you can comfortably and easily hear and understand my voice. You may do this exercise either sitting or lying down. (Wait 10 sec)

When you're ready to begin, please close your eyes. (Wait 10 sec)

To begin this exercise move your body into a comfortable, relaxed position in your quiet place. (Wait 30 sec)

Complete your Preparatory Process, remembering and imagining each of the individual feelings, images, impressions, and details as you do each step in the process. (Wait 10 sec)

Take in Three Deep Relaxing Breaths. (Wait 45 sec)

Take in Three Energy Gathering Breaths to establish the flow from below. (Wait 45 sec)

Take in Three Energy Gathering Breaths from Below. (Wait 45 sec)

Take in Three Energy Gathering Breaths to establish the flow from above. (Wait 45 sec)

Take in Three Energy Gathering Breaths from Above. (Wait 45 sec)

Remember a time when you were feeling loved or loving. (Wait 30 sec)

Let this memory help you to remember and reexperience the feeling of love. (Wait 20 sec)

If the feeling fades that's okay; just remember another time you were feeling loved and let that feeling build. (Wait 20 sec)

Remember, it is okay to pretend during this exercise. (Wait 5 sec)

Take in at least three more Deep Relaxing Breaths. (Wait 30 sec)

Remember the feeling of standing barefoot on warm, dry sand. (Wait 15 sec)

Imagine the feeling of the sand against the bottoms of your feet (wait 15 sec), and the feeling of a bright, warm, summer sun on your body. (Wait 15 sec)

Remember the deep blue of the sky above (wait 10 sec), with small, puffy, white clouds, lazily drifting by overhead. (Wait 10 sec)

Remember the sound of gentle surf in the distance, beyond palm trees. (Wait 15 sec)

A warm, gentle breeze against your skin (wait 5 sec) that carries the sweet scent of flowers. (Wait 10 sec)

Remember the feeling of walking barefoot on the warm sand, toward the sound of gentle surf. (Wait 10 sec)

Remember flowers along your path with their bright colors, shapes, and scents (wait 15 sec), the gentle sway of palm trees in the light ocean breeze (wait 10 sec) as the sound of the surf grows louder. (Wait 5 sec)

Imagine stepping out onto a wide, deserted, moist, sandy beach (wait 5 sec) with its magnificent view of the blue ocean. (Wait 15 sec)

As you stand admiring the beauty of the beach and the ocean (wait 10 sec), remembering the smell of clean, fresh sea air, take in Three Deep Relaxing Breaths. (Wait 20 sec)

Remember the sound of a seagull's call, off in the distance (wait 10 sec), calling as it slowly glides through the air. (Wait 10 sec)

As you remember the graceful, soaring flight of a seagull (wait 5 sec), gliding over the ocean, take in Three Energy Gathering Breaths from Below. (Wait 20 sec)

As you imagine a seagull glide to a landing, on the beach some distance away (wait 5 sec), ask for a Helper to come and meet you, there on the beach. (Wait 15 sec)

Feel for the presence of a Helper, remembering it's still okay to pretend. (Wait 15 sec)

Is this Helper near or far? (Wait 10 sec)

Is this Helper young or old? (Wait 10 sec)

Large or small? (Wait 10 sec)

Male, female . . . or something else? (Wait 10 sec)

Is this Helper beside you, behind you, or perhaps in front of you? (Wait 10 sec)

As you are becoming more aware of the Helper (wait 5 sec), once again, remember the feeling of love. (Wait 20 sec)

Introduce yourself to the Helper, or pretend to. (Wait 15 sec)

Remember the feeling of placing intent, or just imagine you are doing the Silly Little Finger Bending Exercise. (Wait 20 sec)

Reexperience the feeling of placing intent as you say in your mind, to your Helper, **I deeply desire to contact** (wait 5 sec), **to communicate with** (wait 5 sec), **to gather verifiable information from** (wait 5 sec), **and be of service to** (wait 5 sec) **a person in the Belief System Territories needing retrieval.** (Wait 10 sec)

Ask the Helper to guide you to the person in the Belief System Territories needing retrieval (wait 5 sec), and follow the Helper there, or pretend to. (Wait 20 sec)

As you sense your arrival, near this person, is it your impression that you are indoors or outdoors? (Wait 10 sec)

Are there buildings or other structures nearby? (Wait 15 sec)

Feel for the presence of the person and gather in more impressions of your surroundings. (Wait 15 sec)

Is it your impression you are indoors or outdoors? (Wait 10 sec)

Is this person behind you, beside you, or in front of you? (Wait 10 sec)

As you begin to become aware of this person and your surroundings, gather your impressions of this person and the scene they are in, or pretend to. (Wait 15 sec)

Is this person male or female? (Wait 10 sec)

Is this person a child, teenager, young adult, or elderly? (Wait 10 sec)

As you become more aware of this person, gather in more impressions of this person's appearance, how they are dressed, and the scene they are in, or pretend to. (Wait 15 sec)

Gather your impressions of any other people nearby. (Wait 15 sec)

Ask the Helper, "What is this place and what beliefs do the people here share?" (Wait 15 sec)

Ask the Helper to assist you in understanding how these beliefs hold the person here that you are to retrieve, or pretend to. (Wait 15 sec)

What is your impression of the person's situation? (Wait 15 sec)

What is your impression of what this person is feeling and experiencing? (Wait 15 sec)

Do you notice anything unusual about this person? (Wait 15 sec)

How is this person dressed, and what is your impression of what they are doing? (Wait 20 sec)

Ask the Helper for suggestions about how to approach and interact with this person, and if there is a role or character you can play to facilitate the retrieval. (Wait 15 sec)

As you are now more completely aware of this person, introduce yourself in whatever way seems appropriate to you. (Wait 15 sec)

Join into this person's reality, playing your role or character if appropriate, or pretend to. (Wait 15 sec)

Ask this person, "What happened to you and why are you here?" (Wait 20 sec)

Ask this person, "What is your name?" (Wait 10 sec)

Ask this person, "What is this place where we are?" Gather your impressions. (Wait 15 sec)

Ask this person, "What beliefs do most people here share?" (Wait 20 sec)

Ask this person, "How do these beliefs affect what people do here?" (Wait 20 sec)

Ask this person to describe to you some of their favorite things to do. (Wait 20 sec)

Ask this person, "Where are you from?" (Wait 10 sec)

Ask this person,"How old are you and where were you born?" (Wait 15 sec)

Ask this person to show you, tell you, or give you something that would prove to someone they know that you have visited with them. (Wait 20 sec)

Ask this person, "Have things recently happened that conflict with your beliefs?" (Wait 15 sec)

Ask this person if they want to leave this place, and why. (Wait 20 sec)

As you continue gathering your impressions of the person's answers, remember the Feeling of Love, let it build, and then project Love Energy to the person. (Wait 20 sec)

Introduce the Helper to this person in whatever way seems appropriate to you, or pretend to. (Wait 15 sec)

Gather in your impressions of any interaction between the Helper and this person. (Wait 20 sec)

As you observe any interaction between the Helper and this person, this might be a good time to take in more Deep Relaxing Breaths, or Energy Gathering Breaths if you feel the need. (Wait 30 sec)

You will know when the Helper and this person are getting ready to leave—when they do, follow them, or pretend to. (Wait 15 sec)

You will know when the Helper and this person stop moving—when they do, stop with them. Or pretend to. (Wait 10 sec)

As you become aware of where you've stopped, gather in impressions of your surroundings to help you understand where you are. (Wait 20 sec)

What is this place where you've arrived? (Wait 15 sec)

Are there other people here? (Wait 10 sec)

If there are, who are these people and why are they here? (Wait 10 sec)

As you continue to observe these people and your surroundings, you will know when the Helper is getting ready to leave this person with the others. When the Helper moves away from this person, stay with the Helper. (Wait 15 sec)

When you are alone with the Helper, ask the Helper for clearer understanding of the place you found the person and the system of beliefs. (Wait 30 sec)

Ask the Helper what Belief System Territory this is, and to help you understand how and why it functions as it does. (Wait 20 sec)

Ask the Helper what made it possible for the person to leave that place. (Wait 15 sec)

Ask the Helper why this person was chosen for you to retrieve and who made this choice. (Wait 10 sec)

Ask the Helper who those other people were you saw. (Wait 15 sec)

Ask the Helper what this place is where you are, and why this person was brought here. (Wait 15 sec)

Ask the Helper where this person will go next and what they will do there. (Wait 20 sec)

Ask the Helper to show you, tell you, or give you something that will prove to you that this retrieval experience was real. (Wait 15 sec)

Ask the Helper for any other information or guidance you desire. (Wait 20 sec)

If there is some nonphysical place you'd like to explore, or information you'd like to access, ask the Helper to assist you. Take as much time as you need and when you feel complete with this experience, express your gratitude to the Helper, and open your eyes. Then immediately begin to write about your experience and use the debriefing section in the *Afterlife Knowledge Guidebook* to assist you in recording your experience.

(Do not record this note: you may either keep the tape recorder running to leave a very long blank space on the tape, or you may choose to leave a short blank space and plan to turn off the recorder for the remainder of your exercise experience.)

Debrief

Remember to write down every detail of your experience in your notebook, and use State-Specific Memory to remember more. It may be helpful to read portions of the exercise script above to trigger more memory. Pay particular attention to recording whatever the person or Helper gave you that could prove your contact was real. Make sketches of any objects or scenes that were a part of this experience.

Look for ways you might be able to verify the experience.

Spend some time reflecting on what you discovered about the BST you visited, the beliefs involved, how those beliefs are enforced within that BST, and how it is that people become ready to leave it. You might also reflect on your own belief systems and how they affect your existence.

Consider sharing your retrieval experience by posting it on the Conversation Board at my web site, www.afterlife-knowledge.com.

Tips for the Belief System Territory Retrieval Exercise

Many participants report that they had to let the verbal guidance sort of run in the background because their interaction with the Helper and the person they were retrieving provided all the guidance they needed. Follow your experience.

Some participants report that it sometimes takes more than one trip to accomplish a BST retrieval. Their first contact with the person in these cases feels like an introduction that allows a level of trust to build between themselves and the person. Subsequent visits lead to the retrieval.

The same pattern of increasing retrieval complexity that I've observed in Focus 23 retrievals applies to BST retrievals. As you become more familiar and proficient working within the BSTs, as your capabilities increase, you become available to work with more complex situations, and your opportunities to learn more about our afterlife expand.

Some participants report that their BST retrieval exercises were like a visit to learn about how a specific BST functions. Sometimes these visits have a task that is more general than retrieval of a specific person.

Some participants report a retrieval that appears to be from Focus 23 instead of the BSTs. This may indicate that the Helpers are assisting in more training before carrying out BST retrievals.

24

Belief System Territory Retrieval Examples

The Belief System Territory (BST) retrieval examples in this chapter are taken from workshop participant and other explorer experiences. I've included them hoping that you may find similarities between them and your own experiences, and may be encouraged to continue practicing and gain insights into your experiences.

Ryan's Belief System Territory (BST) Retrieval

One of the very first BST retrievals I witnessed occurred during a two-day workshop in Sydney, Australia. Before witnessing this participant's experience I still believed the physically living didn't have much potential for BST retrievals. I'll call him Ryan. While in this account Ryan only observes a BST mass retrieval performed by a Helper, his experience caused me to question my limiting belief.

When Ryan asked for a Helper, he described the Helper as bigger than the large meeting room we were sitting in. This mega-jumbo-sized Helper explained they were going to a different afterlife place than my verbal guidance would suggest, and my verbal guidance should be ignored. Ryan was taken to the balcony of a huge church which the Helper described as being in Focus 26. From his vantage point in the balcony Ryan could see that the church's pews were completely filled by parishioners listening to a sermon being delivered by a preacher in the pulpit. The Helper suggested that Ryan just watch and observe, then floated out over the congregation high above them, near the church's ceiling. The Helper became a very bright light that completely filled and illuminated the church. When those sitting in the pews looked up and saw this light, they suddenly flew upwards and disappeared through the roof of the church. In a short time the entire church was empty, accept for the minister still preaching his sermon to a now completely empty church.

The minister eventually saw the light—the Helper—and asked it what had happened to all the people who had been sitting in his church. The Helper said that they had been waiting for a sign that would show them the way to Heaven, and had seen it and had left. At that point the minister realized he was seeing the sign he had been preaching about and he too lifted up, flew up through the roof and was gone.

I would say that it's likely that the doubts and belief system conflicts of those sitting in the pews had moved them within that belief system to the church in Focus 26. They had come to believe that there was a better place they were going to from there, and that they would be given a sign that would tell them when it was time to leave and where to go. The Helper merely used their belief in a sign to provide the pathway for them to leave their BST and move on to Focus 27.

Ginny's Concentration Camp Retrieval in the BSTs

As I mentioned earlier, not all the individual territories are created around a set of religious beliefs. In this next BST retrieval account, posted at the web site by a woman I'll call Ginny, the commonly held belief was a belief held by mothers that they are responsible for their children's deaths.

When a Helper arrived at my little park in Focus 27, I was told we were going to do a retrieval in the BSTs. We arrived in a bleak, desolate place with rows of small wooden shacks. The Helper let me get acquainted with the place (I perceived voices off in the distance, authoritative voices) and then informed me he (felt like a "he") would stay outside and that I was to go ahead and walk into the first shack on our left, which I did. It was a one-room run-down place, very dirty, hardly any furniture. As I walked further in, I saw a woman over on the other side of the room sitting by a window, seemingly unaware I was there. I approached her carefully, taking note of what little was there, and finally introduced myself. She didn't look my way, she just ignored me. She seemed to be in her 30s, 40s . . . wearing a dress that looked more like rags, brown hair pulled back, pale face with dark circles under her eyes. At a loss as to what to do next I suddenly received an instant "knowing" about her, why she was there.

Her name was Sadie. In the Earth Life System (ELS) she had been imprisoned in a Nazi concentration camp, along with her three children. Somewhere along the line the Nazis had taken her children and killed them, and shortly after that she caused her unborn child to be miscarried because she didn't want the fourth child to be brought into the world she was now in. Her problem was that she felt she had been responsible for her children's deaths . . . if she had only pleaded with the Nazis more . . . if she had only fallen down and begged harder for their lives. Because they died she was to blame. While in the Nazi camp she came to believe that her God had forsaken her . . . that she "deserved" all that had happened to her . . . that she must be totally worthless and evil. And so here she was, in this shack (and I had a strong feeling that the rows of shacks were close to what the ELS camp had been like, or the treatment there?).

I started talking to her and not much seemed to help her open up until I made the statement that she was not to blame for what had happened to her children. With that she stood up and started angrily saying she was guilty, she had killed her own children. She was really upset and all I could do was listen. When she sat down again she started crying, wailing, and I got the idea (Helper) to send her PUL, just as Bruce has taught. This seemed to calm her down a bit but she was still so completely caught up in her sorrow. I asked her if she and her children had asked to be taken to the camp . . . had it ever been her desire to go there? I think she understood what I was asking but didn't answer and continued crying. I then had the feeling it was time to go and left, having a strong "knowing" feeling that we would be back. This was only the beginning of her leaving this place.

A few days later when I had a strong feeling it was time to return, we did, and as we stood outside the shack a "man" approached, walked in, talked with her, and then left (have no idea if he was a Helper or another nonphysical person in that camp). The feeling I got from the Helper with me was one of urgency, excitement. He told me he would remain outside again, but that when Sadie and I walked out he would be in some kind of uniform and for me to not question it (in the past I've found some of their outfits so strange I would say something about it—guess I've been a great source of laughter for Helpers). So I walked into the shack again and Sadie was standing by the window. When she saw me she quickly walked to a tub or sink and tried her best to ignore me. But it wasn't long before she started talking about her guilt, her punishment, but she wasn't too emotional this time. She sat down and I knelt beside her and asked her again if she and her children had wanted to go to the Nazi camp. I could feel she knew the answer was no.

I told her she had been forced to go, that sometimes these things happen, but she was not to blame. The idea of PUL came to me so I sent her some again and she became very calm. I repeated all of it again, how she wasn't to blame. Feeling nervous but I knew I had to do it, I then told her that her children were somewhere else, in a loving place, and she could go with me to be with them. I told her she didn't have to live here anymore. It was never her fault. She started crying but kept looking at me, finally, and I could feel she was starting to believe this . . . she could be reunited with her children.

She slowly calmed down, asked a few questions (where the kids were, etc.) and then she decided she wanted to leave. I could feel she was fearful of whether someone would stop her, but she wanted to see her children so badly that her desire overruled her fear. As we walked outside a car from the 40s (not sure—don't know cars that well) pulled up and out came the Helper, disguised as a chauffeur who had been employed by her long before the Nazis came.

She was surprised and very happy to see him. I stood off to one side waiting for her to go, but she insisted twice I also come, so we got into the back seat and off we went. She became so worried about her appearance, what would her children think, and before we arrived her clothing changed, her complexion, hair . . . she looked younger and healthy. She opened the car door and almost stumbled out, falling to her knees as her oldest daughter came running into her arms, and the others followed quickly. I had a hard time keeping emotions in check but I did. I have no idea where we were at that point and I guess it didn't matter. She was okay now. She was free.

Ginny and the Monk

This next BST retrieval account has an interesting, unexpected outcome. Also notice at the end of her account Ginny refers to this as Focus 23 retrieval. It was clear to me that Ginny's retrievals took place, by Robert Monroe's definition, within the Belief System Territories (BSTs), not within Focus 23. This account is clearly a retrieval from an area of afterlife consciousness inhabited by a group of people who share the same afterlife beliefs. This account, posted at the web site, and a few by other explorers caused me to do some exploring that changed my old beliefs.

The Helper and I arrived at what appeared to be a large opening in the blackness, and I could see beyond to what appeared to be a lush garden. As I moved through the opening into the scene it was indeed an exotic place; trees, flowers, a soft earth feel, sunshine breaking through the overhanging foliage. I felt a presence to my left and saw a man sitting Indian style on a flat boulder. He had a bald head and was wearing a dark wrap or robe with one shoulder covered. He didn't acknowledge me, he just continued staring off into the garden.

As I moved over to him he finally looked my way and offered a courteous, brief smile . . . and I started receiving information. This was the ultimate place after death . . . peaceful, serene, no wants or needs, no struggling or conflicts . . . and he was bored! He was experiencing disenchantment with the garden because there wasn't anything more to learn. He felt alone and discontent, and at a loss as to what to do. He was also alone a lot mainly because of his disillusionment.

At this point—and not clear as to why—I felt an urge to momentarily leave him and move farther into the garden. This was when I noticed other people who were strolling through what seemed like an endless exotic place. They were meandering in pairs or small groups, talking amongst themselves. One or two looked over in my direction but for the most part I went undetected.

I then moved back to the monk and started telling him of a wonderful place where there was much learning, choices, and love. I told him that I had a friend with me who could certainly take him there. He listened, hesitating, and then decided to go. As he stood and starting walking with me towards the opening I originally came through I noticed several Helpers there. One greeted the monk and began communication. I stood off to one side, knowing he was now okay. And then I got a surprise.

Several others in the park approached where the monk had been sitting and they stopped, wondering what was going on. Apparently communication was going on between the Helpers and this group because another garden member then walked toward the opening and followed the monk out. After a minute or two another monk decided to leave and finally approximately ten of them left with Helpers. I later didn't know what to make of this retrieval but at the time assumed it was once again something to do with F23 I didn't understand . . . but no doubt was very happy to see so many leave.

Dora's Jailhouse Retrieval

After Ginny posted her account at the web site of retrieving Sadie, another explorer (I'll call Dora) decided to try her hand at a BST retrieval. Dora's account of retrieval from an afterlife jailhouse, posted on the web site, was another of the very early explorations that convinced me such retrievals were possible for us physical humans.

First I have to thank Ginny for sharing her amazing visit with Sadie. As we discussed her experience both of us came to the conclusion that she had indeed visited a Belief System Territory. I too placed my Intent to somehow visit there, not just because I had become extremely curious, but to be able to find out what the differences are between Focus 23 and BSTs and discuss them. I started the way Bruce teaches with relaxing, Energy Gathering, and PUL generating exercises. I did more than I usually do and put myself deeper than I wanted to. I think I fell asleep for a short while because when I regained consciousness I didn't remember how I had gotten to the place I was.

I found myself in a jail setting, a long building with closed cells. I was amazed at the clarity of my perception and could see a window with iron bars at the end of the building. The floor was immaculately clean and I was seeing the sunshine come through the window. I found myself sitting at a small table next to the right side of the wall, reading a small book that seemed to be the history of the people there. Behind me I felt a male figure explaining to me where I was. It was a juvenile detention center with young people incarcerated there. In front of me I saw a table with two packs of cigarettes—one was my brand and the other was Salem. I remember thinking hmmmm where is this coming from and why? I've never smoked Salem cigarettes in my life. Neither pack was full, there were only a couple of cigarettes in each pack. Then, I heard the voice behind me, the voice of the Helper I never saw, say, "It's time for them to come out."

Next thing I saw were doors opening, somehow from inside. A small group of young males came out from the cells and I could see their confusion when they saw me. They were thinking, *what is she doing here?* I could only see two of them clearly and they appeared to be the leaders of the group. The rest of the group wasn't very clear, but I could feel their presence.

The group formed a circle around me and I could clearly see they were talking to each other. At this point I remember thinking, *oh shit, I have to do something.* I felt a very strong, aggressive energy from one of the leaders of the group. I looked around but couldn't see any Helpers, and then I found myself very intensely looking at the Salem cigarettes. Feeling a little intimidated, I concentrated to feel PUL, and to cover over my feeling, I said to the young man, "Hey, would you like a cigarette?" Using my nicest manners I told him to go ahead, take one of the Salems and maybe the others would like some too.

He said we can get our own cigarettes, but thanks. Then he grabbed the pack of Salems, took one for himself, and then passed out all the rest to the others. Then he came back for my other pack and took that too, but there still weren't enough for everyone. When he came back looking for more I asked him what did he mean, they could get their own cigarettes?

He said if they wanted to they could go out and buy some, but they didn't because they were afraid to go outside for fear someone else might come in. I was getting the impression they all knew they were not in physical world, but is wasn't clear to me if they knew they were dead, but they definitely knew it was something totally different for them.

At that point I told them I saw a small cigarette shop very close by, and that the town outside seemed very quiet. If they wanted to, I told them, I would be happy to lead them to the store and check to make sure no one else was around as we went there. After a short discussion with each other they said okay let's go.

Next I found myself outside, going with them to a small store where someone was waiting for them. Then the whole scene suddenly disappeared and I was left thinking, *what was this?* A Helper came to me at this point and gave me an explanation.

All the young men were former gang members with very violent backgrounds. Each had the intent to change but had no knowledge of how to separate themselves from their past, so they'd isolated themselves from others by moving into the juvenile jail. They'd each closed themselves off in separate cells because they were afraid of each other. In my interaction with them as a group they had been able to make the decision to leave their isolation, and that had been my purpose in being with them. When I asked the Helper where I had been I was told it was one of many Belief System Territories (BST). I thanked the Helper for his experience and drifted off into a deep sleep.

I'm still trying to work out what the differences are between Focus 23 and the BST and I'll post my thoughts on that in the future.

Marla's Alcoholic's Hell Retrieval

In this next BST retrieval we see a place many of us would expect to find in our afterlife, an Alcoholic's Hell. Marla, I'll call her, posted the following BST retrieval account on the Conversation Board at my web site.

I was in the 3-D Blackness, floating peacefully and enjoying the feeling of being there, but I had in my mind the *intent* of doing a retrieval. Peering into the 3-D Blackness I saw a darker point that had movement, like a black cloud that was spinning. I directed my attention towards this cloud and my awareness became absorbed by it. I felt as if I was traveling more deeply inward.

Suddenly, I arrived in a place in which I saw the face of a man very clearly, drinking from a bottle. The image then expanded and I saw like a dark and somber street with many people with bottles, all of them drinking and drunk. It was really a depressing sight . . . oh boy, what a weird place. I had no idea where I was, and then I got the imp [impression] that I was in the BSTs in a place with only alcoholics. All the people in this place were truly and completely alcohol addicts when physically alive.

The man I saw when I first arrived came to my sight again. I *felt* him to be more sober than the rest of the people there, and asked him his name. "Jerry" was his answer. Then I saw him throw the bottle he was holding to the floor and it smashed into pieces.

I was trying to figure out how to approach him when a thought came to mind. Then I said, "Hey, Jerry, why did you throw the bottle on the floor?" He said, "I'm sick of this drinking! At the beginning it was great! I have all the alcohol I could ever want. The bottle never gets empty, and even after I smashed it on the floor, as soon I want a drink another bottle appears in front of me. This place is a drunkard's heaven, but I've just gotten sick and tired of all this drinking. I'm fed up!"

By then I felt the presence of two Helpers nearby. I told Jerry that he didn't have to stay in this place and that he could go to a better place in which he wouldn't need alcohol anymore. I told him that if he was ready go to this better place there were two very loving beings of light standing in front of him who would take him there. I asked him if he could see them.

He hesitated a little and said, "Are you referring to those two balls of light?"

"Yes," I said. "If you look more closely at them you will see that there are people within those lights."

Then he said, "I have seen those balls before, but I was always so drunk and never paid attention to them."

"Well, Jerry," I explained, "they have been trying to help you before and now I'm here to let you know that they are loving beings of light who are ready to take you to a better place."

"Hey, you are right!" he said, "Now I can see them! They are two people with such a beautiful light coming from them."

"Yes," I said, smiling, "Jerry, you may go with them in peace."

I saw Jerry going toward the Helpers and they took his hand. Then the three of them faded away from my perception. I stayed there for a while, thinking about this place, this Alcoholic's Hell. I never thought that such a place existed and felt so much sadness for the people still trapped there. *At least Jerry is out of this place*, I told myself, and that made me feel just a tiny bit better. Then I came back to C1.

Ginny's BST Retrieval and Visiting the Hall of Remembering

In this next BST retrieval account, notice that the Helper is "dressed" in a particular way as preparation for the retrieval. In this account Ginny mentions a man named Harry, someone Ginny knew when he was physically alive and she retrieved after he died. Thereafter a relationship developed between them in which Ginny followed Harry's progress as he entered training to become a Helper. Ginny's exploration of the Hall of Remembering provides a fascinating look at one of the Centers in Focus 27 and how the staff there, Helpers, assist others.

After relaxing, doing my Energy Gathering Breath (EGB) exercise and filling with Pure Unconditional Love (PUL), the idea to use Heart Intelligence came to me, and upon moving the intellect to the heart center I placed intent to meet up with a Helper and go wherever assistance was needed. A woman appeared to my right, surrounded in gold light and wearing a long white gown. I sensed it was now time for a person this Helper had been visiting to leave an area of the afterlife, and I immediately felt "BST" come to me. I asked about her gown and got that she was "dressed for the part," that it would play an important role in helping this person. Placing my hand on her left arm I then felt a mild sensation of movement. I sensed that there were other Helpers behind or around us but I couldn't see them.

We then seemed to be floating over a countryside at night. Below was what appeared to be a kind of crude stone hut or house with what I guessed was a thatched roof. The sky was a deep blue, lots of stars. I then noticed some kind of light source off to my left and I focused on several people holding burning torches, organized in a circle. I could feel the Helper indicate that we should move to that scene, which we did, coming to rest at ground level and a short distance from whatever was going on. I then saw a tall man in the center of the torch circle . . . and he was not having a nice evening. Those surrounding him were throwing accusations and questions at him, claiming he had "broken the rules." Although he appeared scared he was holding his own, answering that he no longer wanted to live where the others were residing. I asked the Helper what was going on and got that she had been visiting him, helping him to slowly work his way out of this "world." She had influenced him in building the stone house. This was a kind of violation of the beliefs there—"being alone" or in solitude somehow compromised the very belief-fabric of that world. She'd also been encouraging him to realize that he no longer needed the beliefs there. I could feel she possessed a strong love for him, that they had been together in other realities. We continued watching and at one point I moved halfway around the circle, becoming a little alarmed about how this would end. I communicated to the Helper that none of the people, including her friend, seemed to be aware of us. They were all intently focused on the "trial" that was going on and it felt as if their desire to return her friend to where he was supposed to be was working. I then got the idea to use PUL (duh!). The first blast seemed to disrupt their focus on her friend, causing several to turn and look around, more PUL created mayhem. I sensed yelling and confusion as the circle broke up . . . a few scattering out into the night. The Helper then approached her friend, who seemed exhausted and beaten down . . . but I watched his face as he seemed to then recognize her. I also got that he had never really known her true identity, and that her appearance was helping him to remember things pertinent to his freedom. A look of hope filled his eyes as she took his hands and I watched as they both began gliding up and away to my right.

I wanted to know what this belief system was all about . . . why people had been drawn to such a place, and in sensing other Helpers nearby I followed the torch people as they were heading off in single file into the night. It wasn't long after we arrived that a tall mountain cliff appeared to my left with what I initially thought to be a large cave entrance. I kept getting that it had been "manufactured" a long time ago, made by others (?). A rope ladder led up to the entrance, which was huge, perhaps 50 to 60 feet high and very wide, almost perfectly round . . . and people in shadow, hunched over, were moving quickly about.

I saw towards the back of the cave a man sitting in what appeared to be a throne type of chair . . . a woman approached and sat near him . . . and I got that they were in charge. People were grouped in lines, holding sacks of something over shoulders and across their backs. Others were scurrying around, intent on their duties . . . and there was a feeling of fear everywhere. One did not question their role or duties here. The throne guy was quick tempered and quite the tyrant.

I started to feel confused about what would draw people to such a place. I watched as so many seemed to be living in silent desperation. The more upset I became the more scrambled I felt . . . and all I got was that they felt a need to obey someone in charge in order to not have to think or be responsible. This didn't make one iota of sense to me. I started sending PUL to those shuffling forward in line, communicating to them that there were other worlds out there—this wasn't the only one and they certainly didn't have to believe a damn thing the tyrant was saying. I watched several of them become confused, their faces momentarily displaying shock. Some remained frozen to the spot, others started scattering and I could feel fear and anger coming from the direction of the throne. I then felt Helpers around me and I knew we were to move away from the entire scene. I was concerned that I had made it worse for those people, for having shared PUL in the cave, and was told it could only help.

The Helpers then gathered in front of me, about five golden humanoid beings, and I knew I needed to discharge some "stuff" I had picked up in the cave. I did this and felt much better. I then knew that by becoming upset at the plight of those slave people I had somehow opened up to the energies there.

Not wanting to return to waking consciousness yet, I asked the Helpers if they could take me to the Hall of Remembering. I wanted to learn more about it and better understand its purpose. And after a sensation of movement I found myself in front of the same building I'd visited before with its wide cement walkways and grassy areas leading to the front entrance. As I walked into the Hall of Remembering I stopped in what must be the main lobby area and took a good look around.

Off to my right was a large open area where Harry had been doing some "studying." [Editor's note: Ginny has visited with Harry during previous explorations.] There were several booths or workstations running along one wall, each station partitioned off for privacy . . . and they seemed to be empty. Ahead of me and across the lobby was a staircase that led up to a mezzanine area with large windows allowing light to flood the entire lower level. Over to my left was a large circular desk and a wide hallway beyond.

I felt I was being escorted but never focused on who was with me. I just felt a gentle presence to my right, answering questions and showing me around. I was aware that others were busy about the place, apparently unconcerned with our tour. I stated that I was very interested in understanding more of what this place was all about.

We then moved beyond the circular information desk and as we made our way along a wide hallway, I saw people sitting in front of what appeared to be huge TV-like screens. I stopped to watch and got that they were either reviewing scenes from their physical lives, or watching (for lack of better understanding on my part) what appeared to be visual productions or scenes similar to "movies" . . . something that helped in the learning process there. As we continued the tour I also got that the Hall of Remembering was much more spacious than what I was currently perceiving. There were areas filled with books, lecture halls . . . anything and everything available to enable all who were drawn there to take the steps in remembering perhaps who and what they really are.

We then came to an entrance to a dark room and I was told that this was where people could "relive" parts of a physical life . . . for better "understanding." Inside was a modern-looking lounge chair that looked like hard plastic surrounding soft, cushiony material on the seat and high back. I got that when I had been with Harry at his workstation he had been in the beginning stages of his "training" . . . and that he and others would then progress to other areas of learning, eventually arriving at this room well prepared to relive anything important.

My tour guide then extended an offer for me to give the chair a try and I didn't hesitate. It was really comfortable and seemed to almost encourage one to relax . . . which I did, and the guide then asked if I wanted to "relive" something. It was my understanding at that point that I would be able to actually "be in" a scene of my choosing. Without giving it much thought I expressed an inability to understand how the slave people in the BST I had visited earlier could allow themselves to live in such tyranny. I asked if could I experience something that would help me to gain better understanding of why others would allow themselves to be treated and controlled in such an ugly, degrading way. I settled into the chair and the next thing I knew I was riding on the back of a galloping horse. Its mane was whipping across my face as I was hanging on for dear life. I was aware that it was me on a horse, I didn't feel that I was someone else . . . and I felt completely out of control as the horse continued charging at full speed along what felt like a dirt road. I was scared and just barely hanging on . . . with a twinge of confusion going through me as to how this could relate to the slave people. Once that thought went through me I was back in the chair again, as if nothing had ever happened. I then felt a "knowing" sweep through me, an understanding (that unfortunately I now can't seem to completely bring back to my awareness) of the fact that possibly the slave people had experienced that level of fear somewhere along the line—upon death?—and that such totally consuming, heart-pounding fear, coupled with a belief or desire to have someone, somewhere just take control of them (or their fear), was what led them to their present circumstances. I don't think I'm explaining this well, but when I received that "knowing" it made much better sense than it does now, trying to put it into words. I then asked the guide if this "reliving" exercise was similar to using State-Specific Memory, and got back a yes, which felt like a loving warmth washing over me, and I wasn't sure whether I was the one who was pleased with this new understanding or the guide was! One or both of us was pleased with the results of the chair exercise.

And then the tour was apparently over because I was outside the building, in soft blackness, with a Helper nearby. It took a couple of seconds to orient myself to the sudden change, and then I asked a question that has been on my mind for quite some time. I asked why my/our presence was needed in BST retrievals. The Helper offered a generous smile and communicated that there was much learning involved for us . . . and then she said something very interesting: when involved in a BST retrieval and PUL is given to an individual, a "scrambling effect" occurs whereby the individual is momentarily suspended, mentally and emotionally . . . allowing Helpers to move in, so to speak, and grab their attention or surround them with love, etc. And with that I got the impression that I had best get on back to waking consciousness, which I eventually did. I felt energized and full of even more wonder.

25

Visiting or Retrieving a Specific Deceased Person

The most effective way of opening your perception beyond physical reality is to gather verifiable evidence through your own direct experience that a nonphysical reality exists. As this evidence eliminates conflicting beliefs and their perceptual blockages, your ability to gather such evidence more quickly and easily will develop at an accelerated pace. As more and more of your evidence is undeniably verified, your perception will continually develop toward the ability to explore any area of consciousness that exists.

Our afterlife is a convenient reality in which to gather verifiable evidence. It's convenient because it is nonphysical and populated by human beings you can communicate with. It is a nonphysical reality in which the Basic Premise can be used to prove that it exists through your own direct experience.

The Basic Premise

1. Find a way to contact and communicate with a person known to be deceased.

2. Gather information from this deceased person that you can have no other way of knowing except via this contact and communication.

258

3. Verify this information to be true, accurate, and real.

4. This verifiable information is evidence that the deceased person continues to exist after death in the place we call our afterlife.

Proving to myself that our afterlife exists took three-and-a-half years of stumbling exploration. The Monroe Institute's Lifeline program taught me how to shift my awareness to various areas of afterlife consciousness and interact with the nonphysical people I supposedly found there, but these people were not known to me, nor to anyone I knew. Along the way I had to learn about the power of my beliefs to block and distort my perception. I had to discover and use concepts like the Perceiver, Interpreter, and Interpreter Overlay to understand the sources of inaccuracies in my perception. Under these circumstances verification of any of the information received from these people was next to impossible. It wasn't until I began attempting to contact and communicate with deceased people known to my physically living friends that I began to make real progress.

Eventually, the deceased father of a friend giving me information that my friend was able to verify (my *Punky* Experience described in *Voyage Beyond Doubt*) was the turning point in my afterlife exploration. After reintegrating my identity, shattered by the ensuing Belief-System Crash, communication with the deceased quickly became routine. Proving to myself through my own direct experience that our afterlife is real eliminated beliefs that had previously blocked and distorted my perception. This ultimately led to understanding how to teach others to explore our afterlife in a two-day workshop, and to this *Afterlife Knowledge Guidebook.*

My goal in developing the workshop was to make it possible for people to have experiences in the space of two days that would prove to them our afterlife exists. I'm happy to say that this goal is now met in every workshop I give. Some participants in every workshop achieve completion of the Basic Premise for the first time. That is, they experience contact and communication with the deceased which is immediately verified. My intent in writing this book is to help guide you to prove to yourself beyond all doubt that our afterlife exists, and to demonstrate the benefits that flow from that knowledge. This next exercise has the greatest potential to fulfill my intent.

Each time you do this exercise you'll learn more about how your Interpreter translates your nonphysical perceptions into awareness, how your beliefs affect your perception, and how the words you choose to share the information you've gathered from the deceased person affect verification of that information. If you practice this exercise, integrating what you learn each time into the way you approach it the next time, you will prove to yourself that our afterlife exists through your own direct experience. In the two-day workshop this exercise is called Getting a Special Message.

Participants in my workshops begin this exercise by writing on a small slip of paper the name of someone they personally know who is deceased. After folding the paper in half twice, each participant puts this slip of paper into a basket. Then each of ten to sixty participants in turn draws one of these slips of paper from the basket and opens it to make sure it's not the name they just submitted. Each now has the name of a complete stranger, known to be deceased, provided by an unknown participant who submitted this name.

As a participant in the workshop exercise your task would be to contact and communicate with this deceased person. During this contact you would gather specific information that could potentially be verified by the workshop participant who submitted the name. At the completion of your visit with the deceased person you would write as complete and detailed a description of your experience as possible, using all the techniques (like State-Specific Memory) you've learned and practiced in previous exercises. When all participants finish their written descriptions of their experience, it's time to begin the group debriefing session.

In the debriefing session each participant, in turn, shares all the details of their experience with the entire group, without disclosing the deceased person's name. As participants describe their supposed contact experience, no one knows the name of the deceased person or who submitted it. After describing your experience in complete detail, in the large group debriefing I ask if anyone believes the description matches the person whose name they submitted. You then reveal the name of the deceased person. The participant who submitted that name then gives feedback regarding the accuracy of the information gathered. This debriefing and feedback process is where the real learning of the Art of Afterlife Exploration is accomplished.

It is the feedback that gives you the opportunity to validate your contacts with the deceased. Some of these validations will be thin and tenuous, allowing you to doubt their validity, and allowing your conflicting beliefs to prevail. Some of them will be jaw-droppingly accurate, and will undeniably verify your afterlife contact and communication. It is through visiting specific deceased individuals and the debriefing and feedback process that you will learn at an intimate, experiential level

how to trust your perception,
the Interpreter function and Interpreter Overlay,
the effects of beliefs on your perception,
the importance of relaxation and Energy Gathering,
the power of Love,
and so much more.

To the extent that you can accept any verification coming from the debriefing and feedback process, old beliefs will fall away, causing your non-physical perceptual abilities and capabilities to improve. This will automatically lead to clearer perception and experiences that are more clearly, undeniably validated, in turn leading to stronger, clearer perceptual capabilities. Before describing this exercise, I'd like to talk about a few things with regard to proving to yourself that our afterlife exists: *alternative explanations for your experience, statistics, failures,* and *inaccuracy by omission.*

Alternative Explanations

This exercise is designed to eliminate ways in which the results can be explained away. Two common "explanations" that skeptics use are cold reading and mental telepathy.

Cold reading is a process in which the "reader" (the person claiming contact with the deceased) asks questions of a person who knew the deceased, and then uses the information gained to fabricate a phony contact. In the workshop, cold reading is eliminated as an explanation since the "reader" does not know which participant provided the deceased's name. Since you will be doing this exercise alone, you will need to exercise some safeguards to eliminate cold reading as an alternate explanation. Suggestions for such safeguards will be given in more detail later. Basically, you will need to ensure that you have as little foreknowledge of the deceased person as possible. Ideally the only piece of information you will have about the deceased before you visit with them is their name.

I find it amazing that skeptics attempt to use mental telepathy to explain away afterlife contact and communication. Not many years ago skeptics preached that mental telepathy did not exist, and ridiculed any purported claims to the contrary. With scientists' research proving the existence of mental telepathy, skeptics now attempt to use it to explain away afterlife contact and communication. For this claim to be a valid explanation the workshop participant would have to telepathically enter the minds of up to

60 different people, sifting through all the memories of each one until they find the person with memories of the deceased person. Then the participant would have to gather information about the deceased that is specifically defined only during the exercise, and then fabricate a fake contact. As hard-core skeptics are fond of saying, extraordinary claims require extraordinary proof. Frankly, I find this mental telepathy alternative explanation to be an extraordinarily fantastic claim. Until some skeptic can demonstrate extraordinary proof of that claim I find it laughable.

Laughing aside, the retrieval experiences of some workshop participants point to evidence that would invalidate this alternative explanation of mental telepathy with a physically living person. In the next chapter you'll read the accounts of explorers who have made contact with specific deceased individuals. One of those accounts in particular, Dora's, appears to invalidate the mental telepathy explanation. A Helper unexpectedly guides Dora to retrieve her former boss. Her old boss asks Dora to give his still physically living daughter, Agnes, a message. His message is that he secretly hid something for Agnes in an old cash register in his bedroom. He had hidden it there before his death, and no person physically living after his death knew this secret. This message turned out to be an amazing verification for Dora.

Statistics

It's easy to fall into the trap of believing that statistical analysis of your exploration experiences is a valid way to judge whether or not those experiences prove that our afterlife exists. In the debriefing and feedback process you might have 99 pieces of information that are not verified as real, and only one piece of information that is undeniably and irrefutably a jaw-dropping validation, so much so that the odds of randomly guessing that one piece of information might be the equivalent of guessing the winning lotto numbers for the next five lotto drawings in one guess. A statistical analysis still shows that you had 99 misses and only one hit. A statistician could still say that your experience does not prove the existence of our afterlife. According to an old saying, *to prove not all crows are black you only need to find* one *white crow.*

If you encounter a thousand black crows before finding a single white one, statistical evaluation of this fact is meaningless to answering the question about all crows being black. My own experience suggests that you'll have to find lots of white crows before you'll be willing to accept that our afterlife exists. That's just the nature of the way beliefs and doubts work. If you're like me you'll have to accept as real as many experiences that conflict with your beliefs as it takes to crash your old belief system. As you practice this exercise, remember, statistics are meaningless when it only takes one white crow among a million black ones to prove your hypothesis.

Failures

Learning the Art of Afterlife Exploration is key in proving to yourself that our afterlife exists. One of the most important things to know about using this exercise, and the debriefing and feedback process to *learn* the Art of Afterlife Exploration, is:

When Your Goal Is to Learn, You Cannot Fail

The person who submitted the name of the deceased person will see inaccuracies as failures. Other participants will see failures. An outsider will see failures. But, when your goal is to *learn* to explore our afterlife, none of your experiences can be failures because each one is a part of the learning process. In the debriefing and feedback process you are really trying to *learn* how to translate images, feelings, thoughts, and symbols into meaningful statements about your experience of contact and communication with a deceased person.

Some "failures" will turn out to be examples that teach you the difference between describing what you actually perceived, and describing what you interpreted it to mean. For example, in your debriefing you might say that when you asked for something that would prove your contact and communication was real, you saw a young man walking on a lighted path carrying an old-fashioned lantern containing a candle that was hanging from a chain. You might say that this person must have died before flashlights were invented because he used this lantern to light his way when he walked at night. The person who submitted the deceased's name might say that nothing you described is true because it was his uncle who died just a year ago at the age of 87. The submitter could say you've obviously failed because his uncle was an old man, and died only a year ago.

But as the debriefing continues the submitter might disclose that when his uncle was a younger man he was a Catholic priest, and at that point you may suddenly realize that your Perceiver was observing the incense burner which priests carry in some Catholic rituals, but your Interpreter didn't make the connection. You may realize that in your debriefing you didn't mention that the lantern you saw gave off lots of smoke but little or no light, because those facts didn't support the Overlay image of a lantern your Interpreter grabbed. You may realize that:

• The uncle was showing you that the path he was walking in his recent life was that of a Catholic priest, and that he entered the priesthood as a young man.

• You shared your conclusions and interpretations instead of only describing what you *perceived* and *experienced*.

• If you had said that you saw a young man carrying something that looked like an old fashioned lantern, hanging from a chain, which gave off lots of smoke and no light the submitter might have recognized the incense burner and the connections to his uncle having been a Catholic priest as a younger man. Then your contact with the deceased uncle might not have been seen as a failure by the submitter and in fact might have been completely validated.

At this realization you might try to convince the person who submitted the uncle's name that you got it right but described it wrong. That person may or may not believe you, but their belief or disbelief is completely irrelevant to your goal of learning. What is relevant is that your experience has taught you something valuable about using the debriefing and feedback process: *describe what you actually perceived as opposed to your interpretation of what you perceived,* and, *always include all the details, especially the ones that don't seem to fit.* Details that don't seem to fit often have the strongest validation potential.

During contact and communication with a Polish journalist who was killed in Iraq during its American occupation, I suddenly saw a man standing against a desert background. In the next instant an airplane flew past the man at very high speed. This sequence of images lasted perhaps a total two seconds in a contact experience that lasted ten or 15 minutes. It would have been easy to leave this small detail out of the debriefing and feedback process. It was of extremely short duration and did not seem to fit with any of the other information received. But, for the young woman who knew this journalist when he was physically alive it irrefutably verified the contact. He had told her that if anything happened to him, "when you see an airplane I will be there." It was a small, seemingly insignificant detail within a much larger contact experience, yet it was the one white crow that provided ultimate validation for this young woman. Do not leave anything out of your debriefing! It is through such realizations, and learning from such experiences that you will learn the Art of Afterlife Exploration and prove to yourself that our afterlife exists. It took me years to understand that *failure is impossible when your goal is to learn*.

Inaccuracy by Omission

Sometimes, even though you let go of the Interpreter's Overlay to the point that the image repeats, the information just doesn't make sense. There's a temptation to ignore or omit this information when you report it, if for no other reason than you don't know what to do with it. Here's another example from my own experience.

During my visits with my friend Rosalie's deceased father, I kept seeing a young woman, in her late twenties or early thirties, standing off to my left. Every time I focused my attention on her I kept getting that she was Joe's mother. That made no sense as Joe was in his mid-eighties when he died and I couldn't see how it was possible for his mother to be more than 50 years younger than Joe. I repeatedly let go of this information and placed my intent to reconnect with this woman again, and every time I did, her image came back as the same woman, too young to be Joe's mother. She was obviously too young to be Joe's mother and I almost didn't tell Rosalie about her because to me this information was obviously incorrect. Then something she asked prompted me to tell her, reluctantly, about the woman who was obviously too young to be Joe's mother. Rosalie laughed and explained, and I learned something about the inaccuracies that can be introduced by omission. Joe's mom had died when he was 11 years old and she was in her late twenties or early thirties. It made sense to Rosalie that at their reunion in the afterlife Joe's mom would alter her appearance to look the way he would remember her. My lack of understanding and afterlife knowledge was the real problem. At the time I didn't know it was possible for those living in the afterlife to change the age they appeared to be.

Through sharing what I believed to be an inaccurate piece of information two things happened. First, since there was no way for me to know that Joe's mother died when she was in her early thirties, telling Rosalie validated for her (and me) that my contact with her dad was real. Second, I learned something about afterlife existence I didn't know before: those living There can alter their appearance. It also led to my discovery that those in the afterlife can alter their appearance in ways other than just age.

So often it's these seemingly inaccurate perceptions that lead to greater understanding, more afterlife knowledge if you will. And this knowledge becomes part of the process of eliminating old beliefs that block perception, opening our perception to information even further beyond those old beliefs. In your own explorations I encourage you to push yourself to report everything you encounter in your experiences. You just never know when some little piece of "obviously" inaccurate information will be the key that opens a new doorway for your perception.

Even though this exercise is done only once during my two-day workshop, some participants in every workshop have their contact and communication with the deceased person verified immediately after the exercise. The experiences you have using this exercise will teach you how verification in afterlife exploration is done. Every concept, technique, tool, and exercise you've read about and practiced so far in this *Afterlife Knowledge Guidebook* has been in preparation for this exercise. One of the challenges each time you do this exercise is to remember to incorporate and use those tools during the experience.

Setting Up Your Exercise

For you to do this exercise as an individual, instead of as a participant in a workshop, you'll need the name of someone known to be deceased, supplied by a physically living person who knew the deceased person well. There are any number of ways to get such a name, one of the easiest being that you talk to friends and acquaintances about this afterlife exploration you are learning to do, and let them know you need such a name. In the early stages of my own explorations I'd talk to anyone who expressed an interest in listening.

To minimize front loading ideally, the only piece of information you should receive about the deceased person is their name. Any additional information you are given limits the opportunities to receive previously unknown information from the deceased. It can also give you reasons to doubt the validity of some elements of your contact and communication experience, causing you to not accept as real *any* of the *white crows* you do find. Often people will want to give you all sorts of detailed information about the deceased person such as how they died, their beliefs and habits, what they looked like, where they lived, names of other relatives, etc. My advice is that you limit the cold reading potential by asking the person to refrain from giving you any information beyond the deceased person's name. The less you know ahead of time the more opportunities there are to receive and verify information you had no way of knowing other than through contact with the deceased.

Even if you do know more, there are still opportunities for you to receive previously unknown information. For example, the close friend of an afterlife explorer, Karen, died, and this deceased woman's daughter asked Karen to check on her. When Karen asked her deceased friend to show, tell, or give her something to prove that the contact was real, the deceased friend showed her a small ceramic broach. It looked like something made by a child and had the words "Happy Mother's Day" on it. During the explorer's debriefing with the deceased woman's twenty-something-year-old daughter, the daughter recognized the broach as a gift she herself had made for her mother years earlier as a project in grade school. Even though the explorer knew the deceased woman well, there was no way she could have known about the broach. So although it's ideal for the deceased to be a complete stranger to you, take every opportunity you can to practice this exercise and the debriefing and feedback process. Once you have the name of the deceased person you are ready to begin the exercise.

One question that always comes up is, *how will I know if it's a visit or if a retrieval is appropriate?* I use several criteria to make that distinction.

• If the person is alone, unaware of any other nonphysical people, or does not communicate with any other nonphysical people, retrieval may be appropriate.

• If the person is experiencing some form of pain, emotional or otherwise, which they are unable to stop, retrieval from Focus 23 may be appropriate.

• If there are other nonphysical people nearby whom the person is aware of, and if those people attempt to resist or interfere with your contact or retrieval, that's an indication of someone stuck in a Belief System Territory (BST), and retrieval may be appropriate.

But a deceased person who is aware of and communicates with other nonphysical people who do not attempt to impose their will or beliefs on the deceased in all likelihood does not need retrieval assistance. If you are unsure about the need for retrieval you can ask the Helper. In the final analysis if you still feel unsure about whether or not retrieval is appropriate, go ahead and try it. The worst that can happen is that you'll learn more, firsthand, about how to tell when retrieval is unnecessary. In my experience, attempting to retrieve someone who doesn't need it can cause no harm, and if it turns out retrieval was appropriate, you've done it. With practice you'll learn to recognize the indicators pointing to the need for retrieval, and you'll learn quite a bit about the inner workings of our afterlife.

Visiting a Specific Person Exercise Description

This exercise assumes you have the name of a specific, deceased person you desire to visit. In the exercise script below this person will be referred to as "Name." After the exercise you will then be sharing the information you've obtained and rigorously documented with someone who might be able to verify the accuracy of that information. In the exercise script below this person is referred to as "Submitter."

Whether you have purchased the set of CDs with this *Afterlife Knowledge Guidebook*, or you are making your own set of tapes, when you hear the word "Name" in the recording substitute the name of the person you intend to visit. When you hear the word "Submitter" in the recording substitute the name of the person you will be debriefing this exercise with and getting feedback from.

As you do this exercise, if your experience begins to go in a direction that conflicts with the recording's verbal guidance, ignore the recording and follow your experience. This exercise will, with continued practice, prove to you that our afterlife exists. Each time you do this exercise it's an opportunity to remember and use more of the tools you've learned in this guidebook.

Visiting a Specific Person Exercise: Script

This is the Exercise to Contact and Communicate with a Specific Person. (Wait 5 sec)

As you get ready to begin the exercise, adjust the volume of this recording so that you can comfortably and easily hear and understand my voice. You may do this exercise either sitting or lying down. (Wait 10 sec)

When you're ready to begin, please close your eyes. (Wait 10 sec)

To begin this exercise move your body into comfortable, relaxed position in your quiet place. (Wait 30 sec)

Complete your Preparatory Process, remembering and imagining as many or as few of the individual feelings, images, impressions, and details as you need for each step in the process. (Wait 10 sec)

Take in Three Deep Relaxing Breaths. (Wait 45 sec)

Take in Three Energy Gathering Breaths to establish the flow from below. (Wait 45 sec)

Take in Three Energy Gathering Breaths from Below. (Wait 45 sec)

Take in Three Energy Gathering Breaths to establish the flow from above. (Wait 45 sec)

Take in Three Energy Gathering Breaths from Above. (Wait 45 sec)

Remember a time when you were feeling loved or loving. (Wait 30 sec)

Let this memory help you to remember and reexperience the feeling of love. (Wait 20 sec)

If the feeling fades that's okay; just remember another time you were feeling loved and let that feeling build. (Wait 20 sec)

Remember, it is okay to pretend during this exercise. (Wait 5 sec)

Take in at least three more Deep Relaxing Breaths. (Wait 30 sec)

Imagine you are standing on a path that leads into a deep, beautiful, ancient forest. (Wait 20–30 sec)

Imagine you begin walking along this path, entering the beauty of this forest. (Wait 20–30 sec)

Imagine the feel of the path beneath your feet and the sounds they make as you walk along this path, through the warm and comfortable air of the forest (wait 20 sec), perhaps the sound of walking on leaves (wait 20 sec), a forest of huge, tall, stately trees with the gentle scent of their thick, deep bark (wait 20–30 sec), trees whose canopy of leaves, high above the forest floor, is so thick it almost completely blocks the sun. (Wait 10–15 sec)

Here and there beams of sunlight find their way through the leaves and reach the forest floor. (Wait 10–15 sec)

Remember the clean, sweet smell of the forest (wait 10–15 sec), the sound of birds calling to each other from high in the trees (wait 10–15 sec), the warm, still air of the forest, thick with the scent of moist earth and leaves. (Wait 10–15 sec)

Imagine walking along this path in the forest, past plants, trees, and the occasional brightly colored flowers. (Wait 10–15 sec)

Remember the sound of a light breeze gently rustling the leaves of the trees high overhead (wait 10–15 sec), the ebb and flow of that quiet rushing sound of the leaves high above. (Wait 10–15 sec)

Imagine stepping over the exposed roots of the trees, and the occasional stone along the path through a forest. (Wait 5–10 sec)

As you walk along the path remember what it's like as you approach the edge of a forest. (Wait 5–10 sec)

More beams of sunlight reach the ground. (Wait 5–10 sec)

Your surroundings get lighter and lighter as you approach the edge of the forest. (Wait 5–10 sec)

Imagine that just beyond the edge of the forest the path enters a small, open, sunlit meadow. (Wait 5–10 sec)

Imagine you continue walking along the path, entering that beautiful sunlit meadow of grass and flowers. (Wait 15–20 sec)

If you are wearing shoes, remove them, and remember the feeling of walking, barefoot, across the soft, warm grass toward the center of the meadow. (Wait 10–15 sec)

Remember the warm, pleasant feeling of sunlight on your skin. (Wait 5–10 sec)

Remember the sweet smell of the meadow's grasses and flowers. (Wait 5–10 sec)

Remember the beauty of the colors of the flowers. (Wait 5–10 sec)

Imagine stopping near the center of the meadow, and the feeling of a light, warm, gentle breeze moving over your face and body. (Wait 5–10 sec)

As you stand near the center of the meadow, ask for a Helper to come and meet you there. (Wait 10–15 sec)

Feel for the presence of a Helper, remembering it's okay to pretend. (Wait 10–15 sec)

Is this Helper near or far? (Wait 10 sec)

Is this Helper young or old? (Wait 5–10 sec)

Large or small? (Wait 5–10 sec)

Male, female . . . or something else? (Wait 5–10 sec)

Is this Helper beside you, behind you, or perhaps in front of you? (Wait 5–10 sec)

As you become more aware of the Helper, introduce yourself to the Helper, remembering that it's okay to pretend. (Wait 10–15 sec)

Remember the feeling of placing intent, or just imagine you are doing the Silly Little Finger Bending Exercise. (Wait 20 sec)

Reexperience the feeling of placing intent as you say in your mind, to your Helper, **I deeply desire to contact** (wait 3–5 sec), **to visit with** (wait 3–5 sec), **to communicate with** (wait 3–5 sec), **to gather verifiable information from** (wait 3–5 sec), **and be of service to "Name"** (wait 5–8 sec), **and to bring back a special message from "Name" to the person who gave me this name.** (Wait 10 sec)

Ask the Helper to guide you to your visit with "Name" (wait 5 sec) and follow the Helper there, or pretend to. (Wait 10–15 sec)

As you sense your arrival, near "Name," is it your impression that you are indoors or outdoors? (Wait 5–10 sec)

Are there plants or animals, or buildings or other structures nearby? (Wait 5–10 sec)

Feel for the presence of "Name" and gather in more impressions of your surroundings. (Wait 5–10 sec)

Is this person behind you, beside you, or in front of you? (Wait 5–10 sec)

As you begin to become aware of this person and your surroundings, gather your impressions of this person and the scene they are in, or pretend to. (Wait 10–15 sec)

Is this person male or female? (Wait 5–10 sec)

Is this person a child, teenager, young adult, or elderly? (Wait 5–10 sec)

As you become more aware of this person, gather in more impressions of his or her appearance (wait 5–10 sec), how he or she is dressed, and the surrounding scene, or pretend to. (Wait 10–15 sec)

Gather your impressions of any other people nearby. (Wait 5–10 sec)

If there are others there, who are these people and why are they here? (Wait 15–20 sec)

Ask the Helper, "What is this place that we've come to?" (Wait 5–10 sec)

What is your impression of this person's situation and location? (Wait 15–20 sec)

What is your impression of what this person is feeling and experiencing? (Wait 5–10 sec)

Do you notice anything unusual about this person's dress, surroundings, posture, mannerisms, or something else? (Wait 5–10 sec)

How is this person dressed? (Wait 5–10 sec)

Ask the Helper if this is a retrieval situation or a visit, and what in your impressions so far are clues to knowing this? (Wait 5–10 sec)

As you are now more aware of this person, introduce yourself in whatever way seems appropriate to you. (Wait 5–10 sec)

And join into this person's reality, playing along with where he or she appears to be, or pretend to. (Wait 5–10 sec)

Ask this person, "What happened to you and how did you get here?" (Wait 10–15 sec)

Ask this person, "What is this place where you now live?" Gather your impressions. (Wait 10–15 sec)

Ask this person, "Why have you chosen this place to live?" (Wait 10–15 sec)

Ask this person, "Where were you born?" (Wait 5–10 sec)

Ask this person, "Where did you live before you came here?" (Wait 5–10 sec)

Ask this person, "How old are you as I perceive you now and why have you chosen to appear to be this age?" (Wait 10–15 sec)

Ask this person to show you, or describe to you, a favorite hobby or special interest. (Wait 5–10 sec)

Ask this person to describe to you a favorite memory of the person who submitted your name. (Wait 5–10 sec)

Ask this person, "What was one of your favorite things to do where you used to live?" (Wait 10–15 sec)

Ask this person to describe to you a physical lifetime scene that both he or she and the one who gave you their name were in together, and would both remember. (Wait 15–20 sec)

Ask this person to show you, tell you, or give you something that would prove to the one who gave you their name that this visit is real. (Wait 10–15 sec)

Ask this person to give you a special message that you can deliver to the one who gave you their name. (Wait 10–15 sec)

Ask "Name" if there is something else he or she would like to show you, or tell you, or give you. (Wait 10–15 sec)

Is there someone else who would like to enter this scene and make their presence known? If so, invite them to enter the scene and gather your impressions of what they express to you. (Wait 30 sec)

Ask the Helper to show, tell, or give you something that will prove to you that this visit is real.

If this appears to be a retrieval situation, introduce the Helper to this person and follow the retrieval procedure you have learned. (Wait 30 sec)

Ask the Helper for any other information you desire. (Wait 30 sec)

Take as much time as you need. When you feel complete with this experience, ask the Helper to show you, tell you, or give you something that will prove your contact with this person has been real. Then, express your gratitude to the Helper and this person for this visit.

Take more time if you feel the need. Then immediately begin to write about your experience and use the debriefing section in the *Afterlife Knowledge Guidebook* to assist you in recording your experience.

(Do not record this note: you may either keep the tape recorder running to leave a very long blank space on the tape, or you may chose to leave a short blank space and plan to turn off the recorder for the remainder of your exercise experience.)

Debriefing the Visit with a Specific Deceased Person Exercise

Remember to write down every detail of your experience in your notebook, and use State-Specific Memory to remember more of your experience.

It may be helpful to read portions of the exercise script to trigger more memory. Pay particular attention to recording whatever the person and/or Helper gave you that could prove your contact was real. Write down any statements word for word to the best of your perception, along with any feelings you experienced. Sometimes a specific word or phrase the deceased person used during their physical lifetime turns out to be a jaw-dropping validation. Make sketches of any objects or scenes that were a part of your visit. If you were shown or given something by the person or the Helper, sketch enough of the details that you will be able to remember and share it with the Submitter.

After you have finished writing down absolutely everything you can remember about your experience, start at the top of your list and read the first thing you wrote down. Then close your eyes, take in 3DRBs, and remember any feelings or sensations you experienced while you were perceiving it. Let the Hemi-Sync Model of Consciousness and State-Specific Memory help you to remember more of your experience. Make notes of anything new you remember. Then continue going through your list and repeat this process.

In the workshop I give participants enough time to write down all they can remember and then ask them to relax and remember any feelings they experienced during the exercise. Some participants discover that doing this results in remembering more information than they had just finished writing down.

When documenting your experience in this exercise it is very important to make a distinction between what you actually perceived versus your interpretation or analysis of what it means. In my own experience of the debriefing and feedback process with the Submitter, if I share only what I perceived, in a sense the *raw data*, we find lots of white crows. If I instead share my interpretation of what I perceived we're lucky to find any white crows.

Consider sharing your retrieval experience by posting it on the Conversation Board at my web site, www.afterlife-knowledge.com.

Tips for the Visit with a Specific Deceased Person Exercise

1. It is so important to make the distinction between what you perceive and your interpretations that I suggest you use some procedure or method of making these distinctions in your written record of the experiences. For example, after completely recording your experience in your notebook you

might go back and underline only the descriptions of what you actually perceived. To be a little more rigorous I'd suggest the following procedure. Draw a vertical line down the center of the page you'll use to record your experience. Label the left side of the page "Perceived" and the right side, "Interpretation." As you record your experience, think about on which side of the page your description belongs.

2. Alternatively, as you record your experience in your notebook, begin by writing the word "Perceived" as a label for what you are about to write down. Then, as best as you can, write only what you actually perceived, not what you interpret or believe it means, not what you assume it means or represents, but only what you *actually perceived*. Then below what you've written as perceived, write the word "Interpretation" as the label for what you write next. Then, document what you interpret, assume, believe, or expect what you perceived means or represents. Using the example of the visit with the Catholic priest I gave above your entry might look like:

    Perceived: A young man, maybe 30 years old who appeared to be walking on a path of some kind through darkness. He was carrying something that looked like a lantern hanging from a fancy chain. This lantern gave off lots of smoke, but no light. It felt like the man's path and this lantern thing were somehow connected.

    Interpretation: The deceased person was obviously a young man when he died. This young man must have lived before flashlights were invented because he used a lantern to light his way while walking at night.

3. Learning to separate what you actually perceive from your interpretation is a very important factor in getting validation in the debriefing and feedback process. The Submitter is in a better position to interpret the meaning of what you perceive. After all, the Submitter knew the deceased person. Keeping what you actually perceived separate from your interpretations will make it far easier to find those white crows. More importantly, making the distinction between the two will make it far easier for you to learn more about how your nonphysical perception works, particularly as it applies to the Perceiver, Interpreter, and Interpreter Overlay. Learning about these influences from your direct experience leads to the ability to perceive more clearly and more accurately during your experiences.

4. You will be tempted to leave out details of your experience which don't seem to fit, which you feel can't possibly be correct, which you feel certain

you fantasized, or seem insignificant. My advice is, don't leave anything out. You never know what will be validated and what won't unless you try, and very often it's the above kinds of things that lead to the strongest validations.

5. It is entirely normal for you to feel that you've pretended or fantasized some or all of your contact experience. You may be tempted to not record your experience because you're so certain you made all or some of it up. My advice is, record it all in detail. An Arizona participant's experience is typical. She began her debriefing by stating that she was certain she had made up the entire experience and didn't see much point in sharing it with the group. She then spent about six minutes describing her fantasized experience in great detail. When she was finished the Submitter began her feedback by saying, "You were visiting my deceased mother, and there isn't a single thing you've said that doesn't fit my mother to an absolute tee." We are so accustomed to using imagination to perceive our fantasies that using it to perceive something real *feels like* we are fantasizing. As you continue to practice, you'll probably discover that using your imagination to perceive real things actually has a different *feeling* quality than using it to perceive your fantasies. As you learn to recognize this *feeling* and remember it at will, you'll find that remembering the feeling allows your awareness to automatically shift toward perceiving real things as opposed to fantasies. You may get to the point where you *know* when you are perceiving real things and when you're not just by the feeling you are experiencing at the time.

Tips for the Debriefing and Feedback Process with the Submitter

Sharing your contact and communication from this exercise with the Submitter can be a nerve-wracking and performance-anxiety-inducing experience. Sometimes I so wanted to be able to give the Submitter something, anything, that would let them know their loved one was okay that I was afraid I'd blow it and not show them a single white crow. Sometimes I was more afraid that everything I said would be validated and my world would crash down around me. Sometimes it helped to think of the exercise as if I were just sharing the data from an experiment I had run in a physics lab. The only way I found to deal with all of this was to just do it. Remember, the Submitter may see failures. Someone else observing your debriefing and feedback process may see failures. But: *when your goal is to learn, you cannot fail by sharing your experience.*

Six Potential Problems of Perception

There are at least *five* ways that it can look like you haven't found a single white crow when you actually have a whole flock of them. If the Submitter tells you that you haven't gotten a single piece of correct or verifiable information, consider the six possibilities described below.

One: Contamination by Touch

In the workshop, the names of the deceased are written on slips of paper and each participant draws one to get the name. Sometimes the name is someone known to the participant. (You'd be surprised how often this happens.) If someone pulls a slip, returns it, and draws another, the person who eventually draws that returned slip can finish debriefing and not have a single piece of information correct. It looks like a completely blown exercise—but it is entirely possible that the information will be a completely accurate reading of the first person who touched the paper. I know this sounds weird, but I've seen it happen many times. To avoid this problem I suggest the Submitter write the name on a piece of paper in your presence and give it to you, or that you write it, and that you don't let anyone else touch the piece of paper once the name is written on it.

Two: Confusion of Targets

If the Submitter thinks of several different deceased people, finally settles on one, and gives you that name, and your debriefing seems to provide no correct or verifiable information, there's a good chance you visited with one of the other people the Submitter was thinking about. This happens often during my workshops. In one workshop in Germany, it was almost comical. Because of time constraints, I had some debriefings done one on one. I listened in on the debriefing given to a woman I will call Greta by a man I'll call Frank. After almost every statement Frank made, Greta said, "No, you are describing my father. I wanted you to visit with my brother!" Frank's debriefing was quite long and full of details that were validated as accurate for Greta's father. But since she had written down her brother's name, Greta considered that Frank hadn't gotten a single correct piece of information!

The best way I know to mitigate this problem is to inform the Submitter, before the debriefing and feedback process begins, that if the Submitter was thinking strongly about more than one person, and then settled of one of their names to submit, it's possible that your visit was with one of those other people. If some details fit with one of the other people they were thinking about, it might be worthwhile to reread your debriefing notes, asking the Submitter to give feedback for that other person.

Three: Deceased Person's Choice

You're not likely to encounter this one when doing this exercise as an individual. If you do, you probably won't know it.

In another workshop in Germany, the Submitter (Julia) had submitted her father's name and said in her feedback that not a single piece of information the Visitor gave in her debriefing was correct or verifiable. A third person (I'll call her Karla) said that the details sounded like her grandfather, the name she had submitted, but *not* the name the Visitor had drawn from the basket. When they went over her entire debriefing again, everything was validated by Karla, including a very long and detailed description of the physical lifetime scene that both Karla and her grandfather had shared and would both remember.

For some reason in a group setting the deceased person will sometimes choose to come through to a person in the group even though that person did not draw that deceased person's name. In a workshop setting the name of the deceased person is not revealed by the Visitor until after a complete debriefing. This requires all participants to listen carefully in case it involves the person whose name they submitted. In all likelihood, the only way you'll catch this one is if the Submitter recognizes that you are describing a deceased person they know other than the one whose name they submitted. The Submitter might say "nothing you've said is accurate for the person whose name I gave you, but it sounds like my friend's dad who just died recently." The way to get around the problem is to inform the Submitter that sometimes the deceased person who comes through *belongs* to someone the Submitter knows.

Four: Someone Whose Name Was Not Submitted

The rarest situation that occurs in workshops is illustrated by this example from a workshop in North Carolina. The Submitter couldn't find a single piece of correct or verifiable information in the Visitor's debriefing. But some of the details had reminded the Visitor of a neighbor's boy her own son had played with years earlier. She didn't know the boy well, didn't know if he had died, and decided to call the boy's mother after the workshop to check on some of the details. When she did, she discovered that the boy had indeed died and that most of the previously unknown information she'd gathered from the deceased boy was verified as accurate. She got things like: his favorite team sport, football; favorite team, the San Francisco 49ers (which she got when the boy showed her a jacket in the 49ers insignia and team colors). The special message was a clincher. The boy said to "tell her that if the cookies were burned on the bottom there was no way I would eat any of them." And indeed, the boy's mother confirmed that if any of the cookies she baked were even the least bit crispy on the bottom her son would refuse to eat them.

When the deceased person who comes through is someone whose name was not submitted by the Submitter, you or someone else may recognize the deceased person, or suspect who the person is. If so, I suggest you do whatever digging is necessary to try to verify the information through someone who knew the deceased.

Five: A Shift in Perspective Is Needed

This one occurs to some extent in nearly all debriefings. One extreme example comes from a workshop in Germany, and illustrates that a shift of perspective is often necessary for the Submitter to see those white crows.

After the Visitor completed a very long and detailed debriefing of her encounter she commented that she was very certain her visit had been real. She described meeting a man who lived on a very small farm just outside a small village. She described the house and a small barn, a garden, and the surrounding countryside in great detail. She described the layout of the inside of the house and its furnishings. Much of her description revolved around the way this man lived and what it said about his patterns of thinking. For example, she described that the barn was built to house sheep but that there were no sheep in the barn, nor was there any evidence that sheep had ever been in the barn. She also described that the deceased man she visited often slept in the barn because he was concerned that someone would come at night and steal the sheep. When she completed her debriefing and disclosed the name of the deceased man, the Submitter (call him Richard) said that the name he submitted was his father's and that absolutely nothing she had said was accurate.

Later that evening she told me she was absolutely certain she had visited with the father and felt that some hidden aspect was getting in the way of verification. The following evening she and Richard spent several hours going over all the details of her visit, attempting to shift the perspective from which the information was viewed. The following morning Richard asked to address all the workshop participants before we resumed the workshop activities.

He explained that he now saw that all of the details were accurate. He had expected to hear details that correlated with his father's physical lifetime. But now he realized that she was describing the ways in which his father had always said he wished he could live. For example, he wanted to live on his own small farm in the countryside and raise sheep. But he was the kind of person who believed others would always try to steal whatever he held dear. Viewing the information from this perspective, it made perfect sense to Richard that his father would have a barn for sheep and sleep in that barn to protect them from being stolen. Richard spent several minutes going over each of the details that had been described in the debriefing, and explained that by viewing these details from the perspective of how his father always said he *would like to live,* instead of how he had *actually lived,* he could verify all of it as accurate.

There is a tendency to believe that the information gathered during a visit with a deceased person will be verified based on the accuracy of details about that person's physical lifetime. This example demonstrates that sometimes verification will come through what is known about the habits, patterns of thinking, and unlived desires of the deceased. In order to see any white crows, a shift of perspective may be necessary.

Six: Uncooperative Submitter

There will be times when no matter how careful you are to accurately describe what you perceived within your experience, the Submitter will respond by saying nothing you have said can be verified. This can happen when the Submitter does not fully understand how the process works, and expects more than you can possibly provide. One of the best examples of this phenomenon occurred during a workshop in Warsaw, Poland. The exercise was of a visit by a ten-member group in a partnered exploring experience.

After each member of the group gave a detailed debriefing of their experiences, some lasting more than five minutes and filled with specific details, the Submitter said nothing was accurate. One member of the group had claimed the deceased spoke of extensive travel in Asia as a physical lifetime special interest. During the debriefing this person had said they were not sure if the deceased meant travel in greater Asia or smaller Asia, but felt it had been greater Asia. Thinking that perhaps travel might be the correct special interest, but that something in her interpretation had given the wrong area of the world, she asked the Submitter if travel was indeed a special interest. At that point the Submitter acknowledged that travel in smaller Asia had been the deceased's special interest, but since greater Asia had been named she counted this as inaccurate.

To have narrowed down the area of travel for a special interest from an almost infinite number of potential locations in the world to Asia was at least a grey crow. The Submitter obviously believed if the information was not precisely accurate, or even close, down to the finest detail it should be judged to be inaccurate. Other members of the partnered exploring group began to question the Submitter in detail. Over the next ten minutes detail after detail was easily found to be accurate within the limitations of minor semantic variation. While I am not certain of the specific reasons for this uncooperative Submitter's behavior, my impression at that time was that it was belief based. This Submitter's beliefs appeared to be hanging on for dear life in the face of accurate feedback, by demanding unrealistically precise details.

If after you complete sharing all the details of your experience with the Submitter, who responds with a simple, flat statement that nothing is accurate, you might consider some gentle questioning about the details. You may discover that indeed nothing is accurate. You may also discover that just a little probing leads to verification of the information you have gathered.

Guidelines for the Debriefing and Feedback Process

Share every detail you perceived. No matter how insignificant or meaningless it seems, if you perceived it, share it. I see it over and over again in workshops. A participant finishes sharing with the group and I ask, "Is there anything you've left out?" Invariably, the participant says, "Well, there were a couple of other little things I didn't share because I'm sure they are wrong." Often these little things turn out to be the jaw-dropper verifications.

When sharing your experience, inform the Submitter that there is a distinction between what you perceived and your interpretation of your perception. Share each of your "Perceived" statements from your notes and ask the Submitter for any feedback, before you share your "Interpretation" statements.

It is especially important when you are first learning to use the debriefing and feedback process with a Submitter that you both approach your sharing with an attitude of trying to find anything that might be even a hint of a white crow. While you're still in the beginning of your learning it's best if you both do whatever you can to find any possible validations. Early in the learning process confidence building is more important than precision.

Some information may not be verifiable, because it is unknown to the Submitter. When the Submitter can't verify the information due to possible lack of knowledge, ask the Submitter to check the information with someone else who might know. And ask the Submitter to contact you, to tell you the outcome. When a Submitter can validate such information, you have both just found a big, fat white crow.

Sometimes when checking information with others, for religious or other reasons, it may be difficult for the Submitter to admit to other family members or friends that they are involved in communication with the deceased. I'd suggest the Submitter begin such a discussion (using the Gramps was a bank robber story as an example) with a phrase like "a friend of mine had a dream that said Gramps had been a bank robber when he was a younger man." The rest of the details can be shared as if they had been obtained during a dream. It is often much easier for people to accept the possibility of getting information via a dream than via an afterlife explorer.

Validation can come in some pretty strange ways, and can come long after completing the debriefing and feedback process, as with the Arizona workshop participant who saw on TV a photograph of a deceased truck driver, described in detail elsewhere in this book.

Remember what you learned about how to deal with the symptoms of a Belief-System Crash. If you notice the symptoms of a Belief-System Crash, be gentle with yourself and allow time for reintegration.

Above all, when you share your experiences from this exercise, remember, *when your goal is to learn to explore the afterlife you cannot fail.*

26

Visiting or Retrieving a Specific Deceased Person Examples

The examples in this chapter are taken from workshop participants and other explorer experiences. You may find similarities between them and your own experiences. These accounts have been edited for punctuation and clarity, and names have been changed.

Linn's Experience

This first account is a perfect illustration of the importance of sharing what is perceived instead of an interpretation.

I was doing a spirit contact for a lady tonight and her young son came through. As I was describing him to her he gave me the word *Pug*. So, I threw in the description to her like this: Well, he also has a short, turned-up nose. His mom said that he did. We continued the reading with lots of things he was doing and he really is happy, etc. All in all it was a really lovely contact but as she was thanking me she said with a sigh, I just wish he had mentioned "Pug." She explained that Pug was her son's pet name for his grandfather, who had passed before her son died. She had hoped her son would let her know if Pug was there with him.

I laughed real hard and explained that actually her son had tried to tell that his grandfather was there with him since the beginning of the reading. Her son had said "Pug" to me at the very beginning, but instead of just repeating what he said, I took it upon myself to think it was a description of his nose. I learned yet again, if they say something to me, just to repeat it out loud and not try to analyze or interpret what they are telling me.

Katie's Contact with Her Son

Katie posted the following account of her experience on the Conversation Board at the web site.

I attended Bruce's Afterlife Communication Workshop in the Boston area on November 18 and 19 in a state of desperation. My only son, Dan, had just been killed in an auto accident on Oct. 28 in California. Fortunately, I was with Dan for the week before his death, having gone to Los Angeles to be there with him for his 22nd birthday, on October 21st.

From the moment of his death and in the following days, I saw Dan in my dreams, and felt his presence near me when I was awake. However, I NEEDED to see and talk with him in the afterlife and to know that he was happy. During the workshop Bruce taught us how to accomplish that communication. It was so startling! It was so simple! While I was *out there* with Dan I asked him to give me a sign for his dad, John, and Dan pulled that one off with flying colors! He specifically said to me, "Tell Dad I put a 'Special Section' in the *New York Times* for him in tomorrow's paper." The *New York Times* is like oxygen to John; he inhales every word of it first thing in the morning. Our workshop communication was on Sunday and that night, after the workshop, I phoned John and he said the most incredible thing had happened. We had a particular candle burning in front of Dan's recent graduation photograph and it had suddenly started crackling and sparking, as John said, "like fireworks." Dan was the youngest person ever to be given membership into the Western Pyrotechnical Association. I told John to check out the *New York Times* in the morning for "something special" from Dan.

Monday, I left Sudbury, Mass. to drive back to the Philly area. To say the least, I wanted to see a copy of the *New York Times*. Every store I went into was sold out! As I drove down I-95, I kept talking with Dan. I'd say, Okay, Honey, I'm going to turn on the radio, send me a message! He did, every single time. Finally, right before I hit the New York/Connecticut border, I said, Dan, where can I find a copy of the *New York Times*? As though he were sitting in the car with me he answered, "On the next corner in a machine, and Mom, I put something in the crossword puzzle for you, too!" I start my day with the *New York Times* crossword puzzle always looking for messages and Dan used to always laugh at me for it!

There was a Special Section in the *New York Times* for John, an actual SPECIAL SECTION entitled GIVING. It was pages long about how to help out the less fortunate in your community and in the world. The night before, when John was home and I was up in Massachusetts, John became overwhelmed with Dan's death, but he was determined to turn it into something good, something that would help kids in need, kids who don't have parents or the great advantages that Dan was fortunate enough to have. When he opened his *New York Times* Monday morning and saw the special section describing ways he could carry out the desire he'd felt so strongly the night before, he KNEW he had gotten his message from Dan!

And what were the messages in my crossword puzzle? *Fourth Estate* (the press)—Dan was intending on becoming an international journalist; he'd been writing and publishing since age 13. *Newsman Rather* (Dan) and *Japanese fighter* (Ninja)—Dan majored in Japanese language and literature, graduating summa cum laude. I used to call him Ninja Dan. *Easy-to-catch hit* (pop-up)—Dan was a mega baseball fan and player. But most importantly there was *Expert* (guru). When Dan was just months old, his first word was "guru."

Phew! I know this is a very lengthy post, but I feel it is very important to share these experiences exactly as they happened. I cannot find words enough to express my deepest gratitude to Bruce Moen for his books, his web site, but most of all, his workshop.

Steve's Experiences

In May 2000 Bruce was in Sydney speaking at the *NEXUS* magazine conference and was hosting a series of afterlife workshops. So this time I went along with an open mind and learned to retrieve people stuck in the wrong area of the afterlife. My first retrieval was of a 97-year-old man. He seemed very confused. I felt the feeling of an innocent confusion, but he was taken to the right place, which made me feel happy for him. Since then I have been very busy with work, but still have the time to do retrievals and other afterlife activities. Here are two interesting ones.

My mum knows that I do retrievals, but her Catholic upbringing makes it difficult for her to fully accept what I do. Recently, I asked her if she wanted me to find anyone that she knew who had passed away. My mum's aunt died a year or so ago and she suggested I visit with her. They were close but had little contact as we live in Australia and she lived in Italy. A few nights later I found her in an afterlife place that told me she didn't need retrieval. When I asked her for some kind of verification for my mum she told me that when my mum was a little girl she'd tease her by calling her a "naughty little girl." When I later phoned my mother she verified that bit of information saying that her aunt always used to say this to her in a playful way when she was little. Then my grandmother, the aunt's sister who died in the early 80s, shows up on the aunt's left side and I get the very strong impression that she wants me to retrieve my cousin who suicided in 1985.

To cut a long story short, I next retrieved my cousin, moving him to the right place in the afterlife. Just as I finished that I got a very strong impression of his mother (she died in the late 80s) giving me a loving smile. Then I got an impression of a huge, perfect yellowbox tree (my favorite tree) in a park. I got the impression that it was something nice for me, sort of a thank you gift for finding my cousin. For me personally you couldn't have given me anything nicer. I was really touched.

My second story is more recent. A Russian submarine sank near Norway in the Arctic Sea in August 2000. A day or so after it sank the story was on the news and I decided to go looking for it to see if anybody was still alive. I started to do my exercises and focused on finding them. Then I'm finding myself moving through blackness towards a submarine on the sea floor. It was leaning on its right side and the whole front was full of water. In that front area was a strong impression of crew who had already died. At the rear there were many survivors all crammed on the very upper deck. The next few days passed and then the news reported that the submarine was leaning to one side, which was making it very difficult for a rescue. The news also reported that if there were any survivors they would be on the rear upper deck right where I saw them. I don't know very much about submarines but this seemed to verify what I saw in my experience. Some people would call it coincidence but in my experiences there seem to be less and less coincidences.

Lenna Visits a Friend's Mother

My friend's mother died two weeks ago. She was so struck with grief, I blurted out I might try and find the mother in the afterlife to see how she was doing, and try to get a message from her. (My friend and I have been talking about these things before but still I felt she might think me strange.) She was eager to grab at anything and trusted I would not try to cheat her, so she said okay. I decided to try to make contact that night.

I had her name and a brief description of how she looked. I sat down, relaxed, and brought the mother's name to my mind. Immediately there was an image in my mind. Now I don't see in the way I look with my physical eyes. It's more like looking at thoughts, a bit like dream images, and I decide to make them visual and so they do that but not completely. I have an overall impression and little details pop up more visual than others.

The image that popped up was of a very tired, middle-aged woman in a hospital being supported on both arms by two male nurses. She was wearing glasses and the shape of her face was longish, but her hair was all wrong. I had been told by her daughter that her mom's hair was short, originally brown, but she had dyed it blonde. This woman's hair reached under her ears and was more like light brown. She looked very sad and said she wanted to come back, this was too quick for her.

I had a little pause believing this was obviously the wrong woman. A few hours later I tried again and again the same woman came to view. This time she stood near me by a lake or by the sea. An old building was there, painted red with white window frames. Another woman came out when she saw us and the first one hugged her tightly. The other woman was older, her hair was short and gray, and her spectacles really caught my interest. They were very big and copper-colored. It could have been metal or then just a copperish shade of brown. The two women went inside the building and I followed.

Inside there were only two rooms, one a kitchen living room and the other a bedroom. The gray-haired woman gave "my" woman a mug of coffee and said she should go and sit somewhere to think about all that had happened. She went out with the coffee and sat on a little pier. I looked at her and saw pine trees and some rocks behind her on the opposite shore. It looked like a lake. No other houses in view, but a feeling there were other people there, in summer cottages perhaps. The woman sipped her coffee and I asked (just in case she was the right person) if she had a message to my friend. She said to me she understood now it was time for her to go, was sorry for leaving her loved ones behind, and wanted to send love to her family. Then she said something that came as a thought in my mind, not a word but a thought of "pepper" or "peppers." I found this to be odd.

It was two weeks before I had the courage to tell my friend about my visit with her mom. I asked about the different hair and she said her mother's hair was exactly like what I had seen, light brown, under the ears. She wore glasses. The shape of her face was longish. She had died in a hospital by a sudden heart attack at the age of 48 (this I knew beforehand). The house is a friend's summer cottage she loved to visit. It has only two rooms, a kitchen living room and a bedroom. It is red with white window frames. It is by the sea, but the small pier is not directed to open sea; it's a bit angularly towards the opposite shore in the little bay. Pine trees and rock were right. No houses to be seen but summer cottages nearby. The woman with the huge copper-colored eyeglasses and gray hair matches a description of her mother's dear friend of hers exactly (still on "our" side of reality). And she said her mother used to call her and her little sister "mom's little peppers" referring to their unusual temperament, a rather "spicy" character.

I suppose the other woman was a helper taking the shape of her dear friend to get her attention. Sorry, this has been long, but I still have problems closing my jaw after it dropped to my knees when my friend confirmed every little detail of my experience.

Dora's Experience

Dora attended a workshop in Payson, Arizona, and has become quite an accomplished afterlife explorer. Dora gave a little background on the man she encountered during this experience, and I've included it.

Visiting or Retrieving a Specific Deceased Person Examples

For 12 years I worked as a manager and waitress in a Hungarian restaurant in Los Angeles. The owner was an old-fashioned, grumpy, stingy man who was a very unpleasant person to work for. He immigrated to the U.S.A. in 1957 and opened his first Hungarian restaurant in 1959. Later he returned to Hungary to marry and brought his new bride back to Los Angeles. At the age of 45 his wife gave birth to a daughter, Agnes, the love of her father's life. When he sold the restaurant and retired he kept the cash register as a memento, displaying it in the bedroom of his home.

It was November 14th, after the recent plane crash, that I placed my intent to help anyone who might need it. Although my intent was to go to the crash site, Helpers took me to the most unexpected place. After going to the usual blackness I found myself standing on a busy street with many small shops around.

When I arrived on the street I was standing at a storefront where all kinds of Hungarian meat products were displayed in the window. There was a tremendous amount of Hungarian specialty sausages. I was really surprised to see this as I had intended to go to the plane crash. I decided to walk into the store and look around. When I did it came as a big surprise that I saw my old boss busy making endless amounts of sausage. I greeted him and in his usual gruff manner he barked out, "What are you doing here?" Thinking he might be stuck and need retrieval I joined into his reality, telling him I'd come to buy some of his special sausage. I invited him to stop working and sit with me and asked him to open a bottle of his favorite wine. He brought out a bottle, poured us each a glass, and began drinking.

I asked him why he was making so much sausage and he explained that he had to deliver it to many customers at their stores. He told me he didn't like living at his store but was waiting for his daughter because he needed to tell her something. I knew that to retrieve him I'd have to get him out of his store, so I suggested that since he'd been drinking it would be safer if I drove him to the other stores to make his deliveries. Arriving at the first store, his daughter, or a Helper who looked like her, was waiting for us in front of the store. They hugged and in the next moment Agnes disappeared. My old boss then told me that he wanted me to get a message to Agnes and make sure his wife didn't know about this. He wanted her to know that he'd saved quite a bit of money and hidden it in the old cash register. A man came out of the store and asked my old boss to come inside. I realized this was a Helper and knew that the retrieval was about to take place. After this encounter I found a phone number for my boss's old restaurant and called, asking to speak with him. I was told he had died in his sleep as the result of a major stroke about a month earlier.

I didn't know how to pass the message on to Agnes and decided to ask Helpers to assist me. The evening of November 23rd I went to bed wanting assistance from a Helper. Without any preparation or prompting I found myself back at the old restaurant. I was putting crystal clear glasses on a shelf that had a mirror behind it. Looking into the mirror I clearly saw my old boss and his daughter standing at a table where a couple was seated. I recognized the couple! They were friends of my old boss who intensely disliked his wife. They live on the same street as my old boss just a few houses away. At that point I clearly heard a voice in my head saying, "You understand?"

I realized a Helper had just given me the solution to my dilemma of how to let Agnes know about her father's message and the money without her mother finding out. For religious reasons I couldn't just tell her I'd visited with her dead father and he had given me a message for her. When I contacted the neighbor I used Bruce's suggestion and explained I'd had a dream about Agnes's father and he'd given me a message for her. I told them Agnes was to look in the old cash register for something her father left her. It was several months before I got any word back.

In late January I finally received a phone call from the neighbor. After receiving my message Agnes visited her father's former home and found a large envelope taped to the bottom of the cash drawer of the register. In the envelope she found money and a letter from her father! I feel like I just hit the verification jackpot!

27

Retrieving an Aspect of Self

In the chapter on changing beliefs, I described how we can sometimes create an Aspect of Self—spin off a portion of ourselves—to hold and enforce a belief. My experience shows we sometimes create Aspects of Self for other purposes. Of all the exercises in this book, Retrieving an Aspect of Self has the highest potential to cause profound changes in one's beliefs, identity, and perceptual ability. It also has the highest potential to cause Belief-System Crashes and strong symptoms of identity crisis. This is not an exercise to be taken lightly. I recommend that you do not do this exercise until after you have had some experience dealing with Belief-System Crashes and the identity reintegration process that follows them. That said, this exercise also has the highest potential for profound healing and growth experiences.

Some who do this exercise will say, "Nothing really big happened, Bruce, what's all the fuss about?" Others will describe it as being similar to going through organ transplant surgery and the difficult recovery process that follows. The latter will also say that the process resulted in a positive, beneficial, life-changing experience that profoundly changed their understanding of who and what they really are.

The origin of this exercise was a participant's experience during an ordinary retrieval exercise at a workshop in Oakland, California. When she asked for a Helper, the one who came told her that if she was willing she would be guided to a profoundly healing, potentially difficult experience instead of the standard retrieval exercise. With the participant's agreement the Helper led her to what she at first took to be a deceased person needing retrieval. Her debriefing was an extremely emotionally charged experience. It took her several minutes to be able to talk about her experience without choking up and breaking down in tears.

As her experience progressed, she realized that the person she was retrieving was actually a part of herself she had abandoned at an early age. She later said it was as if at that age she had separated a part of her that she labeled *her innocence* and had no further contact with this aspect of herself until she retrieved it during the workshop exercise.

When she realized the person she was retrieving was an aspect of herself, she suddenly began to see how her life had been affected by splitting off this part of herself and abandoning it. She felt totally overwhelmed by the insights and realizations that came to her so fast and furiously. The Helper asked if she would like to bring this back into herself, and when she answered yes, she said the aspect of herself moved toward her and entered her body. During her debriefing, she said she then experienced what she could only describe as an extremely ecstatic, overwhelmingly joyful, physically immobilizing state. And that as the aspect first entered her body, and for a time afterward, the volume of insight and information about who and what she really is was so great that it would take weeks of nonstop talking to describe it all.

Without knowing what this participant was going through, I had become alarmed at what I observed at the point in the exercise in which her Aspect of Self entered her body. Her entire physical body began to shake and tremble uncontrollably—not violently, but continuously—for something approaching two minutes. I focused all my attention on her, remembering everything I'd ever heard or read about how to deal with someone having a seizure. As I continued to observe her, I realized that this was not a medical emergency and that I should not interfere. Believe me, it took a *tremendous* level of trust in that perception to allow whatever was going on with this participant to continue. After her body tremors subsided, she relaxed into quiet tears.

This participant is a psychotherapist by profession. She and I continued to correspond via e-mail after the workshop. Her description of the life changes as the Aspect of Self she called *her innocence* reintegrated into her Being and Awareness led me to develop the Retrieving an Aspect of Self exercise. The next several times this exercise was used in the workshop, I witnessed the incredibly powerful effects it had on some participants. I seriously considered removing it from the workshop, but finally I observed and came to understand that it has two built-in safety valves.

One primary safety valve is my implicit trust in Helpers knowing what level of retrieving an Aspect of Self a participant is *ready for and can handle.* My verbal guidance has little effect on the outcome. There is little I can actually do to guide participants to specific Aspects of Self or retrieve them. About all I can do is to assist participants in making contact with the Helper. Once that contact is made, the Helper takes over the guidance in the exercise.

The second safety valve is the click-out experience.

In an earlier chapter I wrote a little about click outs. You seem to be going along just fine in your exploration exercise, and the next thing you know, you are regaining consciousness. The hallmark of the click-out experience is that when you regain consciousness you have no idea when, how, or why you lost consciousness, nor do you have the slightest clue what happened while you were clicked out. This is accompanied by the feeling that you could have been *gone* for three seconds or three hundred years and you have absolutely no way of knowing which. From my own experience, and observing the experience of others, I've come to believe that there are at least two likely causes for click outs: either (1) the experience is totally incomprehensible, or (2) conscious awareness of the experience threatens such a monumental, all-encompassing, Belief-System Crash that survival of the experiencer's identity as a coherent Being would be jeopardized.

1. If what our Perceiver is bringing into our awareness at a subconscious level is so foreign to our previous experience that our Interpreter cannot find a single *nearest similar thing* to allow translation into conscious awareness, the Interpreter is unable to translate any of what the Perceiver is observing into our conscious awareness. We've lost our Balance on the side of the Perceiver, and for as long as it takes for us to regain our Balance we will be *unconscious to the experience,* or clicked out.

2. If allowing conscious awareness of the experience would have the potential to destroy so many of the experiencer's beliefs—and therefore so much of the experiencer's identity—as to threaten its existence, click out appears to be a sort of built-in circuit breaker. As an ever-increasing number of our beliefs sense fast-rising levels of conflicting experience, it's almost like some metaphorical, internal resistor that can't handle the high current level and starts heating up. And just like the sensor in the electrical circuit breaker in your house, when the internal resistor gets too hot, something goes *pop*, and the lights go out.

Here is an example of one form of clicking out most people are familiar with. Have you ever wondered what causes a person who receives *bad news* to faint? The person is fully awake and conscious one moment; they are told of the death of their spouse, say, or their child; and in the next moment they lose consciousness. It's my guess that a person in this situation faints because their response to hearing it is to completely deny the possibility that it can be true as a way of preventing a loss of identity. Often, the person says something like, *no, that can't possibly be true!* just before their mental circuit breaker pops and the lights go out. The spouse or child is a large part of the fainter's identity, and when the spouse or child dies that part of the fainter's identity—part of his or her belief system—dies too. Receiving the *bad news* can be seen as a sudden, massive Belief-System Crash resulting in such a sudden, massive loss of identity. The fainter's beliefs resist accepting the bad news by causing that person to become *unconscious to the experience*, by fainting.

In my view this is what sometimes causes participants doing the Retrieval of an Aspect of Self exercise in a workshop to have no memory of what they experienced during the exercise. Sometimes, full and immediate conscious awareness of our experience during this exercise could be too much for us to handle. I do see a difference between the experience of fainting after receiving bad news and clicking out in the Retrieving an Aspect of Self exercise. Receiving bad news represents a *loss of one's identity*, while retrieving an Aspect of Self represents *adding to one's identity*. It appears that any large change in the status quo of one's identity can be the source of clicking out.

In any event, clicking out, losing consciousness of the experience, appears to be an automatic safety valve that commonly occurs during this exercise in workshops, and in my view this is as it should be. It's important to remember that while you may have no conscious awareness of what happened during the click out, the information is not lost.

(As a side note and bit of personal commentary: It's my belief that the use of certain *mind-expanding* chemicals and drugs in America in the 1960s and '70s prevented the click-out safety valve from functioning properly. Some of these drugs—LSD probably being a prime candidate—forced users to be consciously aware during experiences in which they would normally have clicked out. In my view some users experienced things that caused such horrendous Belief-System Crashes, resulting in an unrecoverable loss of identity, that the phrase *blew his mind on drugs* came into the American English language.)

Workshop participants often voice the concern that whatever happened during their click outs may be lost forever and unrecoverable. There is evidence to suggest that what is experienced during a click out is not lost at all, it's just stored at the subconscious level where the Perceiver put it. In an earlier chapter on the Perceiver and Interpreter, I wrote about the experience of a buddy of mine, Tony, during an Exploration 27 program at The Monroe Institute.

You will remember that Tony, while listening to other participants debrief their experience in the Exploration 27 program, remembered what had happened during a previous click out at the same program a year earlier.

I would say that he initially experienced the click out because his Interpreter had no way of translating his future experience into his present conscious awareness. But as Tony listened to the debriefing session a year later, his Interpreter grabbed the *nearest similar thing*, which was his click-out experience that had been stored at a subconscious level for over a year.

What happens during click outs is evidently stored subconsciously and future experiences or events become the trigger for bringing them to conscious awareness. Those interested in the roots of déjà vu might reflect on Tony's story and the implications of click outs that can occur without our awareness, the memories of which are triggered by things like driving into a completely unknown city and knowing that city like you'd been there before.

Follow-up with participants who experience click outs during the Retrieval of an Aspect of Self exercise suggests that click outs are followed by an equivalent of time-release-memory pills. Memory of the experience comes to awareness over time, in small enough bites that they typically experience a series of small, easily handled Belief-System Crashes. Perhaps something or someone (Higher Self) adjusts the rate of information recovery to a rate the individual can handle and integrate.

Some spiritual or esoteric belief systems teach their followers to use meditative practices with the goal of launching the meditator into a click-out experience that they label "the Void." The meditator is encouraged to turn off the chattering-monkey-mind completely as a means of entering this Void. That chattering-monkey-mind is the voice of the Interpreter, in my view, and in my experience if you do manage to completely shut off the voice of the Interpreter you will click out, or *enter the Void*. The claim of such belief systems is generally that entering this Void benefits the practitioner in a way that is often couched in mystical language. As a practical, engineer-type person I would say that there probably is some benefit to clicking out, or entering the Void. Being clicked out allows the Perceiver to bring in knowledge at a subconscious level as a way of bypassing the belief blockages that would normally prevent entry of such knowledge into awareness at any level.

Whatever the Perceiver brings in then becomes one of those time-release-memory pills I described earlier. But as an engineer my training has been focused on looking for ways to make processes more efficient, less costly, and less time-consuming. In my view the voice of the Interpreter has a useful function, translating the Perceiver's observations into conscious awareness. If I were to assemble a belief system around the Void, mine would be aimed at teaching practitioners how to carry the Interpreter's voice ever deeper into that Void. In my opinion, maintaining the Balance between the Perceiver and Interpreter at progressively deeper levels of the Void is a faster, more efficient way of exploring that Void.

Retrieving an Aspect of Self Exercise Description

As mentioned previously, this exercise is almost entirely Helper driven. While the script for this exercise is intended to facilitate retrieval of an Aspect of Self, the direction your experience takes may conflict with the verbal guidance. If so, ignore the verbal guidance and follow your experience and your Helper's guidance. In this exercise it is important to remember to take in more relaxing breaths on your own if you feel tension during the exercise. Likewise, if at any point you feel the need to charge up your awareness, take in more Energy Gathering Breaths on your own. And, if you are having difficulty understanding or perceiving, remember to feel love on your own, and remember you can ask the Helper for assistance at any time, on your own.

Each time you do this exercise it's an opportunity to remember and use more of the tools you've learned in this guidebook.

Retrieving an Aspect of Self Exercise: Script

This is the Retrieval of an Aspect of Self Exercise. (Wait 5 sec)

As you get ready to begin the exercise, adjust the volume of this recording so that you can comfortably and easily hear and understand my voice. You may do this exercise either sitting or lying down. (Wait 10 sec)

When you're ready to begin, please close your eyes. (Wait 10 sec)

To begin this exercise move your body into a comfortable, relaxed position in your quiet place. (Wait 30 sec)

Complete your Preparatory Process, remembering and imagining each of the individual feelings, images, impressions, and details as you do each step in the process. (Wait 10 sec)

Take in Three Deep Relaxing Breaths. (Wait 45 sec)

Take in Three Energy Gathering Breaths to establish the flow from below. (Wait 45 sec)

Take in Three Energy Gathering Breaths from Below. (Wait 45 sec)

Take in Three Energy Gathering Breaths to establish the flow from above. (Wait 45 sec)

Take in Three Energy Gathering Breaths from Above. (Wait 45 sec)

Remember a time when you were feeling loved or loving. (Wait 30 sec)

Let this memory help you to remember and reexperience the feeling of love. (Wait 20 sec)

If the feeling fades that's okay; just remember another time you were feeling loved, then let that feeling build. (Wait 20 sec)

Remember, it is okay to pretend during this exercise. (Wait 5 sec)

Take in at least three more Deep Relaxing Breaths. (Wait 30 sec)

Remember standing in a beautiful park, on a sidewalk, on a warm, sunny day. (Wait 20 sec)

Remember the warm, comfortable feeling of the sun shining on your skin. (Wait 15 sec)

The deep blue sky above you with small, light fluffy clouds moving silently across the sky. (Wait 15 sec)

Remember walking slowly along the sidewalk, past beds of beautiful flowers (wait 15 sec), the vivid reds, yellows, purples, and blues so bright, rich, and clear, they almost seem to fill the air around the blossoms (wait 15 sec), deep purples, reds, yellows, blues, and vivid whites. (Wait 10 sec)

And as you move along a walkway remember the deep, vivid green of the fresh-cut grass (wait 15 sec), and the smell of fresh-cut grass. (Wait 15 sec)

Remember the sound of a light breeze stirring the leaves of the trees (wait 10 sec), the ebb and flow of that rushing sound of the leaves. (Wait 10 sec)

If you are wearing shoes, take them off and remember walking barefoot across the fresh-cut grass of the park. (Wait 15 sec)

Remember the feeling of the grass against the bottoms of your feet. (Wait 15 sec)

This park has a small playground, with its slide, merry-go-round, and swings. (Wait 5 sec)

Remember walking barefoot across the grass toward a playground. (Wait 15 sec)

Remember the feeling of warm, sun-baked sand against your feet when you step from the grass into the playground area. (Wait 15 sec)

Remember walking toward the swings—big, tall playground swings, big enough for you. (Wait 10 sec)

Remember sitting down on the swing and the feel of your body against it. (Wait 15 sec)

Remember the feeling of the ropes or chains of the swing in your hands, the texture and temperature, and the sounds they make. (Wait 15 sec)

Remember what it feels like to grasp the ropes or chains. (Wait 15 sec)

Do you remember how you start swinging? (Wait 10 sec)

The feeling of your feet against the sand, pushing your body in the swing back a little. (Wait 5 sec)

The feeling of throwing your legs forward, and your hands pulling hard as you lean back to make the swing go forward. (Wait 3–5 sec)

The feeling of throwing your legs back, and your hands pushing hard as you lean forward to make the swing move back. (Wait 3–5 sec)

At your own pace, swing forward and back a few times; feel it! (Wait 15 sec)

You can remember watching yourself swing, or remember actually being in your body swinging. It's much more fun to remember it from the perspective of being in your body as you swing. (Wait 20 sec)

Remember the feeling of the air against your face and body as you swing on the swing. (Wait 10 sec)

Remember how you make the swing go a little higher? Swing a little higher each time. (Wait 20 sec)

In this playground, when you're swinging high enough, you'll be able to safely jump from the swing and float gently to the ground.

On your next swing backward get ready to jump, and on your next swing forward, remember the feeling of jumping from the swing (wait 2–4 sec) and flying through the air (wait 2–4 sec), landing gently on the ground. (Wait 15 sec)

Remember looking around the park and imagine a park bench along the sidewalk, not far away. (Wait 15 sec)

Imagine walking across the grass, barefoot to the bench. (Wait 15 sec)

Imagine sitting down on the park bench and the feel of it against your body. (Wait 15 sec)

As you remember the warm feeling of the sun on your body, sitting there on the bench, remember and take in the beauty of the park. (Wait 20 sec)

And, ask for a Helper to come and meet you there, at the bench, in the park. (Wait 15 sec)

Feel for the presence of a Helper, remembering it's okay to pretend. (Wait 15 sec)

As you are more aware of this Helper's presence, gather in your impressions of the Helper. (Wait 10 sec)

Do you imagine this Helper is young or old? Large or small? Male, female . . . or something else? (Wait 15 sec)

As you are more clearly aware of the Helper, is this Helper near or far, beside you, behind you, or perhaps in front of you? (Wait 15 sec)

As you are clearly aware of the Helper, imagine introducing yourself to the Helper, or pretend to. (Wait 10 sec)

Remember the feeling of placing intent, or just imagine you are doing the Silly Little Finger Bending Exercise. (Wait 20 sec)

Reexperience the feeling of placing intent as you say in your mind, to your Helper, **I deeply desire to contact** (wait 3–5 sec), **to visit with** (wait 3–5 sec), **to communicate with** (wait 3–5 sec), **to understand** (wait 3–5 sec), **and retrieve an Aspect of Myself** (wait 3–5 sec) **as a healing, loving act of reintegration of my being.** (Wait 10 sec)

And, ask the Helper to guide you to this Aspect of Self (wait 5 sec) and follow the Helper, or imagine it. (Wait 10–15 sec)

As you follow the Helper, imagine you are looking for something that looks like an opening. (Wait 10 sec)

It could be a door, or window, the beginning of a path into a forest, a gate, or the entrance to a cave. (Wait 10 sec)

Look for something that looks like an opening and when you perceive it (wait 5 sec), go to it and through it, with the Helper, or pretend to. (Wait 15 sec)

As you continue following the Helper, you will know when the Helper stops moving. (Wait 10 sec)

When the Helper stops, stop with the Helper, knowing your Aspect of Self is nearby. (Wait 10 sec)

Feel for the presence of this Aspect of Self. (Wait 5–10 sec)

As you begin to become aware of this Aspect of Self (wait 3–5 sec), is it young or old? (wait 10 sec) Is it male for female? (wait 3–5 sec) Is it large or small? (wait 10 sec) Is it heavy or thin? (Wait 10 sec)

Gather in your impressions, or pretend to. (Wait 10 sec)

With the Helper's loving assistance introduce yourself to this aspect. (Wait 10 sec)

With the Helper's healing assistance (wait 3–5 sec), ask to know how and why this aspect was created. (Wait 15 sec)

Ask to know when this aspect came into being. (Wait 15 sec)

Ask to know what purpose this aspect's existence serves. (Wait 15 sec)

Ask to know, what part of me do you represent? (Wait 15 sec)

Ask to know, how has my life been influenced by your existence? (Wait 15 sec)

Ask this aspect if there is anything else it wants you to know. (Wait 15 sec)

Ask this aspect to show you, tell you, or give you something to verify that this experience is real. (Wait 15 sec)

Ask the Helper for more insights into this Aspect of Self. (Wait 20 sec)

Ask the Helper to show you, tell you, or give you something to verify that this experience is real. (Wait 15 sec)

As you become more aware of this Aspect of Self, and gather more impressions, remember the feeling of love and let the feeling build and grow. (Wait 20 sec)

Let it expand and grow and fill your entire being. (Wait 15 sec)

Ask for the Helper's healing assistance as you project love into this aspect, and with the Helper's assistance, retrieve this Aspect of Self. (Wait 20–30 sec)

Take as much time as you need and when you feel complete with this experience, express your gratitude to the Helper and then open your eyes. Then immediately begin to write about your experience and use the debriefing section in the *Afterlife Knowledge Guidebook* to assist you in recording your experience.

(Do not record this note: you may either keep the tape recorder running to leave a very long blank space on the tape, or you may choose to leave a short blank space and plan to turn off the recorder for the remainder of your exercise experience.)

Debriefing Retrieving an Aspect of Self Exercise

Remember to write down every detail of your experience in your notebook, and use State-Specific Memory to remember more of your experience. Pay particular attention to recording whatever the Aspect and/or Helper gave you that could prove your contact was real.

Review the *Ask to know* questions in the exercise script to trigger more memory of your interaction with the Aspect of Self. As you read each question, reflect on the answers you were given by the Aspect or the Helper.

This exercise can have far-reaching effects that you may feel and experience in a variety of ways. The effects of this exercise may be sudden, strong, and overwhelming, or they may be subtle and slow acting. In either case the benefit of retrieving an Aspect of Self is something that is enhanced by keeping a journal of your experiences after this exercise. I'd suggest that you use your notebook as a journal for this exercise and record any insights, feelings, experiences, and memories that you feel might be connected to retrieving an Aspect of Self. My feeling is that journaling is a great way to see changes in ourselves that happen over time.

If you experienced a click out during this exercise it may be especially important for you to journal about changes you sense in yourself over time. Clicking out can be an indication that you've retrieved an Aspect of Self at a subconscious level. Over a period of time you may notice subtle or not so subtle changes in who and what you believe yourself to be. Journaling is a good way to be able to look back at who you were a month or year ago and see the changes that have occurred.

Tips for the Retrieving an Aspect of Self Exercise

Some participants report that the Aspect of Self they retrieved was a part of their identity from their present lifetime. They can identify the time, place, and reasons why they split off this part of their identity, and the effects this had on their present lifetime.

Some report that the aspect they retrieved would best be described as from a past life.

Some report that the act of retrieving the Aspect of Self was as if that aspect walked right into their physical body. This is most often reported for retrieving present lifetime aspects.

Some report that the act of retrieving the aspect was more like a normal retrieval. In these cases it was like bringing this aspect to an afterlife environment where they were met by other nonphysical people they recognized. In this kind of retrieval of an Aspect of Self it's more like the aspect maintained its own identity after the retrieval, rather than integrating into the Retriever's present body and identity. These are often past life retrievals.

Some report retrieving Aspects of Self from other planets, other energy systems or dimensions.

And some participants report that the experience of retrieving an Aspect of Self was so powerful that the Belief-System-Crash effects continued for days, weeks, and longer after the workshop. My follow-up with these participants shows that over time they became completely different persons as a result of their experience in the exercise.

28

Participant Experiences of Retrieving an Aspect of Self

The examples in this chapter are taken from workshop participant and other explorer experiences. You may find similarities between them and your own experiences that may lead to greater understanding.

Erika's Power

Erika's experience in the workshop exercise demonstrates both the *healing potential* and the *potential for Belief-System Crash turmoil* that can result.

When Erika asked a Helper to come, she heard a voice from inside her that said, *I am here*. This voice seemed to be a part of her that wanted to help her with the exercise, but she didn't feel comfortable with the Helper's voice coming from inside her. When she expressed this, the voice said that two more Helpers would be there with her. According to Erika, "That is when the Light Beings came. I remember feeling very connected to them from the beginning. It wasn't like when the other Helpers came during the other retrievals."

Erika described these two very bright Light Beings as feeling neither male nor female, just Light. The Light Beings stood slightly behind and on either side of her and gave her a sense of security. When she asked these Helpers to guide her to an aspect of self needing retrieval, at first she felt like she was going somewhere, but could only see blackness surrounding her. As a scene came into view she found herself standing in a field, looking at a big, heavy door that had been slid open to reveal the opening to a cave. Erika and the Helpers approached the opening and entered the cave.

She described that it was red inside the cave and she could see jewels piled high on the floor of the cave. Most of these jewels were red and there were some gold ones also. The cave opening led to a tunnel and she began walking through the tunnel with the Light Beings moving along behind her. As she proceeded she continued to pass large piles of the red and gold jewels. At the end of the tunnel Erika walked into a big room with more of the jewels piled high on the floor of the room.

She then saw a throne in front of her and a king, wearing a crown and dressed in royal robes, appeared sitting on the throne. Another throne appeared and seated on it was a queen, also wearing a crown and dressed in royal robes. As she looked at them she realized that the king and queen were her "power."

She remembered creating them during her present lifetime when she was between the ages two and four years old. She remembered that it had been too hard to keep her own power at that age and deal with the rest of her life. So she had created the king and queen to hold it for her and sealed them in the cave. After this realization she knew it was time for her and the king and queen, her power, to be reunited. The king and queen stood up from their thrones and walked to where Erika was standing. They kissed her cheeks and then one by one each put their crown upon her head. They removed their royal robes, put them around Erika, and then as she described it, *they just kind of came into her.*

Erika then saw that there was now only one throne and she walked to it and sat down. Sitting there, her first thought was, *what am I going to do with all these jewels?* A whirlwind suddenly began and she, both Light Being Helpers, and all the jewels, were picked up and transported high above the Earth. The two Light Being Helpers then assisted Erika in sprinkling the jewels over all the people in her life and every situation that had occurred since she had created the king and queen as a child. When they were done she turned to her Light Being Helpers and hugged them both, feeling great love and deep gratitude. Before she parted from the Helpers they said, "Now, don't be a stranger," and then she returned to the workshop and opened her eyes.

When I contacted Erika via e-mail two days after the workshop she reported that things were pretty chaotic the first day after the workshop, and she was working at *pulling herself together.* She realized these feelings were probably a result of her workshop experience and expressed confidence she would be able to pull herself together. Her choice of words was for me a graphic description of the process of reintegrating her identity after the experience of retrieving her *power*.

In an e-mail one week after the workshop Erika said it was hard to describe how she was doing. "I feel depressed, yet still have a lot of hope without expectations about how things are going to be different." She went on to say, "Here's something interesting that I've noticed: Up until last week I had been putting things that I wanted to get rid of in a pile in our garage. A few days ago I knew it was the time to really get rid of the pile. So yesterday and today I have been collecting all the other items out of our house that I don't want anymore and adding them to the pile until the donation truck picks it up. I can't help but think that what I am doing in my house is a mirror image of what is going on inside me. I do feel like I am discharging something, and that the process is not yet over."

Erika's understanding of the mirroring of her physical life events and the reintegration of her power speaks volumes about the process. She continued describing things in her life now that may be part of this reintegration process:

"Another interesting thing is that some old health problems came back this week. Maybe they are also reappearing until I discharge them properly or deal with them in a better way. Probably one of the most soothing things I did this week was going out to an organic farm with my two young sons. We picked a wheelbarrow full of fresh and free vegetables plus pumpkins for carving. I am anxious to see what the next month will be like."

Gathering "fresh and free vegetables plus pumpkins for carving" and the soothing quality, to me points to part of the process of getting to know this part of self that she retrieved. In some ways it reminds me of the biblical passages that speak about the need to be *born again*. Erika ended her latest e-mail by saying, "feel free to put it (her experience) on your web site and in your newsletter. I hope that it is helpful to someone who reads it."

I want to thank Erika for her willingness to share such a personal and powerful experience with the rest of us. Perhaps through sharing her experience others will recognize something in their own life experience. Perhaps it may help trigger such experiences for some of you who read this story of Erika regaining her Power.

Janice Retrieves Two Aspects

Janice came to a workshop in Boston desperate to contact her deceased husband, Joey, to understand why he'd committed suicide. Joey had fallen back into drug addiction and become horribly abusive after they were married. In his reign of terror he had controlled every aspect of her life with beatings and threats against herself and her children. What she feared most after his gruesome suicide was that his professed love for her had been a lie. By the time we began the retrieval of an Aspect of Self exercise Janice had become comfortable with a Helper she called Wendy, who'd been with her during all the previous exercises. Here's Janice's description of the experience.

This is probably one of the toughest things I have written about because I haven't processed it all yet, it may take months to realize all the implications. I have a lot of conflicting emotions. Sometimes, I get sad, other times mad, confused, doubtful, nervous, you name it. The emotions I feel quite a lot are confusion and anxiety.

After I got the "hang" of exploring, I quickly settled into this next exercise, retrieving an aspect of myself, and settled on the floor surrounded by my new friends. I can't remember everything Bruce said in the beginning of this guided exercise; actually, I don't remember any of it now. I only remember the experience, which is pretty cool considering in the first exercise I couldn't get past listening to Bruce's voice. Also, this third time, I didn't seem to have much control, it was a very spontaneous thing. I remembered asking for my Guides to come and help me retrieve an aspect of myself. I had no idea what this REALLY meant, so I was pretty comfortable and open to whatever happened.

I was suddenly back home at my apartment sitting at my table. I looked over and there was John, a guide I'd been aware of in previous exercises who had been so elusive. Then, suddenly, John became Donny, a fellow workshop participant! I said, "Donny! What the hell are you doing here?" as I smiled happily! He just raised his eyebrows and shrugged an "I dunno!" to me. Wendy was sitting directly across from Donny, wearing the same purple garb I'd seen her wearing previously, and as always she spoke not a word. So I said, "Okay, let's go."

I told them we had to leave the apartment through the living room so we wouldn't disturb the kids. We walked out onto the balcony, then Wendy took one hand and John/Donny took the other. When we moved forward and stepped off the balcony I was afraid I was going to fall. Hello? I live on the second floor! As I realized we were floating in the air above the ground I started to think *this was gonna be fun!*

I could see my whole neighborhood! It was dusk, almost night. We started moving. When I realized where we were going I freaked out a little bit. We were headed right up over the trees and as the crow flies toward my old house where Joey and I lived together. I'd moved away from there as soon as he died. I said, "Hey! Hey!!! Hey wait! I don't wanna go there! I'm afraid of THERE!" Well, tough shit for me I guess because they didn't say anything, they just kept flying me Peter Pan style to my old house. It was so weird and wonderful to see like a bird and feel the absolute freedom of my spirit!

I don't know how to explain the sudden shift in my emotion that happened next. One minute I was floating off my porch, the next feeling happy and fun, the next nervous, then all of a sudden I felt the most intense sense of URGENCY! We were no longer floating blimp-like along, and as we soared through the door and down the cellar stairs, John/Donny and Wendy were no longer holding my hands; they didn't have to. I knew instinctively what I had to do.

I was filled with such a rush of urgency and purpose! I looked around quickly and saw a very young girl, probably 8 or 9, maybe 10. She was huddled up in a fetal ball on the cold stone floor of the cellar with a red cloak on and a hood. It looked kind of like what Wendy was wearing, but red. She was crouched there hiding, but she was in plain sight to me! She peeked ever so slowly out of the corner of her eye around the hood and I saw the outline of her face. It was MY face! HOLY SHIT, MAN! I ran to her and I knew I needed to take her with me but she started to run away! I freaked out again! I didn't want to lose her but feared in my forceful urgency that I was frightening her so badly she would get away. I softened as much as I could and told her, "No, no, please don't run away. I won't hurt you. I am part of you, and you me! I want you to come with me, please! PLEASE!" I didn't give her a whole lot of opportunity to change her mind because I grabbed her and that's when I heard Bruce's voice saying look for a door, but I had already spotted a window and decided that would be my door. It opened up and expanded as soon as I grabbed this little me. It was full of white/yellow light. I got the surge of feeling that I had Aspects of myself left all over that house and the property! I began to feel very, very sad.

My heart ached with the pain of the knowledge of losing such a beautiful and vital part of myself, and at the same time joyously sang at the love I felt for her, this little girl, and having her back with me! I was just flooded with all these emotions! I felt the tears running down my face and I felt the sobs and the *ache my god, the ache in my heart was unbearable!* I started to feel the workshop room around me but the grip of this retrieval had me tight. I fought back the sobs fearing I would disturb the other participants. I returned my full attention to my Guides and the girl. Wendy and Donny/John and I and the girl took hands, or bonded, or something, and we zoomed out of the window and up, up into the night and into the yard surrounding the house. I could feel Aspects of myself EVERYWHERE! Oh GOD! It was awful! It was awful because I knew I couldn't get them all. I felt like I was trying to save all the people I loved the most in the world at the same time from a fire, and desperately knew I was going to fail and lose some of them! The torture of that feeling! But a choice had to be made.

I got a strong sense of someone way in the back of the yard, down by the trees. I flew over there and there she was. She was a full-grown version of me sitting on the root of a tree grown out of the ground that wound around and back into the earth again forming a chair. She was a couple of feet down an embankment that led down to a deep ravine and was all trees and darkness. I extended my hand and pulled her up and out onto the lawn. The three of us stood there, in the night, with John/Donny and Wendy encircling us. I stood there flooded to the brim with emotion of sorrow, loss, joy, and a million feelings I couldn't put into words if I tried for a hundred years. As we stood, the little girl and the adult me each opened their hands and extended their palms out to me. As the moonlight illuminated their hands, I saw each girl had a beautiful, perfect little pearl. I knew that those pearls were beautiful pieces of my heart that they kept for me. I knew the shocking paradox of love and hate, bitterness and joy, freedom and captivity in an instant.

The three of us joined hands as I accepted their gifts for me, and as we did, as our hands became like one, a great beam of white light shot out from the earth between us and high into the heavens. In an explosion of love we all, including Wendy and John/Donny hugged and hugged and the two that were me, melted into me.

I don't remember any more of the scene after that, I think I just couldn't hold on any longer. My eyes opened and my heart exploded. I was breathless with the PAIN! I had to get out of that room and I had to get out fast. As quietly as I could I stepped over the other participants who all were still busily exploring their experience. I ran to the bathroom and sobbed and sobbed and sobbed!

My first reactions were, how could I have let Joey do this to me? How could I have let him cause me so much pain that I lost those two beautiful parts of myself? I was wracked with the implications of it all! I couldn't have imagined this! I couldn't have made it up! It was real. It was shaking me to my soul and I was falling apart! I went outside to breathe the air, hoping desperately for some sort of stability.

When I sat down in the cold night air of the New England November, I was so sad. A million questions raced through my mind. How? Why? How? How could I let this happen? What was I going to do about the rest of the Aspects of myself there? What if I had Aspects of myself all over the place? How the hell was I going to find them all? How would I handle this mentally? Oh my GOD! How could Joey hurt me so bad? How could he hurt me so bad, then say he loves me, then just kill himself and leave me here so lost? How could God allow this to happen?

As I sat there filling up tissues, I began to get answers. Very clear, very simple, concise answers. How could it happen? I had to drop those parts of me; otherwise, I never could've survived that relationship. I remember how lost I knew I was becoming in the violence of the drug-induced rages Joey would experience. I could never leave my kids and he knew it. So I would always try to escape the hours- and hours-long onslaught of verbal and sometimes physical abuse. I would run to the cellar and just cry and cry and cry begging him to stop. I would cry out to God for help. And my God how I just felt like shit and wanted to die! He made me feel so awful and I kept allowing it to happen! When would it all end? How much more could I take? I understood that the little girl in the cellar was my *Innocence*. I remembered the day that I climbed back up those cellar stairs and I knew what I was getting myself into, but felt I had no choice because I loved him. That little girl took that piece of my heart and protected my innocence.

I'd found the second girl in the exact same place I went to one night to escape the onslaught once again. I remember so vividly wishing Joey would think I had run away and he'd leave so I could flee with my kids. I remembered how I couldn't understand how he could cage me like he did. I couldn't understand why I could still love him. I couldn't understand how crazy things had become. I couldn't understand anything, it seemed. I just know I felt so desperately lost and alone. I was afraid. I am not sure what those pearls signify, but I feel it is something yet to be discovered and integrated. I feel that those pearls are somehow connected to the sense of freedom I'm feeling in my life since this retrieval experience. That freedom is what keeps me going and moving toward more change, even though I'm scared to death of it.

This experience has rocked my world to say the least. I have felt very anxious since it happened, but I've made plans to leave the place I'm now living in. I want to move, start again, living in a place where people only see what I am, not what I was. I am going to find the rest of my life.

29

Beyond Retrievals

Partnered Exploration

The techniques you've learned are a form of retrieval-based exploration. By being of service to those who've become stuck after death you've learned how to gather information from the deceased that can be verified by physically living people who knew them. Proving to yourself that we continue to exist beyond death is a huge, life-changing step that leads to a quantum leap in the development of your perceptual abilities. You've no doubt eliminated a number of beliefs that previously blocked perception beyond physical reality. You've also come to know that Helpers who are willing to assist you in your explorations actually exist. And yet, from my perspective, retrieval-based exploration can be thought of as training wheels on a bicycle. A more advanced technique you can use for deeper exploration of our afterlife and beyond is partnered exploration.

In retrieval-based exploration, verification comes through comparing information you've gathered from a deceased person with someone still physically living who knew him or her. But, what if you desire to learn about aspects of our afterlife that no physically living person can verify? For example if you want to know if Heaven or Hell really exists and what human existence is like in those places, is there a physically living person who could validate whatever you discover? If you want to explore the existence of beings who live on other planets, or in other dimensions, who could verify what you believe you've discovered? Partnered exploration offers a means of verification of such exploration experiences.

In partnered exploration two or more physically living people explore nonphysical realities together in a shared experience. After each exploration session all partners separately document their nonphysical experiences in great detail and then exchange notes for comparison. A measure of verification comes when partners find their own experience described in their partner's notes.

My original intention was to include the partnered exploration workshop material in this *Afterlife Knowledge Guidebook*. However, the resulting book would have been too long. I intend to publish it as a separate book in the Exploring the Afterlife Series.

30

Resources

At this writing, the www.afterlife-knowledge.com web site has been on-line for nearly ten years. While it contains much useful information, one of its most vital resources is its discussion forum called the Conversation Board. Here newcomers and seasoned afterlife explorers have the opportunity to share their questions and experiences. I encourage you to visit the Conversation Board and utilize its connection with fellow explorers for the marvelous resource that it is. I visit the Conversation Board regularly, answering questions and taking part in the discussions. Elsewhere on the web site you will find information on many topics, links to other useful web sites, and schedules for my appearances and workshops. There is also an on-line bookstore where you can purchase signed copies of my books, tapes, CDs, and videos.

About the Author

Bruce Moen lives with his wife, Pharon, in Denver, Colorado, where he is an engineering consultant in his own small firm. Curiosity about things metaphysical led him to the afterlife explorations recounted in his first four books, *Voyages into the Unknown, Voyage Beyond Doubt, Voyages into the Afterlife,* and *Voyage to Curiosity's Father.* He has been successfully teaching the workshop this book is based on around the world since 1999. Visit www.Afterlife-Knowledge.com to share your experiences with others and to see a schedule of Bruce Moen's lectures and workshops.

Voyages into the Afterlife
Volume 3: Charting Unknown Territory
Bruce Moen

Moen goes farther than ever before, reaching new realms as he uses Monroe Institute programs to explore Focus 27. Join Moen as he explores the Earth's core, begins partnered exploration, and feels the universe's unconditional love for him and all life.

Paperback · 320 pages · ISBN 1-57174-139-9 · $13.95

Voyage to Curiosity's Father
Volume 4
Bruce Moen

Moen's otherworld quest continues as he considers the benefits of partnered exploration to verify the sights and sounds of other realms, the worlds of Heaven and Hell, telepathic beings, and more.

Paperback · 320 pages · ISBN 1-57174-203-4 · $13.95

Astral Dynamics
A NEW Approach to Out-of-Body Experience
Robert Bruce

This encyclopedic out-of-body masterpiece gives you everything you need to understand the practice and go out exploring on your own. *Astral Dynamics* includes a practical "how-to" guide, troubleshooting advice, and a fascinating theoretical perspective on astral travel.

Paperback · 560 pages · ISBN 1-57174-143-7 · $16.95

Cosmic Journeys

My Out-of-Body Explorations with Robert A. Monroe
Rosalind A. McKnight

Foreword by Laurie Monroe

McKnight was one of the first and most successful out-of-body research explorers to work with Robert Monroe. In *Cosmic Journeys*, she recounts the early days of The Monroe Institute and her sessions in the famed "black box."

Paperback · 296 pages · ISBN 1-57174-123-2 · $13.95

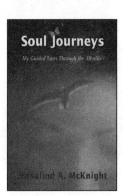

Soul Journeys

My Guided Tours through the Afterlife
Rosalind A. McKnight

In *Soul Journeys*, McKnight relates her explorations of the afterlife with a being she calls Radiant Lady. With Radiant Lady as her spiritual guide, McKnight explores and reports on the nonphysical energies in the afterlife. *Soul Journeys* reveals the inner workings of the other dimensions, including the afterlife, and emphasizes that all of us have spirit guides we can work with at any time.

Paperback · 272 pages · ISBN 1-57174-413-4 · $14.95

Eternal Life and How to Enjoy It

A First-Hand Account
Gordon Phinn

This description of what happens after people die was transmitted directly from Henry, a fun-loving, carefree soul—who just so happens to be dead. Henry describes his "first day dead," the various heavens and hells, and his own experiences as an afterlife guide for the newly deceased. Most importantly, Henry reveals what awaits us all and demonstrates how our beliefs in this life create the reality we experience in the next.

Paperback · 224 pages · ISBN 1-57174-408-8 · $13.95